D0140100

PROMOTION AND MARKETING FOR BROADCASTING AND CABLE

THIRD EDITION

Promotion and Marketing for Broadcasting and Cable

THIRD EDITION

Edited by

SUSAN TYLER EASTMAN
DOUGLAS A. FERGUSON
ROBERT A. KLEIN

*Endorsed by Promax, the association of promotion
and marketing executives in electronic media*

Focal Press

Boston   Oxford   Auckland   Johannesburg   Melbourne   New Delhi

Focal Press is an imprint of Butterworth–Heinemann.

Copyright © 1999 by Butterworth–Heinemann

 A member of the Reed Elsevier group

 Butterworth–Heinemann supports the efforts of American Forests and the Global ReLeaf program in its campaign for the betterment of trees, forests, and our environment.

Library of Congress Cataloging-in-Publication Data
Promotion and marketing for broadcasting and cable / edited by
    Susan Tyler Eastman, Douglas A. Ferguson, Robert A. Klein. — 3rd ed.
        p.   cm.
    Rev. ed. of: Promotion & marketing for broadcasting & cable.
    Includes bibliographical references and index.
    ISBN 0-240-80342-6 (alk. paper)
        1. Television broadcasting—Marketing. 2. Radio broadcasting—
    Marketing. 3. Cable broadcasting—Marketing. I. Eastman, Susan
    Tyler. II. Klein, Robert A., 1928– . III. Ferguson, Douglas A.
    IV. Promotion & marketing for broadcasting & cable.
    HE8689.6.S85 1999
    384.55´4´0688—DC21   98-56532
                                                                      CIP

British Library Cataloguing-in-Publication Data
A catalogue record for this book is available from the British Library.

The publisher offers special discounts on bulk orders of this book.
For information, please contact:

Manager of Special Sales
Butterworth–Heinemann
225 Wildwood Avenue
Woburn, MA 01801-2041
Tel: 781-904-2500
Fax: 781-904-2620

For information on all Focal Press publications available, contact our World Wide
Web home page at: http://www.focalpress.com

10 9 8 7 6 5 4 3 2 1

Contents

Foreword

Welcome to the most comprehensive book written to date about the exploding field of electronic media promotion and marketing. Written by many of the most honored and respected leaders and educators in the field, this textbook will introduce its readers to one of the most competitive fields in commerce today: the fight for viewers between television networks, stations, systems, and program suppliers. The war for consumers and viewers is being waged across the global electronic media complex. This worldwide, interconnected communications industry is populated by some of the most familiar and influential names in media including Disney, Time Warner, Fox, Paramount, Universal, and many others. Their programming products are distributed through instantly recognizable services including MTV, CNN, Discovery, NBC, HBO, ABC, CBS, ESPN, BBC, and hundreds of other brand-name programming providers.

The programs these corporations distribute and promote consist of thousands of daily hours of television watched by billions of viewers around the world. These programs include titles like *Seinfeld, Oprah, Xena, Hercules, Absolutely Fabulous, Sesame Street, Mighty Morphin Power Rangers, 60 Minutes, ER, Law and Order,* and *NYPD Blue.* For sports viewers, there are telecasts of *Monday Night Football,* World Cup Soccer, Wimbledon Tennis, the Olympics, the World Series, and countless other broadcasts of every imaginable competition. At the local level, stations in every major city in the world broadcast locally-originated programming with names like *Eyewitness News* and *Good Morning Denver.* These services provide communities with news, weather, sports, and national network programming.

And at the center of this industry, armed with a remote control, sits the common critical ingredient to the success of each of these enterprises, the viewer. Hundreds of millions of dollars and the success of a multibillion dollar corporation can depend on what prime-time program or channel this viewer watches. Fueling this business with billions of dollars are the advertising clients whose commercial support of a program or channel can leave it an extremely valuable asset or a money-losing drag on its parent company's financial statement.

Into this fierce battle between competing corporations and their program products steps the promotion and marketing professional. Charged with attracting viewers to his or her network, station, or program, this warrior for viewers uses on-air promotion spots, advertising, creative design, public relations, and even contesting to lure viewers' valuable attention for a few minutes or a few hours to targeted programming. The story of this art and science is the basis for the book you now hold in your hand.

For some time, leaders in our field have expressed the need for a comprehensive guide to this process of audience building for television. This book was written in response to this need and explores the evolving marketplace, the industry competition, and the tools and techniques being used to secure profitable viewing audiences in the media industry.

As the world's association of television promotion, marketing, and design professionals, PROMAX has endorsed this textbook as our recommended guide for use by educators and students in better understanding this dynamic profession and preparing for successful careers in the television industry.

With more than 4,000 member companies and individuals from more than 60 countries, PROMAX annually conducts conferences and competitions for promotion, marketing, and design professionals in the United States, the United Kingdom, Europe, Asia, and Latin America. As a source of critical information and expertise, PROMAX and its promotion, marketing, and design members are key to the future growth of every growth-focused television and electronic media company.

We hope this textbook will serve as a valuable resource for you and that it leads to a better understanding and interest in the dynamics of growing audiences through the use of promotion and marketing for broadcasting and cable.

Jim Chabin
President and CEO
PROMAX International
Los Angeles, California
March 1999

Acknowledgments

The most marked change in this new edition is the addition of a third co-author in a seamless tradition. In this and two previous editions, Susan Eastman worked with Bob Klein to envision the direction of this promotion and marketing book. The cooperation of academic and industry voices, now including Douglas Ferguson, has enhanced each edition, especially as Bob has provided invaluable help in securing access to people and materials.

We are indebted to authors contributing to earlier editions: Diane K. Bagwell, Robert A. Bernstein, Symon B. Cowles, Valerie Crane, David L. Crippens, Jerome Greenberg, Lee A. Helper, Gerald Minnucci, Jeffrey Neal-Lunsford, Dick Newton, Charles E. Sherman, Morton A. Slakoff, John L. Sutton, David P. Tressel, Lloyd P. Trufelman, Richard J. Weisberg, and especially Jerry Wishnow.

We also wish to recognize those who reviewed the third edition in preparation and thank them for their generous compliments and useful suggestions. At Focal Press, Terri Jadick efficiently supervised the book's development phase; Jodie Allen employed outstanding copyediting skills to polish and smooth the text; and Marie Lee continued to support us with warmth and wise counsel. We are grateful to all these people for their help, to PROMAX, and to the Departments of Telecommunications at both Indiana University and Bowling Green State University for their support.

Susan Tyler Eastman
Douglas E. Ferguson
Robert A. Klein

Contributing Authors

William Jenson Adams (Chapter 9) is professor of telecommunications at Kansas State University. His main research interests are television programming theory, research methods and audience analysis, media promotions, and media trends. He has written chapters for several textbooks including *Broadcast/Cable Programming* and has been published in such journals as *Journal Broadcasting & Electronic Media, Journal of Media Economics,* and *Journalism Quarterly.* He also writes on media for the popular press. Dr. Adams has received three NAB research grants to study television programming and audience trends.

Robert K. Avery (Chapter 7) is professor of communication at the University of Utah. A former public radio and television administrator, Professor Avery was directly involved in public broadcasting's early promotional efforts as chair of the Board of Directors of the National Association of Educational Broadcasters. He continues his direct involvement with public broadcasting as academic liaison with KUER-FM and KUED-TV in Salt Lake City. Professor Avery is coauthor of four books and numerous articles on the subject of public broadcasting and is founding editor of *Critical Studies in Mass Communication.* He is a member of the Japan–U.S. Telecommunications Research Institute.

Robert V. Bellamy, Jr. (Chapter 10) is associate professor of media studies at Duquesne University. His research interests include television programming, media and sports, and the impact of technological change on industry structure, conduct, and performance. His work has appeared in several edited books and in such publications as the *Journal of Broadcasting & Electronic Media, Journal of Communication, Journalism Quarterly,* and *Journal of Sport & Social Issues.* He is the coeditor of *The Remote Control in the New Age of Television* (1993) and coauthor of *Television and the Remote Control: Grazing on a Vast Wasteland* (1996), both with James R. Walker.

Joseph G. Buchman (Chapter 3) is associate professor in business management at Utah Valley State College. He coauthored two editions of *Broadcast and Cable Selling* (Wadsworth, 1986, 1993), as well as contributing the radio chapter to the previous edition of *Promotion and Marketing for Broadcasting and Cable.* His other publications have appeared primarily in the trade press, and include articles on radio, the Internet, and legal issues in *Next* and *Virtually Alternative.* His research and teaching focus on communication technologies, especially radio news, talk, and promotion. Dr. Buchman has held numerous positions at commercial radio and television stations, including serving as creative services director for WAGT-TV in Augusta, Georgia, technical director for WHAS-TV in Louisville, and radio personality for WBWB-FM in Bloomington, Indiana.

James B. Chabin (Chapter 10) is former president and CEO of PROMAX, now president of the Academy of Television Arts and Sciences, the organization that gives the Emmy Awards. Prior to joining PROMAX in 1992, he served as vice president of national promotion at E! Entertainment Television. His career in radio, television, and cable marketing, sales, and management also includes positions with Chabin Communications (owner of KKIS-AM/FM in Walnut Creek/Concord, CA), CBS Television Stations, CBS Radio Sport Sales, CBS Television National Sales, and KVMT-FM (Vail, CO).

Susan Tyler Eastman (Chapters 1 and 2) is professor of telecommunications at Indiana University. In addition to editing and authoring three editions of this book, she has edited five editions of *Broadcast/Cable Programming: Strategies and Practices* and contributed chapters to many other books. Her teaching and research focus on television programming and promotion for sports as well as entertainment shows, and her studies of on-air promotion have reached wide audiences through such journals as the *Journal of Broadcasting & Electronic Media,* the *Journal of Communication,* and the *Journal of Sports & Social Issues.*

Douglas A. Ferguson (Chapters 1, 4, and 5) is professor and chair of communication at College of Charleston. Previously he was program director of NBC-affiliated WLIO (TV) in Lima, Ohio, from 1976 to 1987. Since 1990, he has taught media management and television programming strategies. His research on television viewing behavior appears in various research journals, such as *Journal of Broadcasting & Electronic Media.* He coauthored the fifth edition of *Broadcast/Cable Programming: Strategies and Practices* (Wadsworth, 1997) and *The Broadcast Television Industry* (Allyn and Bacon, 1998).

Randy D. Jacobs (Chapter 6) is associate professor of communication at the University of Hartford. His research interests include cable television marketing, subscriber expectations, and user satisfaction. His work has appeared in such publications as *Journal of Broadcasting & Electronic Media* and *Journal of Media Economics.* He teaches courses in advertising and promotion campaigns, media planning, and new media technologies. He also is an active marketing communications and research consultant.

Robert A. Klein (Chapters 1 and 6) is founder and president of Klein &, a Los Angeles firm that creates and produces communication concepts. Klein & initiates and oversees design, audio and visual production, copy, and music for promotion. The company has received awards for its work from the top industry societies. Robert Klein has lectured at the University of California at Los Angeles and San Diego, the University of Southern California, the University of Illinois, Indiana University, and for the American Management Association. He has served on the national boards of directors of the Pacifica Foundation and PROMAX.

Bradley A. Moses (Chapter 5) is director of Creative Services at WTVG 13ABC, Toledo, Ohio. His practical experience includes ten years of network-affiliate promotional advertising and four years of corporate promotion within the television medium. He also serves on the marketing board of the regional March of Dimes.

Suzann Mitten Owen (Chapter 7) is a practitioner in the field of promotion. She is director of Public Information at WTIU, the PBS station licensed to Indiana University. She is also a lecturer in the Department of Telecommunications at Indiana University, teaching courses in promotion and writing. She has been a publications and promotion specialist, mostly for professional organizations, higher education, and broadcasting, since 1968. Her television promotion work has broadened to include new nonbroadcast technologies and services that complement broadcasting services.

Ronald J. Rizzuto (Chapter 8) is professor of finance in the Daniels College of Business at the University of Denver. His research and teaching interests include capital expenditure analysis, mergers and acquisitions, and cable telecommunications finance. He just completed a book with Dr. Michael Wirth, *Costs, Benefits, and Long-Term Sustainability of Municipal Cable Television Overbuilds.* Dr. Rizzuto has conducted numerous workshops and conferences for professional managers in the cable telecommunications industry. He has authored numerous case studies on cable telecommunications as well. In addition to his normal teaching responsibilities, he serves as codirector of the Bob Magness Institute at the National Cable Television Center and Museum.

Michael O. Wirth (Chapter 8) is director of the School of Communication and professor and chair of the Department of Mass Communications and Journalism Studies at the University of Denver. His teaching and research focus on cable, broadcast and telecommunication economics, policy, management, and regulation. Professor Wirth has coauthored one book, *Costs, Benefits, and Long-Term Sustainability of Municipal Cable Television Overbuilds,* and he has written numerous scholarly articles and essays that have appeared in such periodicals as *Journal of Economics and Business, Telecommunications Policy, Quarterly Review of Economics and Business, Information Economics and Policy, Journal of Broadcasting & Electronic Media, Journal of Media Economics,* and in scholarly books. Over the years, Professor Wirth has provided consulting services for a dozen major national corporations.

CHAPTER 1

Marketing the Media: Scope and Goals

Douglas A. Ferguson, Susan Tyler Eastman, and Robert A. Klein

Because of the exorbitant costs associated with mass media programming, promotion is a vital component of broadcast and cable strategy. Promotion is a primary marketing function enabling competitive positioning of stations, networks, and systems in their markets. Because the public understandably regards television programs, radio formats, and some networks as nearly interchangeable, management must find ways of luring viewers or listeners to its particular stations or channels. Promotion is the indispensable tool for creating and exploiting differences— that is, for *positioning* by convincing the public that one network, one station, one cable service or system, or one particular program differs substantially from its competitors.

Part of the larger field of marketing, *promotion* is the term commonly used in selling media images, programs, and personalities to audiences. (*Promotion* generally is considered a "smaller" term than marketing, but the broadcast industry continues to use *promotion* while the cable industry uses the term *marketing*. This book generally combines the terms or uses them interchangeably.) *Marketing* refers collectively to advertising, promotion, direct mail, and direct sales. Together, marketing and promotion encompass such diverse elements as the on-air spot or *promo*, print advertisements in program guides and newspapers, billboards and other signage, web pages on the Internet, customized merchandise for listeners and subscribers, the ever-present car bumper sticker, community activities for publicity, and media public relations.

Promotion and marketing also facilitate the sale of programs by syndicators, the licensing of cable networks, and the sale of advertising time by stations, systems, and networks. They have become crucial to the success of television and

Figure 1–1   *Types of Promotion and Marketing.*

radio stations, the commercial broadcast networks, public broadcasting, the major pay and basic cable networks, and the on-line services that are beginning to imitate mass media services. Each marketing situation calls for a particular set of strategies to gain and hold viewers or listeners and advertisers or underwriters. Command of marketing strategies is one of the major attributes demanded of outstanding professionals in the fields of broadcasting, cable, and the web. In addition, promotion has become a new path into executive management for college graduates, especially when combined with an understanding of programming strategies.

The most important division among types of promotion and marketing lies between promotion to audiences, to advertisers, and to affiliates (see Figure 1–1). Audience promotion is directed toward viewers, listeners, and users; advertising promotion is directed toward clients, that is, advertisers (or potential advertisers) and their agencies and to sponsors, usually called *underwriters*; affiliate promotion is directed by networks to stations and cable systems and by program syndicators to stations and cable program purchasers. Audience promotion is initiated by the station, system, or network and is intended to increase or at least maintain ratings; its cost is usually borne by the promotion department.

Marketing has the goal of selling a program or commercial time, and its costs are covered within the station, service, syndicator, or network's advertising rates or marketing budget. In radio, a sales promotion intended to get a group of advertisers to purchase commercial time may involve an elaborate audience contest as a lure to get advertisers to participate. Although its real purpose is to sell advertising time, a sales promotion contest may sound like audience promotion to most listeners. *Merchandising*, a way to gain visibility with audiences, advertisers, and affiliates, refers to such giveaways as T-shirts and coffee mugs. Mugs are particularly useful in displaying a station's name on the desks of potential advertisers. T-shirts help disseminate a particular image throughout a community. Shirts and tote bags might come from The Weather Channel or Disney to cable operators. Local stations and cable systems can use community service activities to tie together elements of audience and advertising promotion.

Distributors and syndicators purchase a great deal of trade advertising and direct marketing to lure station affiliates into licensing their product. Trade advertising in magazines like *Broadcasting & Cable* attracts station affiliates as well as gains sales for programs. For example, syndicators use print ads to brag how their first-run and off-network shows have had high ratings with target demographic audiences. Many ads provide a list of affiliated stations for a particular syndicated program to create the necessary momentum to attract new buyers and also to reinforce the decisions of those stations already on board. Direct marketing mailings accomplish the same goals but allow the distributor or syndicator to target specific stations with elaborate presentations. Some of this promotional effort goes beyond simple print advertising, providing videotape samples of programs and unique gifts. For example, a promotional package for a sporting event might include team merchandise that the station's prospective sponsor can pass along to his or her children at home. Similarly, new cable networks use trade advertising to attract the attention of cable operators with the goal of expanding their affiliate lineups.

Public relations, another category of activity related to promotion, is conducted by media companies of all kinds. It is directed toward media representatives, such as journalists and editors, to opinion leaders, such as local officials and community leaders, and also to competing stations and networks, advertising agencies, syndicators, and program producers. The purpose of public relations is to build visibility and a positive image for the station, service, or network, so it usually is allied to other promotion. In addition, many publicity and community service duties fall under the purview of promotion departments, along with image-building activities that other departments are too busy to handle.

Marketing a station, system, or network on its own air or its own channel is *on-air promotion*. It is budgeted and planned differently from paid advertising. Purchasing or trading for ads or signs in other media or trading spots with other stations or cable is *outside media*, also called *external promotion* to draw attention to the use of media outside the station's, system's, or network's own resources.

INFLUENCES ON PROMOTION

The importance of the study of promotion and marketing lies in six continuing developments in broadcasting and cable economics: the decline of the influence of the commercial broadcast networks, increases in program costs, education of management about marketing, pressure from new competing media, the removal of some federal impediments to open competition, and new digital delivery technologies. These six influences have combined to bolster the status of the job of marketing programs and images.

No broadcast network can be sure of dominating the ratings for any great length of time, especially as cable networks nibble away at audience shares. Consequently, network position no longer automatically determines a local affiliate's market ranking or its local image. Affiliates of any of the networks hold top position in some markets, generally on the basis of their newscast's popularity. Local promotion thus directly influences station positioning.

Programs now cost as much as some station or network is willing to pay for them, and the sky is the limit. Affiliates, independent stations, cable networks, and even some cable and DBS systems compete head-to-head for the same programs and movies. Off-network series can cost thousands of dollars per episode in large markets, running the total cost of the most popular series into the millions of dollars—while only filling a half-hour or so per day. Therefore, managers are more eager than ever to get their money's worth out of every program and movie, and promotion is the tool to accomplish this—to get and maintain ratings or subscribership.

Persuaded by program consultants and scientific research about broadcast and cable marketing, many in management have become educated to the subtleties of program decision making and the crucial role of effective promotion and marketing. Research into images and programs conducted by such influential "news doctors" and consultants as Frank N. Magid Associates has been reinforced by frequent media reports about image advertising in political campaigns, community service campaigns, and national product sales, increasing the salience of marketing to all professions. Media executives now generally accept the need for professional promotion to maximize profits and neutralize undesirable publicity.

Fierce competition has evolved among broadcast, cable, and satellite networks as well as through consumer electronic delivery via cassettes and discs. Although the total amount of media use increases steadily from year to year, the number of competitors for viewers, listeners, and web users also expands, slicing the pie thinner and dividing advertising dollars more widely. Effective promotion helps stations, networks, and systems keep a piece of the pie.

Beyond generally opening competition for viewers and listeners to many new media, several decisions by the Federal Communications Commission have particularly affected media promotion. These included lifting restrictions on local station identifications (IDs) and loosening limits on changing station call letters and on airing lotteries. The commission also dropped its processing guidelines covering the quantities of nonentertainment material (such as news or public affairs) aired by broadcast stations and dropped hourly limitations on the number of commercial minutes. Federal regulations also have eased restrictions on the cost of new delivery systems. Relaxed rules have increased local flexibility, in turn giving greater salience to each station's or system's marketing of programs, formats, and images.

The sixth and final influence is the changeover from analog to digital standards in both television and radio and the growth of the web. The convergence of computer and telephony with electronic mass media is certain to change the way people receive entertainment and information. On the one hand, marketing and promotion will play a pivotal role in the implementation of new delivery systems. On the other hand, strategies of audience promotion, sales promotion, and public relations will be influenced by digital convergence of media.

All of these changes add up to increased importance for promotion in the twenty-first century. Professionals trained in the strategies and techniques of marketing will be in great demand in the decades ahead. A growing number of college courses and industry seminars now are addressing the need for informed practitioners of broadcast and cable promotion.

PROMOTION TO AUDIENCES

The most important concept in audience promotion for all entities—except the largest broadcast networks within prime time—is that not all viewers or listeners are the *target audience*. Only those viewers or listeners likely to be interested in the message should be targeted with promotion. Trying to go after everyone in a single message will result in reaching no one very closely. Using more messages, each targeting a different demographic or psychographic group, is more likely to be effective than frequent repetition of a single message addressing all.

In promotion, *on-air* collectively refers to prerecorded television and radio spots, called *promos*, radio *filler* material, *IDs*, and *logos* that identify stations or networks, on-air billboards of upcoming shows, and live *teases*, *bumpers*, and *tags* appearing on a channel's own air time.

There are two basic types of promotion and advertising content: topical or *tune-in promotion* and *image promotion* (also called *branding*). An on-air spot or print ad in a program guide that promotes a particular episode of a series on a particular day, as in Figure 1–2, is program-specific promotion. The ad in Figure 1–2 refers only to 7 P.M. on some particular Monday; the ad could be used only for the few days preceding that Monday's show. Topical on-air promos and newspaper ads that promote that evening's headline stories on a newscast also are using a *specific* strategy. These are attempts to get viewers or listeners to tune in at a specific time on a particular day. Most network and local television promotion is tied to the daily content of individual series episodes and news stories. Networks refer to these tune-in promos as *topicals* or *episodics*.

Figure 1–2   *Program-Specific Newspaper Ad. Courtesy WGBO-TV.*

In contrast, promotion and advertising that focus on the overall qualities of a station, system, or network, not tied to any day's individual episodes or news stories, are *image* promotion (see Figure 1–3). They position the service by telling what is important about it and creating a "brand" in people's minds. The promo or ad may feature a particular image for the station, the beginning of a new entertainment series, or perhaps a new anchor for the newscast. Television stations, for example, periodically produce or purchase branding promotion to create an updated image for their evening newscasts. Specialized cable networks typically promote themselves in relation to particular programming formats, tying their names closely to their overall programming.

TV and Radio Promos

Commercial and noncommercial television stations and networks make heavy use of prerecorded promotional spots (*promos*) on their own air, usually producing them in their own studios. Promos are prerecorded in standard 15-second and 30-second lengths; 10-second, 20-second, and 60-second spots also are useful to fill odd lengths of air time. Promos may be scheduled daily in predetermined time periods (*fixed-position* promotion) or in unsold commercial time (*leftover availabilities*).

Promos usually spotlight an upcoming program or a news or talk personality. Some feature the station, system, or network more generally as part of an identity campaign. Most distributors of syndicated series and movies supply edited segments of each episode or film; the local station or cable system adds its own identification and the show's air time.

Because local newscasts are so important to television station ratings and revenue, the time, staff, and budget are available to videotape daily news promos highlighting upcoming news stories. Most topical news promotion, however, consists of live news anchors announcing upcoming news stories (*stand-ups*). Stations may produce generic promos highlighting the personalities or professional skills of their newscasters as part of a campaign to bolster news ratings, but routine, daily news promotion always is specific to that evening's newscast.

The major broadcast and cable networks devote large budgets to producing on-air promotional spots for their entertainment programs. Every fall, the commercial networks create elaborate developmental campaigns to introduce new programs and encourage viewing of prime-time series. On-air promotion of network entertainment series (and local news) is especially active during the fall season introductions and during the November, February, and May ratings periods. Similarly, cable network promotion follows the broadcast network pattern, while system promotion should be continuous.

13 Action News, committed to complete coverage of the stories that affect your life.

If it concerns you . . . we're there.

Morning after morning.

We'll help guide you through the morning maze of traffic.

Day after day.

Figure 1–3   *General Image Promotion. Courtesy WTVG 13ABC.*

Giving you a daily dose of health news on medical minute.

Night after night.

Ready with complete weather coverage right where you live.

13 Action News . . . working harder to bring you more.

Figure 1–3   *(continued)*

On-air for radio stations consists of a broad spectrum of live and prerecorded talk directed to listeners by disc jockeys or talk hosts. The focus often is on repetition of the station's identifier and slogan. For music format stations, on-air filler typically includes giveaways and contest activities such as prize announcements, statements on contest rules, and telephone calls taken over the air. News and talk radio stations, however, use more prerecorded spots than music stations to promote their upcoming feature stories. Promotion for specific programs plays a lesser role in radio because most stations adhere to continuous formats rather than discrete programs. Because the major markets are nearly always being rated (as many as 48 weeks a year), radio promotion is almost constant.

Identifiers

In addition to preproduced promos, stations and broadcast and cable networks schedule brief IDs (identifications) during program breaks (see Figure 1–4). These state the way the network or station wants to be known (*identifier*). Identifiers may be only auditory or both auditory and visual. Networks and systems merely state their names, with or without a theme. For TV stations, the identifier nearly always is a channel number. For radio stations, it usually is a combination of letter (from its call letters) and frequency, as in Q-95 or "Power 95" for a station operating at 95.1 MHz.

Television IDs are seldom more than 3–5 seconds long, and they have become useful devices for reiterating a promotional theme or advertising an upcoming program. When split between mentions of a program and the station, it is called a *shared ID*: "This is WXXX in Hometown, the station that brings you *Seinfeld*." Television stations (and most cable networks) routinely include an ID of some kind in half-hour and hourly breaks, and the ubiquitous identifier in the lower corner of the screen during live programming provides continuous promotion.

Teases, Bumpers, and Tags

Another type of live on-air spot used commonly in both television and radio is the *tease* or *bumper*, a brief auditory plea for viewers to stay tuned through a series of commercial announcements. News teases placed toward the close of a 5:30 P.M. show, for example, tantalize local television viewers with glimpses of sensational footage from upcoming news stories to entice them to watch the 6:00 P.M. newscast. Radio DJs use audio bumpers just before a commercial break, naming

Figure 1–4   *Broadcast Network Logo. Courtesy Fox Broadcasting Company.*

the song or artist to be played just after the break to induce fickle listeners to stay with the station.

While teases and bumpers are live visual and auditory elements that announce upcoming program titles, *tags* usually refer to something visual stuck on the end of the preceding program or spot. Tags include prerecorded visual material, such as a station or network identifier, and insertion of the day or time and channel of the next episode in a series. Tags, then, usually are on top of preceding material, whereas teases and bumpers stand alone.

GOALS FOR ON-AIR PROMOTION

On-air promotion ultimately is the best place for most stations and channels to extend viewership or listenership and build loyalty. There are two persuasive arguments for on-air promotion: in highly competitive situations, stations and channels that do not promote cannot dominate in viewership or subscribership; and the more successful promotion is, the more likely advertising rates can be increased. Although advertising dollars may be invested in other media to attract sampling, the payoff is in what the stations and channels say to the huge flow of viewing audience on their own air. Therefore, on-air promotion must present a message in harmony with the external advertising that attracted the viewer in the first place. It must deliver on the promises made in the other media. It must be consistent.

GOALS FOR CABLE SYSTEMS AND NETWORKS

For most system operators, the overriding goals are getting and retaining subscribers. Acquisition of subscribers requires a traditional product and service marketing approach using conventional media campaigns, concluding with a direct phone number to call in order to subscribe. The various media are measured in terms of their cost per inquiry and their cost per subscriber. The most productive marketing media receive most of the cable budget. Commercial television probably gets more than its share of cable media dollars because its known reach surpasses that of all the other media.

The second main objective—keeping subscribers—involves strategies that are still in the process of evolution. This objective becomes the most important priority by far once most homes passed (by the feeder wires) have been signed up. One retention device common to all services is the program guide, usually a monthly publication displaying the complete program schedule, promotional materials on the programming, and teaser promotions on upcoming programming. A substantial responsibility for lowering the rate of disconnects (called *churn*) falls to on-air promotion. Cable systems often add their local identifiers to national messages and reserve about a quarter of ad time for self-promotion, including promotion of networks and services.

Some MSOs (multiple system operators) initiate development of special identity campaigns that their systems can use to enhance local viewer perception and provide top-quality packaging for their cross-channel promotion. The majority of media investment relating to cable comes from the major pay networks, especially HBO/Cinemax, Showtime/The Movie Channel, MTV, and Time-Warner/Turner's CNN, TBS, and TNT.

Web Pages

With the advent of the World Wide Web connecting the domains of the Internet, all organizations (even noncommercial ones) are occupying spaces, called *web sites*, where products, services, and ideas are displayed. The formal purpose is to provide yet another *address* for accessing information, beyond the usual street address for mail, telephone number for questions, and fax number for document exchange. Another purpose is to widen the distribution of their images and to do additional program promotion. By 1997, nearly all media had been linked to a web site, including networks, their affiliates, their studios, their suppliers, and many audience groups.

At the most basic level, broadcast and cable web pages provide an access point, a gateway to information, a feedback loop for audience members, who receive media messages, direct sales of merchandise, and a directory of resources. Most media outlets go beyond a mere catalog listing to provide *multimedia* content that combines text, graphics, audio, photos, and full-motion video. One particular site (www.promolounge.com) permits television viewers to download on-air program-specific promos from the networks.

Advertising

In promotion and marketing, *advertising* refers to paid or traded promotion external to the station, system, or network, as contrasted with the service's own air. Paid advertising for programs and images includes ads in newspapers, magazines, and program guides, outdoor billboards, cab-top signs, cards inside and signs outside buses, trains, and subways, even call letters painted on hot-air balloons, and other imaginative methods of promoting listening, viewing, or subscribing.

The broadcast and cable networks purchase large amounts of space in program guides such as *TV Guide* to promote their new fall seasons. Local television stations make heavy use of newspaper and magazine advertising during ratings periods, usually promoting their news specials in newspapers and their entertainment programs in program guides. Radio stations, having much smaller budgets than television stations, usually seek to trade some of their air time for time on local TV stations. They frequently use billboards when there is a change of format or morning personalities.

All marketing plans must contain a strategy for using other media. Although media planning for specific broadcast and cable needs is addressed in subsequent chapters, a number of basic views are commonly held among marketers and appropriate to most situations.

Newspapers are playing a decreasing role in broadcast and cable promotion while radio has surfaced as an effective targeting device for both commercial and public television stations and cable. Television advertising is the major medium for achieving increased sampling. Many radio stations consider television advertising too expensive, although syndicated campaigns are available that reduce costs, and most media will consider trading time between radio and television and between radio, television, and cable, either on a pure promotion basis or a part trade–part cash basis. Equivalence can be determined by time (30 seconds for 30 seconds) or total rating points. Outdoor billboard advertising can be effective in those markets with extensive billboard coverage, provided the signs reach the right target audience. And *TV Guide* remains the giant among magazine guides to programming and is crucial to topical network promotion and image promotion of stations. It is increasingly becoming a tool for cable services, along with various customized cable guides.

Newspapers

Newspaper readers tend to be older than the typical mass television audience and the dominant radio audience. They also tend to be economically upscale. These two facts limit the use of newspapers as a major advertising medium for mass broadcasters. On the other hand, newspapers reach an influential, opinion-making public and a news-interested audience. Newspaper readers (especially subscribers) tend to be more serious about the content and quality of their news, and they also tend to voice their opinions strongly on reported issues. Consequently, they can be effective as an institutional medium for communicating overall identity and for promoting news specials.

Because of the influential individuals they reach, newspapers traditionally have been used to launch major campaigns and new seasons, programs, services, and formats. Still, the use of newspapers is considered supplementary to on-air promotion and, in many cases, to radio. The weekend TV supplements produced by most newspapers are the major exception to this rule. In many markets, they outdraw *TV Guide* readership.

Promoting Television on Radio

Radio is an ideal medium to supplement television's own air. It is especially effective for topical advertising. Some television stations use live radio spots, generally during the late afternoon traffic periods, to promote their early evening news. If a station's objective is to increase the quantity of specific day-to-day program promotion, radio probably is the most flexible medium. Stations can be selected that pinpoint the very audiences that television is most interested in reaching at the times of day when listening by the target audience is at its peak.

Moreover, radio allows for piggybacking of two different messages within one 30-second spot. This practice is especially desirable for promoting the lead-in or lead-out for local evening news (early fringe to news to access programming), a time period that is the highest revenue-producing time period for most television stations.

Promoting Radio on Television

Television generally is regarded as the highest-impact medium for radio advertising. Most radio formats can be sold very effectively on television in 15 seconds or less, and the medium excels at creating awareness and generating sampling of new programs by large numbers of viewers. Many radio stations emphasize television spots using animation, graphics, and laser art to stress the "look" and "feel" of their sound. Others promote their personalities in "Face Behind the Voice" campaigns.

Television time is expensive, however, as is television production; a radio station's message competes for attention with national and regional spot commercials combining high creativity, sophisticated production values, and big budgets. To meet this problem, spot campaigns have been developed for syndication that market specific radio formats that can be adapted by a change of identifiers at low cost.

Promoting Cable Television on Broadcast Television

Both national cable services and local systems make extensive use of on-air spot advertising on commercial television stations. Many network-affiliated stations, viewing the cable services and systems as direct competitors, have refused to accept cable tune-in advertising. However, most stations now accept generic cable advertising. On-air television still can serve the dual purpose of informing current subscribers about upcoming movies while urging other viewers to subscribe in order not to miss out.

Magazines

TV Guide and the weekly television supplements in newspapers are the publications essential to commercial television networks and stations and PBS. They are the publications most viewers read, and their readership is made up wholly of viewers. There is no waste circulation.

Some cable systems distribute printed cable guides. Their effectiveness is the subject of considerable disagreement. In their current forms, guides provide an outlet for national program publicity as well as detailed cable channel listings. Some customized guides are produced for local systems and thus provide extensive opportunities for system promotion as well as advertising sales. But most guides are produced nationally and provide little flexibility for localization. Several national services also produce monthly magazines for cable subscribers. Some, like the *Disney Channel Magazine* combining feature stories and listings, are sent out free to all subscribers; others, like *A&E* distributed by the Arts & Entertainment cable network, are sold on an annual subscription basis. The national services that publish their own magazines consider them to be important, basic marketing tools. Generic cable-only guides, on the other hand, which list all the most popular national channels but lack local system identification, have more problematic value. Viewers complain when cable-only guides lack listings for the local broadcast stations.

Outdoor Advertising

Outdoor advertising is expensive and one of the least flexible of all advertising media. However, it is extremely effective in establishing programs, personalities, and themes in markets that are heavily posted and heavily trafficked. Unfortunately, most broadcasters use outdoor advertising so seldom that they lack expertise in making the space work for them to maximum advantage. It is advisable to consult outdoor companies and to take advantage of their recommendations in preparing copy and art.

An old truism claims that an outdoor message cannot contain more than six to eight words and still be effective. By and large, that probably is true, but it does not deal with the fundamental challenge of how to design an outdoor message that makes a memorable impact on the passing viewer, one that avoids the usual passive message.

A number of publications can prove helpful and challenging in the use of outdoor advertising and all the graphic arts. Ultimately, however, broadcast marketers must become students of all outside media—to become knowledgeable about each medium and its dynamics when combined in a media mix, to tailor the most relevant messages for each.

Merchandising

Merchandising refers to the aspect of marketing concerned with premiums (items of merchandise). A broadcast station or cable system gives away such premiums as T-shirts, baseball caps, and a seemingly infinite variety of other small merchandise, all labeled with the service's identifier. Stations do this to remain popular with their listeners or viewers and advertise to others. The most popular items can even become a revenue stream for the media, as the broadcast networks and The Weather Channel have done by selling items with their logos.

Networks, stations, and cable systems also flood potential advertisers and buyers at advertising agencies with customized premiums to keep the service's name highly visible. The offices and homes of a station's long-term advertisers usually are glutted with calendars, coffee mugs, pens, posters, clocks, radios, and what-have-you, all intended to reinforce a positive, ongoing relationship. Merchandising becomes an aspect of audience promotion when it is directed toward viewers and listeners; when it is directed toward advertisers, it becomes sales promotion.

Stations also receive merchandise and services in return for unpaid use of their air time, called *tradeouts*. Local businesses occasionally provide such goodies as shipboard cruises, restaurant meals, and slightly used cars in exchange for on-air mentions. Radio stations commonly trade air mentions for concert tickets to local events, benefiting both the concert promoter and the station who then has highly desirable prizes to give its contest winners.

SALES PROMOTION

Anything that helps sales executives sell commercial time on a broadcast or cable network, a station, or a cable system is *sales promotion*. Networks and stations usually distribute customized brochures of printed sales materials to potential advertisers. Local brochures contain maps of the station or system's coverage area and detailed analyses of its best ratings or best satellite channel audiences. They also may contain testimonials from advertisers about previous successful advertising campaigns and photographs of television stars and local news anchors. Syndicators of off-network and first-run TV programs and radio features also use sales promotion materials to market their programs to stations and cable networks.

In radio, audience games and contests designed to attract the public into the premises of a retailer are a major part of sales promotion. Many advertisers want a measurable return for their advertising dollars; potential customers who come into a store to guess the number of beans in a jar or to drop off an entry blank provide the chance for sales and, at a minimum, assure the advertiser that these people know exactly where the store is. These sales contests provide *added value* to on-air commercials and foster positive, ongoing relationships between the station or system and advertiser.

PUBLICITY AND PUBLIC RELATIONS

Unpaid mentions in newspaper columns and magazines or on other stations are *publicity*, a way of getting one's name out that can be more valuable than paid advertising because publicity is visibility that comes from a presumably disinterested (unpaid) source. Stations participate in parades and concerts and sponsor charitable fundraising activities to generate positive publicity for themselves.

Public relations and publicity often are intertwined, but we commonly distinguish formal activities such as writing press releases and making speeches to organizations and groups as *public relations*. A press release is a written announcement of some event mailed or delivered to members of the press. Stations send out press releases describing new and ongoing shows or to announce an unusual event such as a TV star coming to town, or when the station/system sponsors a new activity. Writing a daily or weekly press release usually is an activity of the promotion or marketing department at a station, cable system, or network.

Public relations also refers to management's interactions with the press, government, pressure groups, and the public on a broad scale. In broadcasting and cable, two specialized forms of public relations are crucial to the industry: trade press relations and community relations.

Trade Relations

Trade press relations involve unpaid publicity and paid advertising in trade magazines and newspapers intended to influence executives in advertising agencies, media buyers, advertisers, and to a lesser extent, federal and state government officials. An expensive page in the *Wall Street Journal*, for example, targets other media and advertisers rather than merely audiences. The networks devote whole departments to public relations quite separate from their daily on-air and print promotion departments. Publicists doing trade press relations make use of printed mailers, press releases, and gifts of merchandise, much like sales staffs do, but their success depends largely on their network of personal contacts.

Community Relations

Community public relations targets the station or system's hometown audience, incidentally including, of course, advertisers and local government officials who, after all, are members of the local public. Community service promotion has two aspects: personal participation by the station or system's staff in local events or organizations and station support for charities and other nonprofit organizations and causes through on-air campaigns. Joining local civic groups and participating in local events gives the station or system's employees a visible and positive role in the community and keeps management in touch with local needs and issues. Tackling on-air public service campaigns demonstrates the station or system's commitment to serve the community and can help to foster social change. Stations and systems commonly get involved in service campaigns for educating about AIDS or substance abuse or encouraging the use of bicycles or public transportation.

MARKETING STRATEGIES

Marketing experts frequently distinguish between advertising as a means of informing and promotion as a means of persuasion. In broadcasting and cable, this distinction is not clear. Promotion staffs at local stations and marketing departments at cable systems handle both print advertising and on-air promotion with the aim of informing and persuading in all their efforts. Promotional materials, however, target two separate groups. The first of these are audience members who do not now watch, listen to, or subscribe to the station or system. To reach this group, the station or systems must use external media and educate viewers about the programs and services. A marketing effort to encourage program sampling or new subscriptions uses an *acquisitive strategy*. For a television station, the most important visual and auditory elements in acquisitive promotion are the day and time of the programs and the identifier of the station. For a radio station, the most important elements in acquiring new listeners are promotion of its format and identifier. A cable system, on the other hand, must promote its multiple services in combination with its name and phone number to acquire new subscribers.

   The second group that a station or system wants to inform and persuade consists of people who already listen to, watch, or subscribe to the station or system. The goal is to retain these people by keeping them satisfied with the station or service through a *retentive strategy*. To this end, radio stations constantly give away records and tapes and concert tickets, either as prizes for easy-to-win contests or just for being "the seventh caller." Cable systems, pay-cable networks, and public broadcasters provide program guides, devices that keep subscribers knowledgeable about their viewing options and thus, it is hoped, pleased with the service. This kind of promotion uses a long-term retentive strategy. Stations and networks also use short-term retentive strategies intended to maintain audiences for more viewing or listening in the next hour or day part.

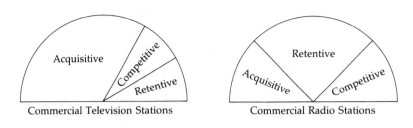

Figure 1–5 *Models of Promotional Strategies.*

The broadcast television networks annually adopt new promotional themes to foster excitement for their new fall seasons (see Chapter 4). Many of these themes, however, retentively target affiliated-station executives and advertisers more than they acquisitively target viewers. Nonetheless, overall, the networks' promotional efforts are primarily acquisitive (see Figure 1–5), whereas established radio stations playing popular music concentrate on retention, as do public television stations. The trend in cable marketing has begun to shift from acquisitive to retentive techniques such as community identity campaigns, media advertising, and extensive cross-channel image promotion (see Chapter 6).

Competitive strategies, sometimes called counter-promotion or guerrilla promotion, are attacking warfare, intended to disable competitors' promotion efforts. A radio station may create a contest sounding very much like a competitor's contest with the goal of confusing listeners. A television station may begin promoting its weather radar merely because a competing station is doing so. Such strategies are intended to undercut the effectiveness of competitors' efforts and are considered unethical when they are extreme or frequent.

Positioning campaigns may have a mix of acquisitive, retentive, and competitive goals, but individual items of promotion usually are most effective when they have either a solely acquisitive or solely retentive goal, because the strategy changes the content and medium to be selected. Acquisitive promotion requires external media; retentive promotion can use a station's own air or a system's own channels. Competitive promotion wastes time that could be devoted to acquisitive or retentive efforts, and time for promotion usually is scarce.

Overall promotional and marketing strategies have five major aspects to their design:

1. Building program popularity.
2. Generating loyalty that results in extended viewing and listening.
3. Appealing to the entire coverage area.

4. Identifying the specific service with the needs and interests of its community.
5. Developing a competitive position in relation to the other media in the market.

Comprehensive marketing plans covering all five of these objectives are *total identity concepts* and involve collaboration between management, programmers, and promotion personnel in backing a coordinated strategy over a considerable period of time. A station or network's unified approach then is reiterated in all on-air, display, print promotion, and public relations materials; ideally, this effort has a cumulative effect on the audience. Reinforcement through repetition and congruence are the most basic tactics of a comprehensive marketing plan.

Image and Identity

In addition to programs, the development of image or identity in the marketplace is the other principal consideration in broadcast marketing strategy. Unfortunately, the words *image* and *identity* are too often used interchangeably to refer to the character of a network, station, or service as it would like to be perceived by the audience. Marketing experts, however, make a distinction between the two terms: *Identity* is the true nature of the product or service, namely, its programming in the cases of TV, radio, and the web. *Image* is a manufactured and marketed identity. *It is better in the long run to create ways to market a real identity than to struggle with a false image.*

The objective of a branding strategy is to develop long-term audience loyalty to an image that matches a particular broadcaster, cable service, or web site. Elements of image occur in identifiers in thematic concepts, and in music and graphics. The ID is one of the most demanding elements of promotion. It provides the possibility of summing up all the station or service's attributes in a single symbol, a theme, a line of copy, a sound, and attitude, and it has to be communicated to viewers or listeners in as little as 3–5 seconds. A slogan is not enough, especially if there is no differentiation between the service that adopts the phrase and a competitor who does not. Instead, marketing people try to create a *unique selling proposition* that sets one product or service apart from its competitors and communicates most effectively with consumers.

Balancing Priorities

The two main goals of a broadcaster's marketing efforts are to support programs or personalities and to build an overall image. Research has demonstrated the strong impact of a station's overall personality and service to the local community in developing and sustaining audience loyalty. The *umbrella* concept of promotion refers to having a unifying promotional concept that ties together all of a station's or network's identity strategies under a theme, style, and attitude. A unifying concept should be related to community involvement, leadership, or uniqueness of service.

Tying into a network's theme (e.g., NBC's use of "Must See TV") has become less and less satisfactory for station strategy for these reasons: (1) the widening gap between the networks' main strategic objective of increasing prime-time sampling and their affiliates' objective of building local news viewership; (2) the unpredictability of competitive standings among the four largest networks; and (3) the continuing proliferation of new media choices. The best strategy for local broadcasters is to seek a strong local identity designed to exist independent of, but complementary to, network image, within a total marketing plan.

A parallel issue about marketing strategy exists in cable television. Local systems must decide how much emphasis to place on nationally promoted services and how much on building local identity. While the cable networks each seek to build a unique identity, local systems have begun to establish identities that claim credit for the totality of services they offer.

LEGAL CONSTRAINTS ON PROMOTION

Promotion is governed by the legal restrictions on advertising when it is paid but falls into a special classification when it is unpaid (and not traded). The Federal Trade Commission (FTC) is the government agency traditionally responsible for eliminating deceptive advertising practices. Promotional spots on a station's own air involve no payment to anyone, but the same promotional announcements placed on another station's air or in print may be paid advertising. Although promotion obviously is a form of self-advertising, it has never come under the scrutiny of the FTC because no one has seriously attempted to prove that economic injury resulted from on-air promotion.

However, certain promotional and marketing practices can present a minefield for the media practitioner. See the material in Box 1–1 for a delineation of some of the more prevalent concerns.

BOX 1–1 Legal Concerns: Promotional and Marketing

Lotteries

Few legal issues affect only promotion practices; most are shared by all producers (copyright) or other businesses (fraud). One area of unique legal concern to broadcasters is that of lotteries, because many states continue to prohibit the advertising of privately run or charity lotteries but have declared lotteries otherwise legal. Indeed, a special law had to be passed by Congress to permit the reporting of state lottery results on television and radio in the states where they are permitted. Each state determines whether (1) lotteries are legal within state boundaries and (2) whether they can be advertised.

Broadcasting information about a lottery is legal under federal law if the lottery is not prohibited by state law and if either (1) the lottery is conducted by a charitable organization (charitable organizations are those that qualify as tax-exempt under Section 501 of the Internal Revenue Code) or (2) the lottery is conducted by a business where the lottery is "a promotional activity and is clearly occasional and ancillary to the primary business of that organization." Lotteries are legal in most but not all states, but advertising them is more restricted, leaving stations in states permitting lotteries and advertising able to air some contests that are lotteries without penalty and leaving other stations under strong prohibitions.

The manager of a contemporary music format radio station needs to be an expert in what constitutes a lottery. Specifically, any game involving a valuable prize, a just-above-minimal cost for entering the contest (called *consideration*), and random chance (not skill) is a lottery. Deciding whether a contest activity requires skill or random chance is sometimes difficult, as is deciding if an effort reaches the level called *consideration*. Promotion managers should consult station management or legal staff about potential lotteries to learn which laws and station policies apply.

Contests

A *contest* is simply a lottery with one of the three elements missing. Contests may be freely promoted and advertised by all broadcast stations. Common contests are those that involve a valuable prize and chance but no consideration (as in giving concert tickets to the tenth caller) or involve a valuable prize and consideration but require an element of skill rather than chance to win.

Whenever contests are conducted by broadcast stations, care should be taken to assure that the contest is not false, deceptive, or misleading. For example, a contest to win "the keys to a brand-new car" should include the car (unless it's clearly stated that only the keys are being awarded as a prize). Specific elements of all contests that should be disclosed to potential contestants include (1) how to enter, (2) entry deadlines, (3) when the prize will be awarded, (4) how the winner will be selected, and (5) tie-breaking procedures. Station contests that are not broadcast to the public are not covered by these rules. For example, sales department contests among account executives or clients may be pure lotteries and are restricted only by fair practices and station policies. Finally, whenever a winner of a contest (listener, viewer, salesperson, or client) is awarded more than $600 in prizes, the station must file a form 1099 with the IRS, on which the station reports the prize as income for the winner.

Sales Practices

Any practice that is illegal or unethical in selling goods or services—such as systematically discounting for certain buyers among competing companies—also is illegal in selling broadcast time. Federal laws relating to sales practices can be enforced by the FTC and the FCC.

Federal law explicitly enjoins broadcasters and networks from unfair trading practices in the sale of time. The shift from prepublished station rate cards to flexible patterns of time pricing (since there now are several ratings books from which to choose audience estimates) has blurred time sales transactions. However, many broadcast network discounting practices that traditionally favored major advertisers such as Procter & Gamble (and tended to create monopolies) have been eliminated in recent years due to investigative efforts by the FCC and FTC and the networks' pressing need for increased revenue.

Another sales practice that occasionally affects promotion staffs is that of cooperative advertising in which a manufacturer and a retailer share advertising costs. FTC guidelines on co-op advertising now prohibit a wide variety of practices. Although these regulations apply more directly to sales efforts rather than to promotion, an employee seeking cooperative contracts for public service efforts, for example, should consult the station or system's legal advisor to see if the arrangement falls within the FTC's guidelines.

Copyright

Two other areas of legality relating to promotion are *trademark* protection and *copyright*. Network and station logos, wordmarks, and slogans can be registered as trademarks to receive protection within the United States. Moreover, many attention-getting symbols, characteristic sounds, original program titles, call letters, and distinct personalities may be protected. Advice on what a station can protect is available from the National Association of Broadcasters.

Copyright looms as an important concern to all producers of local materials. Contracts for materials produced by production resource companies spell out the limitations on a station's use of the materials supplied. Generally, the station licensing a program, jingle, or copyrighted slogan may make unrestricted use of it for a designated period of time (such as one year). After that time, the station loses the right to air the materials except under a renewed contract.

All music registered with the American Society of Composers, Authors, and Publishers (ASCAP), Broadcast Music Incorporated (BMI), and the Society of European Stage Authors and Composers (SESAC) is protected from use without payment of fees. Similarly, photographs and drawings not created by station employees must be purchased (or leased) from the copyright holders before they can be incorporated in promotional productions. However, the fair use provision of the Copyright Act allows a station to use a creator's work (a book cover, for example) as illustration in a promotion that advertises that person's presence on a program (a talk show), without seeking explicit permission. Moreover, syndicators of movies and series conditionally incorporate in licensing contracts permission for the stations or networks to use clips and stills in on-air and print promotion to audiences.

Release Forms

Release forms permitting the use of someone's face or voice are required before the likeness may be broadcast in programs or promotional spots. This stipulation applies to both hired actors and members of the public; it does not apply to news footage, celebrities, or public officials. Shots of people participating in large-scale public activities, such as rallies, parades, or fairs, are exempted from the need for releases. Recognizability is the criterion determining when a signed release must be obtained from a casually recorded member of the public (who did not seek recording and was not participating in a mass activity). In producing promotional spots, it must be assumed by management that payment may be required if members of the public are asked to be on camera or to take direction of any kind. Certainly, a release form must be signed, and it is best to check with the company's legal counsel, the Screen Actors Guild (SAG), or the American Federation of Television and Radio Artists (AFTRA).

Hypoing, Phony Testimonials, and Payola

Promotion departments always share ethical responsibility with other employees for the social effects of both the broadcast programs and the commercial advertising messages. Quantities and types of violence and sexual content on program promotions are issues of broad social concern that reach far beyond quibbles about good taste or puffery. They have resulted in loss of audience and sales for media companies. Another fundamental social concern is the long-term effect of mass consumerism projected in broadcast programming when many people in the world do not possess even the necessities of life.

Four practices relating to audience promotion should be considered unethical despite their frequent occurrence: (1) the use of excessive hypoing to boost audience ratings; (2) the creation of erroneous impressions of program content or the conditions for winning prizes; (3) the airing of phony testimonials by celebrities, actors, or members of the general public; and (4) the toleration of payola or plugola.

The rating services that measure audiences actively discourage practices classified as *hypoing*, which constitutes flagrant artificial inflation of the viewing or listening audience to maintain audience allegiance and drive up the measures on which advertising rates are based. Prohibited are on-air mentions of diaries or ratings (particularly in connection with the station's call letters) and the conduct of field surveys (about programming, news, or viewing preferences) during a rating period or the preceding four weeks. Scheduling documentaries or news interviews about ratings during this period is especially discouraged by the rating services. Unfortunately, such prohibitions have little effective force. Creating an erroneous impression in on-air promotion also is unethical. Promotional spots sometimes make misleading suggestions regarding the importance of roles played by celebrities or use titillation as a come-on to series episodes. Using an actor to pose as a celebrity or a public figure is obviously misleading, as is false testimony solicited by producers of spots; both practices may violate FTC regulations. These practices may not harm the public, but they can minimize the effectiveness of other promotional efforts. A more serious concern, for radio stations especially, is misleading information about on-air contests. The FCC requires broadcasters to disclose periodically all the terms of a contest on the air.

Other practices may not be so obvious, however. Public display of microphones and television cameras influence people's responses in subtle ways in "man-on-the-street" interviews, a common means of gaining content for local promotional spots. Most people tend to give positive responses if they anticipate some reward, such as a giveaway. Also such interviews are prone to biases arising from the subject's assumption that any negative responses will be edited out of the broadcast material. Thinking that the wool can be pulled over the public's eyes is generally unproductive; the audience usually sees through contrived testimonies.

The dividing line between promotion and advertising becomes blurred when stations join with advertisers (for example, in a promotion for a rock concert) in any fashion that promotes the interests of both the advertiser and the station. Both radio and television management must be watchful for instances of staff payola and plugola. *Payola* refers to illegal payment for promoting a recording or song on the air. DJs who accept free merchandise or other bribes for playing particular songs are guilty of taking payola. *Plugola* is the variant in which material is included in a program for the purpose of covertly promoting or advertising a product without disclosing that payment of some kind was made. For example, mentioning the name of a restaurant as if it were a personal favorite of the DJ, instead of something he or she has been secretly paid to do, constitutes plugola. The penalties for violating payola or plugola regulations include fines up to $10,000 or a year in jail or both for each offense, and ethical managers will promptly fire DJs when there is evidence that payola or plugola occurred.

The subject of ethics for promotion usually involves questions of personal and social values rather than purely legal issues. Ethics are a matter of concern throughout the industry. Many articles in PROMAX publications have addressed borderline promotional practices and exhorted promotion managers to adopt high standards.

SETTING GOALS

When setting promotional goals, commercial broadcast marketing managers deal with an uncertain commitment on the part of the station's management. Promotion is the most discretionary budget a broadcaster has to manage. Moreover, many broadcast station managers lack adequate training or experience in marketing and design of marketing materials. Therefore, a large part of the marketing manager's efforts must be devoted to educating management and working toward practices that place a high priority on marketing strategy.

At most television and radio stations, the promotion manager reports to the station manager. At stations where promotion receives a high priority, it usually is because the promotion manager serves as a catalytic force among the other department heads involved in the process of setting station goals. The same holds for marketing directors at cable MSOs and systems.

The aggressive promotion executive takes the lead in tying together the views of management, programming, news, sales, public affairs, and public relations by organizing them into a coherent marketing plan. Having involved the department executives in the process, the manager should try to enlist their support before presenting a marketing plan and budget to the station manager. A thorough and businesslike approach is the best way to counter the high degree of subjectivity that typifies reactions to creative concepts. And a marketing plan, to a considerable degree, is a piece of creative work. In the ideal situation, the marketing director, each year, guides the department heads and top management toward agreement on a set of goals for the coming year.

The first goal in promotion and marketing is to define the audience a station, network, or service wants to attract. Commercial broadcasters and cable channels are strongly influenced by the requirements of their advertisers and tend to define their audiences as those that are most salable. Cable operators and cable network executives also must deal with three other groups: the total audience to be wired, the total audience to be sold on pay and basic services, and the many special-interest audiences to be attracted to programming designed to appeal to them. Public broadcasters tend to divide their audiences into three groups: the loyal core group, the occasional viewers or listeners, and the potential but thus far uninvolved growth group.

There are two approaches to defining a salable audience; one is quantitative, the other qualitative. Since no single message can reach everybody, commercial broadcasters attempt the next best thing—reaching the largest number of viewers or listeners consonant with advertisers' needs (the target audience). Commercial television broadcasters usually seek a mass audience measured in gross numbers and demographics. Gross numbers represent total numbers of viewers or listeners; demographics represent the major age groups and sexes.

In radio, stations pursue more specialized mass audiences via such special-interest formats as talk or news and popular music of various types. These larger categories break down into a dozen or more variations—thus popular music becomes adult contemporary, album-oriented rock, beautiful music, and so on. Each of these formats appeals to a specific demographic portion of the mass audience spectrum. Radio stations offer programming to fractions of the mass audience because it is profitable. Some basic cable networks also offer specifically formatted services such as all-news, all-sports, all-weather, all-popular music, or all-children's programming because they target specific, salable demographic groups.

The major objectives of marketing are common to all the profit-making entities involved in broadcasting—service, stability, and profitability. Without service, no broadcaster, no cable operator, and no program supplier can retain the audiences it attracts. Service is the "better mousetrap" that audiences and advertisers want. Stability comes from managing and marketing the service in such a way that it is consistently and competitively appealing to its audiences and, usually, growing.

BEYOND THE MEDIA

Beyond the use of paid advertising media, marketing links up with the great traditions of theatrical showmanship. Publicity demands exploitation—involvement in everything from rock concerts to 10-kilometer runs, from circuses to squiring stars. No textbook can teach promotional exploitation. The best way to learn it from books is to read about P. T. Barnum and the circus or Ziegfeld and vaudeville; read the exploits of the flamboyant flacks of Broadway and Hollywood who turned their shows into front-page events and created stars on assignment. Today's promotions are the direct descendants of the circus parades, carnival come-ons, and personality buildups that have been the stock-in-trade of theatrical showmanship for generations.

Exploitation in broadcasting usually falls within the purviews of both the promotion and the public relations departments. The subject is examined in several chapters of this book. The PROMAX organization and the annual radio workshops of the National Association of Broadcasters give a sense of what broadcasters are doing. The Cable Television Advertising and Marketing Association (CTAM) tells what the cable industry is doing. Trade publications such as *Variety, Cable Marketing,* and *Billboard* often report on special promotions in entertainment and communications. Reading about the exploits of the great showpeople can supply a background and respect for the craft, but imagination and a little craziness are required if one is to create new and effective promotional exploitations.

CHAPTER 2

Designing On-Air, Print, and On-Line Promotion

Susan Tyler Eastman

New marketing managers need to be able to defend their decisions about promotional materials and say why one design is more likely to be more effective than another. Unfortunately, the preferences of general managers, the ideals of news directors, and the inclinations of the art directors frequently clash with the needs of the promotion manager. General managers tend to favor the familiar and prudent in promotional design, but what seems safe to them too often targets the wrong audience or at least too broad an audience for maximum effectiveness. News directors tend to want their important news stories presented with heavy-handed seriousness (and talking heads) rather than with a light, active touch, although humor and sensational action are known to attract more viewers.

But in-house and out-of-house art directors usually present the greatest problems for marketing and promotion managers. Art directors want to win awards for promotional design. Acknowledged or not, there is peer pressure among commercial designers to come up with award-winning ideas. And awards seem more likely to come for trendy themes and innovations in multilayered logos than for hackneyed slogans and very simple logos. Moreover, awards seem to come more often for polished *TV Guide* advertisements than for routine newspaper ads. After all, *TV Guide* is printed on high-quality paper that permits the use of subtle shades of the gray scale and more complex design, and the designer often gets a full page to work with, whereas newsprint is nubby and gray already, limiting the contrast that can be achieved, and few television ads are large enough to stand out from the surrounding commercial clutter. A regular tug-of-war goes on between the understandable desire of the art director for "good design" by artistic criteria and the promotion manager's urgent need for promotional effectiveness.

Figure 2–1   *WEVV's Paid Advertising for a Basketball Game.*

So the criterion the promotion manager must hold out before others is "likely effectiveness with the target audience." And KISS is the paramount idea that always applies to design that is effective for promotion. KISS stands for "Keep it simple and stupid" (or alternately, "Keep it simple, Stupid"). That means valuing *simplicity* over intricacy. That means seeking *easy readability* over clever lettering. That means prizing *tried-and-true themes* that have been shown to work in similar markets over untried promotional concepts. Adhering to KISS means the promotion manager must find the strength to send sample artwork back to the art department whenever "art" has undermined simplicity. Too many billboards and signs easily can be comprehended by a consumer standing in front of them but are incomprehensible at 40 or 60 miles per hour. Many innovative concepts can be decoded with a little thought but will be incomprehensible to most people who merely give them a passing glance. Figure 2–1 exemplifies ready understandability without excess complexity.

No one is obliged to look at promotional advertisements or on-air spots. People won't bother decoding or deciphering some ad they just happen to see. Trade reports estimate that the average person is flooded by some 8,000 commercial messages every day. Why should anyone put effort into figuring out a piece of promotion? It is the obligation of the promoter to make the message come through to a casual glance, despite the lack of attention given to ads and spots.

Of course, original ideas have a place in promotion. Implementing a new idea for a contest or a humorous twist on a plot line for a sitcom spot is vital to keeping promotion exciting for audiences and morale high for the promotion staff. Achieving a *breakthrough* indeed is crucial to advertising success, and the ads that break out of their environment to capture immediate attention win awards and are likely to be highly effective with viewers. And there are some exceptions to the rule that consumers will not make an effort to decode promotional ads: A radio contest may intrigue a teen listener who will call the station to learn what's needed; a sports fan will find the time and channel of the game no matter how confusing the ad. But the day-to-day battle in television promotion revolves around getting people to watch ordinary television shows—particularly the local news and a couple of stripped series that already are familiar to most viewers from previous years on a network. At the network level, it revolves around prime-time shows competing with similar shows on other channels. The practice of effective promotion is more a matter of efficiency and productivity than extraordinary innovation. The ability to capture the essence of a routine news story or the twist in a familiar sitcom plot is the skill of value to a promotion manager. And this is a skill that novices can learn.

EVERYTHING COUNTS

The first rule of the TV screen is that nothing is there by accident. Everyone is aware of the millions of dollars spent in producing major television commercials. Every second of time and every frame of a spot's design have been scrutinized for maximum impact and maximum appeal. No details of background or foreground or sound are left uncontrolled. Sets are built, costumes are constructed, hair is sprayed and faces painted to create exactly the effect wanted. And viewers know all this, perhaps unconsciously, but they recognize the carefully structured nature of commercial messages. On-air spots touting programs (*promos*) are merely more commercial messages, usually produced in a shorter time with far smaller budgets. Their ultimate goal is to make money for the station (or network), and viewers recognize that fact. Therefore, program spots must be constructed as carefully as their competition—the commercial spots—to have a chance of effectiveness. Every detail must contribute to the desired effect or be eliminated. Saying "that's close enough" is rarely good enough to win the battle for viewers. Visual and auditory control are the essence of effective promotion.

PRIMARY TOOLS

Logos, wordmarks, and themes are three of the tools promotion uses daily. A *logo* is the *graphic identifier* of a network or station, a two-dimensional design that represents the name of the company in abbreviated form. Nowadays, logos appear

WHDH-TV

Lifetime®
Television for Women™

Figure 2–2   *The TV 7, CBS Eye Logo, and the Lifetime® Wordmark. The Lifetime logo is the exclusive property of Lifetime Entertainment and is used with permission.*

on-screen in large size between programs and a "bug" in the corner of the screen during local shows to remind viewers where they are in an increasingly cluttered television environment. Logos are used on giveaways like T-shirts and pens; and for the major networks, they have become important brand identifiers to be protected from duplication and imitation because of their potential for worldwide recognition.

A local television station or cable network may have a logo but is more likely to make use of a *wordmark*, a particular way of writing the station's channel number or company's name, and it has the same copyright protection as a logo and serves the same communication function. The smart television station adopts an easy-to-read wordmark that works in print and on-the-air, whether blown up large or squeezed very small, whether reproduced in black and white or in color, whether in motion or still. It then uses that wordmark constantly in one standardized form to keep its name in front of potential viewers and advertisers. One failing at some stations occurs because of management's refusal to settle on only one wordmark. Having more than one design for the way the company's name is printed (or stated) means that ads and promos do not reinforce each other; a different way of writing the company name appears to the casual eye of disinterested viewers to represent a different company. Figure 2–2 illustrates a highly successful network logo, a typical station logo, and an effective cable network wordmark.

When used on the air, logos and wordmarks usually are animated and accompanied by a soundbed. The on-air version of the network, station, or service's identifier is called a *signature*. An effective signature is thus an enhanced version of a two-dimensional logo or wordmark incorporating motion and sound but simultaneously triggering recall of the basic logo or wordmark.

Reinforcement is a primary goal of promotion. The name Disney, for example, always appears in exactly the same form, whether the reference is to The Disney Channel, a Disney movie, or some other Disney subsidiary. Advertising research has shown repeatedly over the decades that seeing or hearing a single message rarely gets through to anyone; it rarely changes behavior. The traditional rule of thumb is that it takes at least three repetitions to affect behavior. That means the same invitation to watch a program needs to air repeatedly to have a chance to increase viewing. It also means that signatures must be consistent to have optimum impact. Whether used on stationery, trucks, bumper sticker, billboards, on the air, or in newspapers, the logo or wordmark should remain consistent in design (and color when possible).

The third tool of promotion, *themes*, are phrases that characterize a station's programming, and they play a big part in on-air identification and image creation. Radio stations tend to call their themes by the more casual name of *slogans* because radio stations tend to change them nearly as often as one changes socks! New owners, new formats, and bored announcers generally want new slogans (or mottoes) to say on the air.

Television stations more commonly commit to a good theme for the long haul, and some of the best-known stations have had a single theme (or variants thereupon) for decades. WCCO in Minneapolis/St. Paul, for example, has long been known as the "Good Neighbor." "WGN is Chicago" has been employed for 40 years. KMOX in St. Louis uses the theme "The Voice of St. Louis" to embody its commitment to its community. WRTV in Indianapolis called itself "The News Leader" or "Your number one source for news" for many years. In Washington, D.C., WUSA has consistently used "The one and only TV 9" to incorporate its channel identifier.

On the broad international level, NBC is attempting to brand itself as "The Network of the Olympics." Domestically, it is attempting to position its Thursday night programs as "Must See TV." Correspondingly, the ABC network has long marketed "TGIF" to brand its Friday night programming. When they work well, such themes become permanently embedded in the public's image of a media company and in the self-perception of the staff. Of course, to be successful, a theme must capture an essence of the station or network's programming. A disjuncture between the programming and the image the theme attempts to create always will be unsuccessful.

Once management decides on a logo or wordmark and theme, they need to be embodied in virtually every piece of the daily on-air and print promotion of the station or network. Promos, teases, and tags are the everyday tools of on-air promotion. A *promo* is a short preproduced spot that usually urges viewers to tune in to a particular episode of a show. A promotional *tease* is a brief live spot intended to lure viewers to a newscast that usually shows an anchor reciting a bite from the night's highlighted story. Typically located toward the end of a promo or tease, or recited over end credits, a *tag* is a line that gives the crucial information of *where* and *when* the program or newscast can be seen. A *bumper* is a very short message intended to "bump" viewers or listeners into the next segment or program.

Historically, the information in bumpers often was stuck at the end of preproduced and reused spots and, in the early years of television and radio, was merely a vocal line saying something like "Stay tuned for the next episode of X." But promotion has become more sophisticated, and bumpers and tags more often are incorporated within promos and repeated both visually and auditorily so that viewers cannot miss the messages. The "where" and "when" of promotion are so vitally important that they have been called the *essential messages* of promotion. What channel a TV program is on—in other words, the number *identifier* used by the station—and what *time* the show begins generally are more important to implant in the viewer or listener's memory than any program's name. Big billboards that scream the name of a show or its stars and bury the channel location and time of the show largely are wasted advertising. They make money for the billboard company but do little to lure viewers or listeners to the station. Because the public is flooded with so many commercial messages, the best the promotion manager can hope to do is to get someone to remember when and where a desirable show comes on television. If the viewer remembers vaguely that "tonight at 7:30 there's a show I want to see on Channel 6," the job of the promotion manager has been accomplished. That viewer need not recall the program's name. If the viewer remembers only the program title, then a hunt for the right channel and time becomes necessary, a second step when a good promo would have left a memory of that information. Effective topical promotion focuses more on the where and when of programs than on the titles of shows.

The radio promotion manager and the creative services director of a narrowcast cable network have somewhat different problems from the promotion director of a television station. In radio and cable, there may be no specific programs (or very few) to lure listeners or viewers to, so the message to convey is the *format* of the station or network (all-news, top 40, all-shopping, all movies, etc.) and the *identifier* of the service—which is, in the case of a radio station, some permutation of its dial position, and in the case of a cable network, its name. Radio stations typically use identifiers like X100 or Magic 101 that combine some hint of their formats along with their dial positions. Even people who have never heard of X100, for example, are unlikely to think that the station is all-news, easy listening, or classical music. Qs, Zs, Xs, and so on are a convention for rock formats targeting young listeners that most people unconsciously recognize. And the 100 represents an approximation of an FM dial position, somewhere between 99.5 and 100.5.

Unlike television and radio stations, networks lack a promotable channel number. The affiliates of broadcast networks have different channel numbers in different markets, and most cable networks have the vexing problem of having different channel positions on many of the nearly 12,000 different cable systems. Networks therefore are left with only their names, themes, and program titles to promote. With the exception of a few regional pay services, broadcast and cable networks are national entities and their promotion must be suited to use in hundreds of markets, whereas stations (and cable systems) are local entities and have local identifiers. Most often, cable focuses on telling subscribers (and potential subscribers) how much good programming there is to watch on cable, trying to build viewer satisfaction so that the monthly bill is paid when it arrives. Most cable operators reserve 25 percent of their availabilities for local promotion of network shows, image messages, and spots touting service advantages (for example, discounts or other specials).

MEDIA FOR PROMOTION

Promotion make uses of "free" internal media as well as paid or traded external media. *Internal* refers to spots airing on the station's *own* air. On-air on *another* station, or any kind of print, is *external* to the station because it is paid advertising (or traded media that must be reported to the Internal Revenue Service by their dollar value). The internal medium has the terrific advantage of reaching current viewers or listeners via the most effective means ever devised—*on-air television.* And messages can be repeated until they get through to viewers or listeners. However, it is a great mistake to think of the station's own air as "free." Every promo that airs displaces a commercial message. Instead of income for the station, airing a promo represents a loss of revenue. Management is well aware of the importance of airing promos to attract and maintain audiences, but the wise promotion manager understands that positive value (in increased ratings or a better image) must result from the collective impact of that airtime. It is too valuable to treat casually.

The function of external promotion is to reach people who are not now the station's viewers or listeners or subscribers. The ability to attract *new* audiences or acquire *new* subscribers justifies the cost of external media. Whenever possible, broadcast stations make considerable use of trades with the opposite electronic medium, and co-owned AM/FM/TV stations have an advantage in the ease with which they can cross-promote each other. But all local electronic media utilize each other when permitted. Television stations can effectively promote their newscasts to evening commuters listening to car radios; radio stations use TV spots to reinforce a new format or changed call letters (the two often go together). At the same time, the print media play special roles. Newspapers are ideal for promoting sporting events and news specials because sports fans read the sports pages and committed news viewers tend to consume printed as well as electronic news. However, a quarter-page in a local newspaper easily can cost as much as $800—and that's just for one small ad for one day. A national newspaper such as *The New York Times*, utilized primarily by major broadcast and new cable networks, has the staggering price of $70,000 for a full-page ad for one day.

TV Guide and other program guides, as well as the weekly TV supplements in newspapers, are ideal sites for promoting entertainment. Just as a supermarket display is perfect for selling a food product because shoppers are looking for ideas for meals (called *point-of-purchase* marketing), so a television program guide is perfect for luring viewers to a program. Program guides tend to be left near where viewers sit to watch TV, and people use them (especially older viewers and women) to locate the channels and times of programs. Thus, viewers' attention is open to being captured by an intriguing ad for a program they may not have intended to watch.

Figure 2–3   *Sticker from KKBQ-AM/FM's Morning Show Called Q-Zoo. KKBQ/FM. Used with permission.*

City magazines—the ones named after a particular big city—as well as *People* and its ilk also are good locations for ads for television programs. Their readership is very broad, and the topic of television shows is highly popular, thus creating a positive environment for ads for specific shows. But only on rare occasions can stations afford the thousands of dollars one such ad costs.

Billboards are popular in areas with extensive commuter traffic, provided the station's target audience happens to be commuters. Top 40 stations targeting the young listener generally avoid the expense of billboards in favor of sponsoring concerts and outdoor activities of appeal to their listeners. But broadly appealing morning shows on radio, as well as news-oriented radio and television stations, are well suited to billboard advertising. Billboards are part of the larger class of *outdoor* advertising that includes signs on buildings, buses, subways, trains, cabs, window posters, and so on. Effective communication via a billboard or another outdoor medium takes account of the fact that people generally see the messages when they are in motion (either the bus moves or the car drives by), and therefore the content should be no more than eight words (counting a graphic as a word). KISS is absolutely essential in effective outdoor communication (Figure 2–3).

Bumper stickers belong to the class of items called *giveaways* in the media business. Because they are relatively cheap (perhaps $2,000 for 50,000 of them in two colors), they can be handed out at concerts, races, and local fairs; passed out to children and adults touring the station; and dispensed on any other occasion when a giveaway has a chance to make a small positive impression on the recipient. Inexpensive pens, pencils, balloons, and keychains imprinted with the station's logo or wordmark serve a similar purpose.

A huge range of items from inexpensive coffee mugs and soda-can huggies, to moderately expensive T-shirts and baseball caps, to very expensive briefcases and windbreakers are available from companies who will be happy to imprint them with the station's logo or wordmark. The daily mail inundates promotion staff with glossy brochures of imprintable merchandise that can be purchased for contest prizes or giveaways, but the neophyte promotion manager should be wary of expending too much of the year's budget for such items. The more expensive items may be useful for giving to selected advertisers either as reminders to purchase ads (a desk calendar or coffee mug usually serves this prompting purpose effectively) or as rewards for exceptionally large purchases (a briefcase or jacket, perhaps). KISS and reinforcement are the rule in designing such items: Use the standard logo or wordmark, not a variant; use the station's established colors whenever possible; and don't clutter up a small item with more than a very simple message; otherwise, the item probably has very little impact.

The newest external promotional medium is the web site, usually a mix of programming and promotion. While a web site can provide many kinds of information to potential viewers and advertisers, it should serve primarily as a vehicle for promoting the desired image. Secondarily, it may be a tool for tune-in promotion and may have a tertiary function of supplying background information on the network, station, or system and its staff. While the Internet may someday provide full-fledged and distinct mass-audience programs that compete directly with stations and cable systems, today it is best thought of as a new tool for promotion. Streaming video and sound on the Internet are tools for promoting programs carried on the broadcast station or cable network. For example, ZDTV on-line stresses its ZDTV cable channel as part of its web service.

Industry experience has revealed some guidelines for effective promotion via the Internet. For example, the first frames of a web site should be designed as carefully as an on-air promo or print ad to attract on-line users and to convey the station's image. The design should avoid commencing with a long list of links because they readily can take the user *away* from the station's site and primary message. Instead, an effective site begins with the station's logo or wordmark and theme and, in graphic fashion, supplies a few links to pages that each open with a variant on the station's overall image promotion (for example, see www.wrtv.com). Only later move to details about some aspect of the station, such as talent bios, program listings, station history, and so on. In other words, no matter where the user goes, the station's identifier and theme should stand out, and only after going a long way into a site should the user be invited to link away from the station (to a network, a producer, a sports team, etc.). An effective web page strives for congruence of color, typeface (fonts), graphics, and sound with the station's programming and the rest of its promotion. No matter how an Internet user scrolls through a station's web site, the logo, theme, and "feel of the station" should be constantly on-screen.

BASIC MESSAGE CONCEPTS

In designing promotional messages, as noted in Chapter 1, it is essential to distinguish between tune-in and image promotion. However, another distinction is similar but not identical—that between generic and specific promotion. *Generic* (or "general") promotion may be about station or network image or it may be about a program, but it is not tied to any particular episode or any particular airdate. A radio or TV spot that urges viewers to "Watch *Rosie O'Donnell* every day at 4:00 on Channel 6" is generic. In contrast, a *specific* (or episodic or tune-in) spot will urge viewers to "Catch the Judge breaking his gavel today at 4:30 on Channel 8." Much of radio promotion, when not tied to contests, is generic because it promotes the overall format of the station. Outdoor billboards and bumper stickers, for example, claiming that a station airs "all the hits, all the time" or "all the news, all the time" are generic promotion.

A specific promo, however, is tied to a particular episode (or movie or game) to be shown on a specified date and can be used for only a short time, whereas a generic message is for the whole program (or whole station or service) and can be reused over a long period of time. Billboards, for example, are inherently generic; newspaper ads usually are specific. Experts agree that specific promotion for programs is much more likely to be effective on broadcast television and should be utilized whenever possible. KABC-TV in Los Angeles, for example, airs its *Oprah* billboard daily to list upcoming topics in that afternoon's show. While wise promotion managers will devote most of their activity to producing and scheduling specific promotion, having a few generics tucked away for emergencies makes sense. Once in a great while, a brief power outage, a camera malfunction, or some other technical disruption can be turned from (promotional) disaster by hauling out a stash of generics for the shows.

Cable television, in contrast, has effectively used generic promotion and often cannot create specifics. Major cable networks appear on thousands of different systems with varied channel numbers, and their programs even appear simultaneously in different time zones. Therefore, they cannot promote the "where" and "when" of their programming as concretely as broadcasters. Nonetheless, specific promotion about programs is probably more valuable than generic promotion wherever possible.

Another distinction in television is in the structure of the promo or ad. On the air, a promo can be a single or a multiple. A *single* is a spot promoting just *one* TV program. The networks create many singles for their new fall series, and local stations acquiring new syndicated shows usually promote them in singles until most of the audience has a chance to become familiar with their presence and location and time. News, entertainment, and sport specials also are promoted in singles much of the time.

In contrast, already familiar programs and dayparts often are promoted within *multiple* spots, advertising two or more shows. In particular, an evening's two-hour lineup of four situation comedies commonly appears in one multiple, and the spot typically ends with a billboard listing the titles and times of each show in order of appearance on the air. Such multiples serve to promote the various shows, link them together, and teach the audience what time they appear. Another strategy is to link a new show with an established hit by pairing them in a *double* (a multiple of just two shows). Multiples are the primary way much of the audience learns the order and times of programs, especially in the fall when network (and station) schedules change. Indeed, the scheduling of promos throughout a daypart should follow the order of the program lineup and thus painlessly teach the audience when shows are scheduled. Print advertising sometimes employs a kind of ad comparable to a multiple: Called a *stack ad*, a single guide or newspaper advertisement can include photographs, titles, and times for several programs succeeding each other on a network. Such stack ads are common in *TV Guide*, and the shows may be piled vertically or spread horizontally. Sometimes a local program, such as the 11:00 late news, appears at the end of an ad stacking two or more network programs, showing viewers the order of the lineup and visually linking the local program to the network programs. The goal of multiples and stack ads is to promote the flow of programming to minimize tune-out.

Rosser Reeves, an advertising genius of the 1950s and 1960s, coined the phrase *unique selling proposition* (USP), which has since embedded itself in the practice of advertising and promotion. A *USP*, generally translated nowadays as "unique selling point," refers to something that can be said about a program (or station or network) that cannot readily be claimed about its competitors. For example, most cable networks occupy narrow niches, making it easy for them to claim that they have unique content, while the broadcast networks (and some cable networks like USA and TNT) try to offer something for everyone, so their claims generally are tied to individual programs or nights of shows. A television station can promote the fact that it is the only station in its market with a 10:00 newscast, or the only one carrying a recent off-network hit, or the only one with the most advanced weather radar. Radio stations usually hold up their formats as USPs: "WXXX, the station with the hottest hits" or "the station with soul-country," and so on. Finding that USP and embodying it in promotion is one key to successful promotion. Ideally, a theme should state a station's overall USP, and every promo about any program should emphasize what is special about that program: "WXXX, always first with the news" and "Watch *Friends*, with the relationships you treasure."

A related, and sometimes identical, idea in practice is the concept of a *benefit*. Promotion needs to be consumer driven, not product driven. An effective piece of promotion usually tells viewers or listeners what they will get out of tuning in to the promoted program. What they will get typically is something relatively mundane, such as an opportunity to laugh a lot, an opportunity to be first to know what's happening in the city, or an opportunity to hear the hits before listeners to competing stations. Whatever the precise benefit, conveying it in promotion tells the viewers what they will get out of watching (or listeners from listening) and answers the not-very-hidden question of "why *should* I [do what you want]?" Merely telling viewers that "this show is the greatest" is an example of telling what the product's value is to the station, hardly a matter of interest to consumers. They want to know what benefit from viewing the show will come to them.

Finally, all promotion coming from a single source needs to be *congruent*. In other words, each item of promotion needs to reinforce the other items. Just as the various pages in a web site need to promote the source in the same general way, so billboards, bumper stickers, and on-air spots need to be congruent with each other. They need to use the same colors, same typefaces, same messages. To fail at congruence is to waste the opportunity for mutual reinforcement. Because the messages of small media companies easily can be lost in the clutter of media communications inundating an audience, sticking to a simple design with the same colors, same typeface, and same theme is prudent. But national media entities that already are well established have more freedom to vary what they do, although a high degree of congruence appears in their promotion. Analyze the on-air messages of the cable network MTV for an excellent example of congruence of a very modern video sort. No matter how many variations of the network logo viewers see, they all share a common essence that "reads" MTV, and that congruence also appears in the network's print advertising. MTV has successfully utilized variations on the basic design of its signature without compromising consistency of impact.

DESIGN CONTENT

Artists and psychologists have long studied the movement of the human eye as it scans a two-dimensional design. While artists often sought complexity and impact, psychologists wanted to understand cognition and the behavior of the

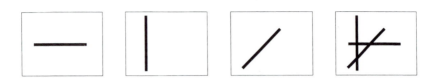

Figure 2–4   *Simple Graphic Vectors (Horizontal, Vertical, Diagonal, and Combined).*

brain. Decades of study in this area have led to elaborate eye-tracking equipment for research, but the designer of promotion can use simpler methods in implementing messages. The first lesson from history is that organization matters. The layout of the elements in any design is crucial to the movement of the eye and thus to what is seen and not seen by the reader or viewer. Factors such as the relative size of elements, the colors of elements, the contrast between background and foreground or lettering, the amount of white space, and the vectors incorporated into a design profoundly affect what is seen and thus what has at least a chance of impacting the viewer's behavior.

It is pretty obvious that elements on a TV screen or in a print ad that are larger than others are more likely to capture attention. Designers often designate larger items as foreground and smaller as background elements, though this distinction makes little sense when speaking of something as small, for example, as a bumper sticker or a baseball cap. Nonetheless, the rule of size clearly holds: Bigger probably snares more attention than smaller. It also is obvious that bright, strong colors attract attention more than dull ones or ones that contrast poorly with the background against which they occur. Solid masses of white space (or black space, for that matter) can be used by the designer of a message to steer the eye in a particular direction. But the most useful concept for understanding how the eye tracks, and thus how to *control* how the eye tracks, may be vectors. As explained by scholars of video design such as Herbert Zettl, based on the work of scholars of two-dimensional print such as Arnheim and others, a *vector* is a direction of force. Because all elements on a TV screen or in a print advertisement are presumed to be present on purpose (not by accident as in real life), any appearance of a vector influences how the viewer's eye moves.

Fundamentally, vectors have three directions: horizontal, vertical, and diagonal. A set of three scribbled lines inside some framed shape (like a TV screen) on a piece of paper or chalkboard will easily demonstrate their relative strengths (see Figure 2–4). In attracting your eye's attention, you can see that a horizontal line is weaker than a vertical line, and a vertical line is weaker than a diagonal line, though the effort is minimized when one line bisects another.

Figure 2–5   *Examples of Index Vectors.*

The relative strength of vectors is a visual phenomenon that can be used by designers of promotion in creating on-air promos and print ads. Its wide acceptance can be recognized in the common tactic of slanting the radio or TV station identifier on many billboards and bumper stickers. Slanting one word or line out of many gives that line a kind of dynamism or "off-centeredness" that grabs attention. The fourth example in Figure 2–4 shows the impact of a little slant in such a mundane thing as a line.

Another distinction important to understanding how vectors function is that they come in three main types, usually called *graphic* (or line) vectors, *index* (or pointing) vectors, and *motion* vectors. *Graphic vectors* are those that have the appearance of horizontal, vertical, or diagonal lines. They may be in the background and thus broken and interfered with by foreground lines. Or graphic vectors may constitute most or all of the forces in an entire advertisement. Consider, for example, a web page consisting of a logo and a lot of lines of print in various lettering fonts. Each line of print is a separate horizontal graphic vector. The logo also is a graphic vector, but it probably is not horizontal. Probably, it has one main directional thrust (if circular, that's a variant on diagonal).

Most vectors in print ads (and on the air) are graphic, but occasionally one has the characteristics of a *index vector*: It points. Clearly, an arrow or pointing finger aims the viewer's attention in a specific direction. The screens in Figure 2–5 illustrate index vectors with different directions of force. It is easy to see how the diagonal index vector rivets one's attention, and it would even if there were other elements on the same screen.

Pointing vectors set up the expectation that what is at the end of the index vector is important. The eyes in a face and the nose on the human profile are thought to point, and so do many other design constructions that may or may not be easy to name. For example, a band of color in a rainbow that narrows at one end can be seen to point toward something; a sloping arm in a photograph may seem to point either up or down; a contrasting necktie or a partly revealed white shirt inside a dark jacket sometimes appears to point like an arrow to some other part of an advertisement. Ideally, designers use index vectors to force the viewer's eye to the essential message—the where and when of the program. In Figure 2–6, a reader can see about five main horizontal vectors, a few weaker vertical vectors (minimized by the background stripes), and two strong index vectors created by Bachman's tie and Carrigan's blouse that draw the eye powerfully toward the NBC News and WHO-TV 13 lines (themselves powerful because of their diagonal placement).

The third type of vector comes from motion, and as all television and movie viewers will recognize, *motion vectors* are far more potent in capturing attention than any kind of line or arrow on a screen, and motion gives on-air video a big advantage over any printed advertisement. The energy of motion confers most of what makes television such a powerful communications medium. However, motion vectors can be horizontal and thus relatively weak (but still stronger than any graphic and index vectors); they can be vertical and dominate over any horizontal motions; or they can be diagonal (or come toward the viewer, thus also enlarging in size), and overpower the rest of what is on the screen. While motion vectors are always stronger than index vectors, which are in turn stronger than graphic vectors, inside each ad or spot the motion (or index or graphic) can be predominantly horizontal, vertical, or diagonal and thus have varying degrees of strength. Analyzing a promo for a television sitcom (for example, *Frasier*) in terms of vectors will show how the star achieves overwhelming prominence—even in an appearance lasting just seconds.

It is important to understand that every promo, every ad, and every web page has vectors. They may be simple or complex, weak or strong, reinforced or minor, but they are there. The fewer the items on the screen or in an ad, the more powerfully the few vectors present affect the viewer's or reader's eye.

Moreover, vectors function differently in designs of different shapes. One conception of a design will not serve in different media, because they all have different *aspect ratios*. Magazine pages normally are oriented vertically—they are taller than they are wide. TV screens, in contrast, are horizontally oriented and wider than they are tall. Presently, any television screen has a ratio of 3 units high to 4 units wide (high-definition television will alter the proportions to 9 high by 16 wide). Billboards, on the other hand, are very horizontal and rectangular but variable in proportions; some are less rectangular than others, but none is as nearly square as a regular TV screen's shape. Contrast the typical billboard with the typical bumper sticker; the latter is wholly horizontal (and skinny), usually in a one to four ratio. The standard bumper sticker is 3 inches high by 12 inches long, a very different proportion than that of billboards (more commonly a 1 to 1.5 ratio). The important point about aspect ratio is that the placement of the elements in each medium must vary, just to fit in or fill up the space, and thus the vectors become altered.

Figure 2–6 *Joint NBC/affiliate News Anchor Ad. WHO-TV. Used with permission.*

Figure 2-7   *Example of the Edge Effect.*

Another, related, concept in two-dimensional design is the *edge effect*. This term refers to the tug out-of-the-frame created by placing any item too close to (or touching) an edge. Figure 2–7 illustrates the difference between placing a block of type or a logo (or a rabbit) too close to the screen or ad edge or, for comparison, positioning it well away from the edge. (The hypothetical block of type in Figure 2–7 is shown with a rectangular shape, but it could be any size or shape.) The closer the elements are to each other in an ad, the more they seem to relate to each other; when too far apart, they seem unrelated, and the eye does not travel easily from one to the other. The larger or more colorful the item in relation to the other elements in the ad or on the screen, the more powerful is the positive or negative effect.

An item near a frame edge creates a vector that pulls the eye away from the rest of the content and off the frame. The purpose of a piece of promotion normally is to emphasize the essential message, but the presence of an edge effect completely distracts the reader or viewer and pulls the eye away from the essential message.

Keeping the preceding guideline in mind, try the exercise in Box 2–1.

Promo Environment

Several characteristics of the environment in which a promo is placed seem to affect its potential impact on viewers. Promos commonly appear in *pods* (breaks inside a program) along with commercials, public service announcements, and occasional news headlines. Long considered important in advertising sales, a promo's *location* inside the pod may affect its impact. In Europe, some advertisers pay a premium for last position, presuming that "recency" matters to impact. In America, however, many advertisers refuse the last position for their spots, wanting instead to be first or in the middle of a pod. How much it matters where pro-

BOX 2–1   Creative Exercise

As an exercise, prepare the following 12 items on a white background:

- A logo in three sizes.
- A theme in three sizes.
- A profiled face in three sizes.
- Several lines of type in three different sizes.

Cut out all 12 items. Then draw the outlines of a billboard, a bumper sticker, and a magazine advertisement. Arrange any 4 of your 12 items within each of three shapes. Discuss the changes in types and strengths of vectors and any edge effects that occur with different positions of the elements.

mos are located is not clear from research, but the networks traditionally have followed different patterns. UPN places a large percentage of its promos at the beginning of its pods (thus favoring primacy), while Fox places more than half its promos at the close of pods (favoring recency). The traditional big three tend to place their promos in the middle of pods, surrounding them with commercials. Contracts with affiliates often give them last position in one or more breaks, making those positions unavailable to the networks.

A similar variable is the promo's *position* within a program schedule. Promos can be scheduled in the breaks within shows, in the end-credit segment along with producers' and actors' credits, or in a transition between programs. Because the networks generally want a smooth flow from one program into the next, fewer commercials and promos appear within transitions these days. All have been moved into the breaks inside the programs or to the end-credit break.

Because advertising messages long have been thought to be less effective when surrounded by too many other messages, promos also probably benefit from a *less cluttered* environment. Just how many ads, promos, and other messages is too many is not known, and the trend in television is to cluster more and more short ads and promos in the breaks within programs. Radio stations, however, are able to vary in structuring nonprogram material: Some air long sweeps of songs, followed by long breaks containing many ads and promos, much like television networks and stations; others air just two or three songs and then two or three ads, and more songs, and more ads, and so on. Still others stick a prerecorded promo between a pair of songs and save the breaks for commercials. It is likely that this third pattern most benefits promotion because each spot has a better chance of capturing full attention.

Finally, one last variable that probably affects the potency of promos is their *distance* from the program being promoted. Promos that tout the next show ("Coming up next is X") or the next episode in the same show ("Tune in next week when . . .") probably are far better triggers of viewer behavior than promos for shows airing in two or three weeks. Getting viewers to stay tuned for the next show in a sequence when they already are watching television is a far easier task than getting them to remember to watch on a given night in the future. However, a substantial proportion of promos are for programs scheduled two or more weeks away because their value lies in building excitement for an upcoming event. Such promos signal the importance of an upcoming movie or special by far-in-advance notice of the event. The final episode of *Seinfeld* received extensive promotion, beginning months before the airdate to raise the number of homes-using-television (HUTs) far higher than would have occurred with a regular episode.

Print Environment

Ads in newspapers need to be large enough to grab attention. Too small is the kiss of death, as is too gray. High contrast, using large sections of solid black or white (or even gray) often stand out better from a welter of other advertising and news text. Indeed, designers of print ads sometimes shift to *reversal* printing (white lettering and images on a black background as opposed to the more common black letters and black/gray images) to stand out in a program guide or newspaper environment. While most newspaper ads are vertical rectangles, ESPN often employs strips across the bottom of sports pages as a way of reaching readers in nonstandardized fashion. Such ads run the full width of the newspaper's page and are wide enough to contain the essential message as well as artwork, so they catch the reader's attention.

In *TV Guide*, full-page ads attract the eye and can be powerful promotion. Very small ads, however, can be effective, provided the promotion manager gives the audience time to learn to recognize the source of the messages, and no other media competitor uses the same size and style. TBS, for example, promotes in very small ads in program guides, using the smallest size sold. The cable network has standardized on tiny vertical rectangles and stuck with one shape and a narrow range of design for enough years that readers can easily identify a TBS ad. An habitual design that becomes the expected pattern for promotional messages can help a station's (or network's) message stand out from the clutter of messages.

PACING AND COMPLEXITY

MTV had a terrific impact on commercial artwork for advertising and consequently promotion in the 1980s. Its first effect was to greatly speed up the pace of commercials (and promos), increasing the amount of content in a short period of time. Wide adoption of fast-paced messages contributed to shortening commercial messages on television from 30 seconds to 15 seconds in the 1980s, and many promos on broadcast television now are just a few seconds in length. Promotion managers have found that a very brief image of a familiar character with star power is enough to remind viewers to watch a favorite show. Thus two phenomena—the increased pace of content and the need to occupy less saleable time—have combined to shorten many promos.

Cable television has stuck to the 30-second spot, however. The cable networks typically keep the whole transition between programs for themselves (explaining why there is no local system identifier between shows on cable), and the networks usually allot a total of 2 minutes per hour to local systems to carry local advertising and promotion. Those 2 minutes usually come as 1 minute in the first pod in each half hour, and half the time normally is used for a 30-second promo, not shorter ones, because most cable systems lack the technical ability to subdivide the time into 10 seconds and 15 seconds.

When targeting very young viewers, art directors recently have adopted other aspects of MTV-like design that are byproducts of advanced computer capability. For example, *morphing* (changing one image into another as viewers watch) and *multilayering* in designs (building up images consisting of semi-transparent layers) have become recognized conventions of video. While morphing has a comic or horror aspect and appears more commonly in commercials than promos, multilayering has been valuable to add a sense of depth and complexity to images. Computer software permits the various layers to move independently and to spread splashes of color or amorphous shapes across the boundaries between words, photographs, and graphics. Some multilayering in advertising messages is as simple as placing a single object over another, accomplished merely by chromakeying people and titles over a different background. But using sophisticated design programs, art directors can create other kinds of multilayering that involve five or more layers of content, usually in motion and sweeping across, between, and inside the main design. While some older viewers may find very complex advertising designs require decoding (and thus too much exertion to grasp), young viewers usually discern the essential message with little effort. It follows that the style of design selected for promotion must take account of the target audience, defined in terms of age, gender, and lifestyle.

Because network television programs target very broadly, seeking local audiences in the hundreds of thousands and nationwide audiences in the tens of mil-

Figure 2–8   *Shared ID, Promoting the Station (WRTV) and the Program (Good Morning Indiana).*

lions, their artwork must easily reach all kinds of viewers. When there is disagreement between art directors and promotion managers, focus groups can provide answers. Generally speaking, if the target audience is broad, simple and straightforward designs are best. If the target audience is narrow and has special characteristics (like young people, for example), then cutting-edge design may be highly effective.

Another consideration that profoundly affects design is the length of time the promotion manager has for the message. A 15-, 20-, or 30-second spot has the time to develop an idea. A typical series spot begins with a come-on (the *hook*), which is followed by a short scene with lines of dialogue, and ends with the punch line accompanied by the essential message. Promos for network situation comedies often follow this pattern. In promos for movies or dramas, bits of two or more scenes might pass the viewer's eyes, accompanied by a mix of sound effects and dialogue. Such promos convey the content of the program slowly to give the viewer time to get emotionally involved, and they are generally classified as *soft-sell* promos.

When only 5 or 10 seconds are available to promo in, the message must be sold hard and fast, and "the message" always consists of the essential message of where and when. Called *hard-sell* promos, very brief spots generally show the mer-

Karen Rowe   Kevin Doran   Elissa Lynn

est motion and often sound effects rather than words, accompanied by voice-over narration that tells what the program is and, most important, paralleled by on-screen text, gives the essential where-and-when message. When networks combine several programs in one multiple spot, some segments may be very hard sell and others less so (typically, the new and thus unfamiliar programs get more time).

When local stations show their station identification and give part of the screen over to promoting a program (in a corner box or split screen), they are using *shared IDs,* a valuable tool that greatly increases the total amount of program promotion possible in a single day. A 3-second identification that splits the screen between program promotion and station ID appears in Figure 2–8. The typical affiliate might have about twenty 30-second spots (or fewer) available for promotion in one broadcast day. Many of those fall outside the best times for promotion. Often, too few people or the wrong demographic group is watching for promotion of key programs (local news, early fringe, and access-hour shows). Using shared IDs on the hour, and sometimes the half hour, can effectively double the number of programs that can be promoted by the station. Shared IDs are especially useful for promoting familiar shows, especially stripped off-network series that have been scheduled on the station for many months.

How is digitalization going to affect the design of promotion? It already has profoundly altered the processes of creating artwork and producing on-air video. Promotion has benefited from the infusion of new technology at networks and stations, just as news departments have. As technology gets smaller, faster, and cheaper—as it is expected to in the twenty-first century—promotion departments and outsource companies will become more efficient. More of promotion will be produced in-house, often right in the promotion department rather than by art departments, because assembling the elements will become a matter of computer manipulation within a range of standardized designs. Art departments may have a major role in creating those standardized designs, but the digitalization of media will bring the implementation of promotional messages right to the desktop computer of the promotion producer or to the latest AVID-type editing system. This means that more promotion targeted more precisely for a particular audience watching a particular show can be produced quickly and efficiently enough to move in minutes from conception to a scheduled position. It will mean that promotion managers will have more choice about which spots to schedule where and be better able to tailor them to particular needs. It also suggests that fewer people will be needed to create and distribute promotion at broadcast stations—or that better and more diverse promotional campaigns can be handled by the individuals who know most about promotion.

SUMMARY OF CRITERIA FOR LIKELY EFFECTIVENESS

The principles of design articulated in this chapter are merely guidelines for promotion. Following these guidelines can help in the process of creating and implementing on-air, print, and web promotion that effectively reaches the target audience. But promotion always is a guessing game: The promotion manager must commit to a design style and message and must commit to scheduled positions for spots (or publications or signage for ads) in advance of knowing whether the promotion will work. Ratings improvements or weaknesses always are revealed some days, weeks, or months later. The guidelines summarized in Box 2–2 only suggest what to do and what to avoid; they are no sure thing, because promotion remains part art and part science (and the money and time for adequate science rarely is available).

BOX 2–2 Promotion Guidelines

1. KISS should guide all promotional design.
2. Control every minute aspect of the screen or ad.
3. Grab readers' and viewers' attention because it won't be given casually.
4. Adopt a logo or wordmark and theme, and stick to them in all promotion.
5. Reinforce every message as many times as possible.
6. Focus every promo, ad, or web page on the essential message.
7. Remember that on-air reaches only current viewers or listeners, while external media reaches new people.
8. Use specifics more often than generics for programs.
9. Use multiples, stack ads, and shared IDs for programs familiar to the audience.
10. Schedule promos and ads for series close in time to the airdate.
11. Incorporate a USP and a benefit in most promos and ads.
12. Create vectors in promos, ads, and web pages that lead the eye to the essential message.
13. Avoid the edge effect.
14. Protect promos and ads from cluttered environments when possible.
15. Employ styles of design that target the exact audience wanted.
16. Aim for effectiveness not awards.

CHAPTER 3

Commercial Radio Promotion

Joseph G. Buchman

MARKETING RADIO

The marketing of radio is unique among all marketing of media. Unlike managers in virtually every other business, radio station managers have almost no influence over four of the five basic elements of marketing. Other business managers can control the way their products or services are distributed, the prices charged, the characteristics of the products themselves, and the postpurchase services offered. But radio managers have very little, if any, control over any of these.

For example, radio station managers cannot control the place where their station's programming is consumed because listening can occur anywhere—in homes, offices, cars; at beaches and playgrounds; along the street; and anywhere on earth over the Internet. One recent study indicated over 40 percent of all radio listening occurs in cars. Radio station managers cannot control the price charged for their product because radio station listening is virtually free to the consumer. Moreover, for most formats, station management has very little control of the product as well. Music-oriented stations rely on the decisions made by music companies or satellite-distributed syndication services. Even news and talk stations are driven by events beyond the direct control of station management. In other businesses, postpurchase service includes items such as warranties, service contracts, and the like. For radio station managers, postpurchase service is limited to responding to listener complaints.

Of the five elements of marketing, only one—promotion—can be controlled by radio station managers. So, from a radio management perspective, when it comes to attracting an audience, promotion is marketing. Radio, however, has one special marketing advantage over other businesses—the ability to promote itself on air.

Radio Marketing History

The role of the radio station promotion manager has changed dramatically over the past half century. Before 1950, very few stations engaged in significant promotional activities. Competition among local stations was very limited and most programming was delivered by the networks. By the mid-1950s, radio stations developed specialized formats to regain audiences that had been lost to television. To make the public aware of these programming changes, positions in promotion were created at many stations. But early promotion managers did little more than process contest entries and produce a few on-air promos. These promotion managers often worked only part-time, had other secretarial or production duties, and had little impact on managerial decision making.

By the 1960s, as competition among radio stations intensified, promotion managers began to develop specific identities for their stations. Station images often were closely tied to call letters (for example, WAKY in Louisville, WILD in Birmingham, KIVA in Santa Fe), and attention was paid to creating a consistent image both on air and in external advertising.

In the 1970s, as increased listening to FM doubled and sometimes tripled the number of commercially viable stations in a market, promotion managers developed strategies to position their stations competitively against others in their market. The 1980s saw a refinement of these image-oriented positioning strategies, with greater reliance on ratings information and other customized research in making promotion decisions.

By the 1990s, radio went through a strong reconsolidation. The elimination of the duopoly rules and increase in the number of stations one company could own significantly increased the power and authority of radio promotion managers—now called *marketing managers* or *promotion directors*. With multiple stations with similar formats in a market, cross-promotion and strategic positioning of station images became vital. Distribution options increased with the advent of real-time Internet audio delivery. Promotion managers in the 1990s increasingly were called on to create and manage event-driven marketing including the acquisition of revenue from nontraditional revenue (NTR) sources.

Promotion managers today commonly influence decisions regarding sales, station image, format, personalities, news, research, and general management policy. Radio station general managers increasingly want to fill promotion management positions with highly motivated individuals who have both academic and professional experience in all the following areas: marketing, ratings analysis, media buying, research design, positioning, creative copy writing, technology innovation, and sales promotion. Filling their promotion management positions with the best possible talent is seen as critical to the overall success of virtually all stations outside the very smallest markets.

RADIO PROMOTION GOALS

Radio station promotion has five distinct goals:

1. Audience acquisition—give prospective new listeners a reason to tune in.
2. Audience maintenance—give current listeners a reason to stay tuned.
3. Audience recycling—give listeners who must tune out a reason to tune in again later.
4. Sales promotion—give advertisers a reason to buy time.
5. Internal promotion—generate excitement and motivation among the station staff.

Radio station promotion managers have only three channels through which they can achieve these goals: external media (print, television, outdoor, direct mail, Internet, etc.), internal media (on-air), and on co-owned stations in the same market (also called *sister stations*). Successful promotion managers generate strategies using these three channels to achieve each of the five promotion goals already identified. Potential listeners may be persuaded to listen to the station because of effective media buying, event broadcasts, station-sponsored community events, mail-out and call-out contests, publicity, and word-of-mouth campaigns. Current listeners may be given a reason to stay tuned or tune in again later because of effective on-air contests, cross-promotion between dayparts, and cross-promotion across commonly owned stations. The goal is to cross-promote in such a way that the listener's desires match with benefits offered by a particular station in the group and thus increase overall time spent listening (TSL) to the whole group of co-owned stations. Promotion managers may give potential advertisers a reason to buy advertising time on the station through sales promotions that involve tie-ins with on-air contests, live broadcasts from the advertiser's place of business, or cosponsorship of station-generated community events. Promotion managers also may call on advertisers directly to barter for giveaways and contest prizes. Finally, many promotion managers produce internal newsletters, recruit other station personnel to assist in promotional activities, and distribute specialty merchandise items to station employees in an attempt to generate excitement and create an esprit de corps among the station staff.

POSITIONING

Listeners' perceptions of what a radio station represents can be vastly more important than the reality of the station's programming. The important thing to remember is that the listener's perception of the station is all that matters. If the listener perceives the station as sounding better, then, for that listener, the reality is that the station does indeed sound better. For example, a station that heavily promotes commercial-free time blocks may be perceived as less commercial, even when (counting all dayparts) it carries more commercials than its competitors. Successful promotion managers produce campaigns designed to create these perceived advantages. This perceived competitive advantage is created not only in relation to other radio stations but also in relation to other media consumption or leisure time activities that are not compatible with radio listening. Such leisure time activities as jogging, driving, and spectator sports are compatible with radio listening. Successful marketing managers of all kinds focus on the image or perception of their product or service in the minds of their consumers. In marketing, perception is reality.

Tom Peters and Bob Waterman (in their series of books including *In Search of Excellence*) identify this characteristic of successful companies as "Staying close to the customer." Rick Sklar in a spin-off book titled *Radio in Search of Excellence* refers to "Keep[ing] a listener's ear view of radio." He continues, "We radio people, promoting a medium that you can't see, touch or feel, must keep a listener's perspective to win listeners." Successful promotion managers stay close to their listeners by focusing on these perceptions. They rely on such research strategies as call-out surveys and focus groups to identify both perceptions of their station and listeners' perceptions of their competitors.

Most information on radio listening, however, comes from diaries, the highly criticized source for radio ratings. Conventional industry practices regarding audience size, flow, recycling, and maintenance presume that diary keepers can accurately record or remember all their radio listening. This is a significant and problematic assumption. Many diaries are filled out some time after listening has occurred by diary-keepers who attempt to remember the call letters and times of day that they listened for all the stations they heard for the past week.

Actual station listening that is unreported because of inaccurate diary keeping, forgetfulness, or uncertainty regarding the station heard, is called *lost cume*. Because of the delay between listening and reporting, many promotion managers and broadcast marketing consultants believe that the positioning of a station relative to the positions occupied by its competitors is vastly more important for ratings success than actual station listening. Because they are unlikely to recall all their listening accurately, Arbitron diary-keepers are likely to record the station that presents the image with which they most closely identify. In other words, the station that they perceive as closest to their desired lifestyle is likely to be the one that they report listening to, whether they actually listened during their diary-keeping week or not. Therefore, occupying the position most compatible with the desired lifestyle of your target audience is more important for ratings success than influencing actual listening behavior.

Armed with this understanding of how radio is perceived and used, the promotion manager also needs to be aware of how the radio programming itself is scheduled. The real experience of listening (who, when, and where) suggests programming strategies that must be supported by promotional tactics.

AUDIENCE ACQUISITION, MAINTENANCE, AND RECYCLING

While diary-based ratings success can be generated by an effective positioning campaign, the station's long-term profitability ultimately will depend on its ability to generate results for station advertisers. To do this, a station first must attract as large an audience as possible and then maintain that audience across commercial breaks. Promotion managers aim audience acquisition strategies to increase the *cume* (cumulative) rating of the station by increasing sampling of the station by nonlisteners. Stations that benefit most from audience acquisition promotion are those with high AQH (average quarter hour) ratings but low cume ratings (in other words, these stations have extended time spent listening among a small, loyal group of listeners). Because the target audience is not listeners to the station, stations must use external media for audience acquisition promotions.

Maintaining listeners through a commercial break requires a variety of promotion techniques. Practically speaking, some of the audience will be unable to easily change stations; for example, those at work or involved in other activity (a volleyball game, for example). Others will be in a position to easily change stations, especially when driving a car. Therefore, many stations promote upcoming traffic and weather conditions just prior to commercial breaks, topics of interest to drivers. Audience maintenance strategies aim to maximize the AQH rating of the station by increasing the average listener's TSL. Stations benefiting most from audience maintenance promotion have a high cume rating but low AQH rating (short TSLs). In other words, the station has a large, disloyal audience that listens for relatively short periods of time before, perhaps, shifting to another station. Maintenance promotion, specifically on-air promotion, targets this large, disloyal audience.

Audience recycling strategies aim to increase the overall station AQH ratings and the cume for a given daypart. Their target is the station's current audience. Stations that benefit the most from an audience recycling strategy have high cumes in one daypart but low cumes in another. Audience recycling can be either *vertical* (later in the day) or *horizontal* (same daypart later in the week). Vertical recycling is achieved when a given daypart's audience returns to the station later on the same day. For example, the morning drive audience returns to listen in afternoon drive. Horizontal recycling is achieved when a given daypart's audience returns to listen to the same daypart later in the week. For example, Monday's morning drive-time audience listens on Tuesday morning's drive. Vertical recycling recycles audiences across dayparts; horizontal recycling recycles audiences across days of the week.

Eight basic promotional strategies are used in radio to achieve all audience acquisition, maintenance, and recycling goals:

1. Contests and giveaways
2. External media buying
3. Merchandising
4. Publicity and public relations
5. Direct mail and telemarketing
6. Event marketing
7. On-air promotion
8. Cross-promotion on co-owned stations

Contests and Giveaways

Contests may be designed to achieve audience acquisition, maintenance, or recycling goals. Careful analysis of a station's ratings will provide vital information on the best way to design its contests. For example, if analysis of the ratings shows that the station enjoys high TSLs but has a low cume, an audience acquisition contest like that shown in Figure 3–1 should be used. Notice how the requirements to "Set all your radios to LA's Magic 106" and "Listen each morning," and "Display this sticker on your vehicle" are designed for audience acquisition. Win-

HERE'S HOW TO WIN:

STEP 1: Set all your radios to LA's Magic 106 on your FM dial.
STEP 2: Display this sticker on your vehicle.
STEP 3: Listen each morning at 7:10 for your license number to be announced.
STEP 4: Also at 7:10 each morning we will be announcing other times during the day when the contest will be played.

Front   **Back**

Figure 3–1   *Bumper Sticker for LA's Magic 106 FM Contest. KPWR-FM. Used with permission.*

WIN · CASH

KMOO AM 158

COUNTRY

MUZ▮K

JERRY REED	KENNY PRICE	MERLE HAGGARD	TOMPALL & GLAZER BROTHERS	JIM REEVES
TAMMY WYNETTE	SUSAN RAYE	FREDDY WELLER	JODY MILLER	DICKEY LEE
JIM ED BROWN	WEBB PIERCE	TANYA TUCKER	JERRY LEE LEWIS	SAMMI SMITH
DON GIBSON	BOBBY BARE	BILLY WALKER	FARON YOUNG	BRIAN COLLINS
FERLIN HUSKY	ELVIS PRESLEY	ROGER MILLER	DAVID ROGERS	LYNN ANDERSON

©1972 Wm. D. TAYLOR

WXYZ "COUNTRY MUZIC" RULES

1. This is your free "COUNTRY MUZIC" card. Each week there is a different color card and you must have the correct color card to win. To avoid confusion, destroy your old card at the end of the week.
2. Turn your radio on, listen to WXYZ at 1230 on the AM dial.
3. Playing "COUNTRY MUZIC" is almost like playing Bingo. But instead of calling out numbers, WXYZ will play records.
4. When a record by an artist on this card is played, keep track by using buttons or other small objects to cover the squares. DO NOT write on, mark or tamper with the front of this card.
5. Just like Bingo, you must complete a line across, down or diagonally to win. A new game is started each hour, just after the news. Records played during one hour cannot be counted toward a win in another hour. Clear your card at the end of each hour.
6. Upon achieving a winning card you must call WXYZ at 321-1230 immediately. The game is over when there is a winner. No records past the winning record will count towards additional wins. NO PURCHASE NECESSARY!
7. The amount of the cash jackpot will vary from hour to hour. WXYZ will announce the amount of the jackpot at the start of each game. In case of multiple winners, the money will be divided equally. No checks will be issued until all cards are verified.
8. Winning cards must be brought to WXYZ studios at 1230 Radio Ave. within seven days of winning. You may mail your card, however, WXYZ cannot be responsible for lost cards.
9. Only one card per person. You must be at least 18 years of age. Employees of WXYZ or the participating sponsors and their families are ineligible.

WXYZ's music is selected for its entertainment value. At no time will WXYZ intentionally present it's music in manner that will make winning impossible. However, there are programming factors, both natural and planned which will effect the odds, and your chances of winning will vary from game to game.

Name ____________ Phone ________

Address ____________ City ________ Game No. ___

Figure 3–2 *Sample Contest Card and Sample Rules for Music Bingo. Courtesy Bill Taylor.*

ning the contest requires listening to the station for only short time periods. This obviously is a station that enjoys high TSLs. The promotion manager has determined that the best strategy for ratings success is to increase sampling of the station by nonlisteners; TSLs will come automatically.

On the other hand, a station that enjoys high cumes but low TSLs might design an audience maintenance-based contest similar to that shown in Figure 3–2. Winning requires listening to the station for several hours at a time, thus increasing the TSLs and AQH ratings of the station.

Ratings analysis could show the need for an audience recycling strategy. For example, a station's afternoon drive daypart might be performing well, but mornings are dismal. In this case, you could design a contest that is heavily promoted in afternoon drive time but requires listeners to listen during morning drive time to win. This strategy assumes that nothing inherently is wrong with your morning drive-time programming. One of the worst mistakes a station (or an advertiser) can make is to heavily promote a bad product. When morning daypart is dismal because of bad talent or poor programming, promoting morning drive time may hurt afternoon drive-time ratings rather than help morning ratings. Listeners who are turned off by your morning drive-time programming may decide not to tune into the station at all. The next time you hear a radio station contest, ask yourself whether the contest has audience acquisition, maintenance, or recycling goals.

Giveaways may be designed to appeal to light listeners of the station ("I've got two free tickets for the first person to call in") or heavy listeners ("You could win $1,000 if you hear the following three songs played back-to-back anytime this month"). It's important to provide balance between these games and giveaways. Too many complex contests that necessitate long TSLs to participate (or even understand) may leave light listeners feeling completely left out (and give them a reason to tune out). Contests and giveaways also can be designed to increase vertical recycling (as in "We'll give away this digital cell phone sometime this afternoon") or horizontal recycling ("Your next chance to win will be at this same time tomorrow").

Horizontal recycling needs are more difficult to determine. Specific day-of-week listening estimates are supplied by specialized reports such as Arbitron's Fingerprint. Once this information has been examined, similar horizontal recycling strategies can be employed. For example, if midday listening is lowest on Tuesdays, contests and promotions can be heavily promoted on other weekdays, with the winners announced on Tuesdays.

Very few of a station's listeners actually participate in station contests or giveaways. Even fewer win. Therefore, all contests and giveaways should be designed to be entertaining for nonparticipating listeners. Contests and giveaway announcements should not become a tune-out factor for most of your station's audience.

Big Prizes

For the vast majority of stations, promotion budgets for contest and giveaway prizes is very limited. To increase the value or number of prizes, sales promotions commonly are used. Frequently, these promotions will be tied to the generation of new business accounts for the station. For example, the promotion manager at an El Paso station wanted to design a $10,000 giveaway but lacked the money in the budget. In conjunction with the sales manager, the promotion manager designed a month-long spot schedule at $1,000 each for 12 clients. The spots were scheduled to run during the first quarter, when inventory pressures were low. Out of the total $12,000, $2,000 covered sales commissions and expenses, leaving $10,000 for the contest prize. (All clients had to be new businesses for the station; no retailer that recently had advertised on the station could participate in this special package.) As part of the promotion, each client received a free remote on one of 12 consecutive Saturday afternoons. To participate in the contest, listeners had to register during the broadcast from the client's location. The result was a $10,000 cash contest prize, motivated listeners, 12 new clients who saw the station's drawing power demonstrated live at their locations, a happy general manager, a contest that cost nothing, and at least one very satisfied listener.

Can you generate the excitement of a $10,000 giveaway without actually giv-ing away the money? One station in Seattle created a promotion that did just that. Wanting to promote their more-music format, they offered this guarantee: If any listener ever heard less than 51 minutes of music during any one-hour period, the station would pay $10,000. The promotion made enough impact to receive cov-erage in the local paper. It also generated a lot of excitement among listeners and increased significantly the station's AQH ratings and TSLs. The free coverage in other media caused a slight increase in cume ratings as well. There are some risks for this type of promotion, however.

Important considerations to keep in mind include

1. Establish a time limit for the promotion. What happens if your station changes format to all-talk next year?
2. Include disclaimers. What happens if the station has a power outage?
3. Have the money ready just in case.

Little Prizes

Often contests need not have valuable prizes to generate effective promotional value. During a debate over legalizing gambling in Tennessee, WSIX-AM in Nashville offered listeners a free trip to neighboring Kentucky (where gambling on horse racing is legal) to "Watch for signs of organized crime, pin-striped suits, violin cases, . . . and other gambling related dangers." KNOW in Austin offered the listener with the ugliest car a free paint job, body work, a new sound system, tune-up, new tires, and an oil change. The total value of the prize was around $3,000. All of the items were traded with local retailers in return for free mentions in the contest (*tradeouts*).

Can a contest generate ratings for your station even when the station is off the air? KFMW in Waterloo experienced some technical problems that kept it off the air for an extended period. They created a "Down but not out" contest. Prizes included down comforters and down jackets, and the first listener to call the sta-tion when it went back on the air won $108.

Sometimes the station need not offer any prize at all to have an effective con-test. WSEN in Syracuse thrilled listeners with an April Fool's extravaganza in a classic takeoff on an old holiday prank. Winners were to receive a free tour of the Salt Museum (closed for the season), a tram tour of Onondaga Lake Park (closed until June), a tour of the French Fort (opens Memorial Day), a guided walk around the Burnett Park Zoo (closed for renovations), and a ride on the famed roller coaster at Suburban Park (famed mostly because it burned to the ground in 1969). The contest generated numerous entries, received free press coverage in other local media, and helped to reinforce the station's not-too-serious, good-natured image. Obviously, this contest would not suit a station concerned with creating an image of high credibility.

Contest Problems

Finally, remember a contest (or any other advertisement) that involves a prize, chance, and consideration is considered a lottery and may be illegal on your radio station. Any combination of two elements is allowed (giving a prize for a drawing is okay); but when all three elements are present, the contest comes under rules governing lotteries (spelled out in Chapter 1). Broadcasting information regarding a lottery (except certain state-government-sponsored lotteries) may subject your station to a fine or loss of license in some states.

Also, contests that may cause harm to the community or risk injury to the participants have been determined by the courts to be inconsistent with the "public interest" obligations of broadcasters and so should be avoided. Todd Storz is credited with developing the prototype of questionable "public interest" contests in the 1950s on his innovative Top 40 stations. The most common was a "Treasure Hunt." Typically, a check for $100,000 was hidden somewhere in the community. Obscure clues were given out on the air (obscure because the station hoped the check would not have to be paid). After a certain date the value of the check decreased to a more modest sum, such as $500. Treasure hunters arrived from hundreds of miles away to listen to the station for clues and hunt for the check. While treasure hunts certainly achieved audience acquisition and maintenance goals, the results sometimes backfired. First of all, the increase in cumes, AQH ratings, and TSLs from this type of promotion usually is temporary and seldom generates results for station advertisers. Also, ill will can be created because of the unclear clues, and when the check is not found in time, many treasure hunters feel cheated.

Occasionally, however, the clues have been only too clear. One radio station in New Orleans was blamed for causing extensive damage to the public library when the contest clues indicated that the check was hidden in one of the library's books. Excited treasure hunters ransacked the library. The station paid for restoration of the books, the staff had to help with clean-up, and the station threw a party for the stressed-out librarians. And the DJ was fired.

External Media

Promotion managers make nearly all of the external media buying decisions for their stations, regularly purchasing space and time in other media. Salespeople from competing media in the market regularly call on radio station promotion managers, attempting to secure a fair share of the radio station's advertising budget. Some stations insulate themselves from these sales pitches by hiring an outside agency to do their media buying. Nevertheless, promotion managers should have a thorough understanding of the advantages and disadvantages of each competing medium in their markets. Evaluation of these other media will depend on a station's format, target audience, image, positioning, and marketing goals. For example, it makes more sense for a talk, sports, or Big Band station to advertise in a newspaper than for a Modern Rock or Heavy Metal station because of the increasingly older demographics of typical newspaper readers. However, having an elaborate Internet site that carries the station's music makes good sense for rock stations targeting younger listeners.

It is also important to have a complete understanding of the cost structures of competing media. Effective media buying requires the ability to show the salesperson why a proposal is too costly and why your counterproposal should be accepted. For audience acquisition, the most efficient media buy will be the one with the lowest cost per thousand (CPM) for nonlisteners in the station's target demographic. Typically, paid external media is for *acquiring* new listeners.

Television stations that use customized ratings reports such as Tapscan and Strata may be able to calculate appropriate demographic-based CPMs for nonlisteners of a radio station. Of course, the overall effectiveness of any promotional campaign will depend not just on efficient media buying but also on the creativity, execution, and overall appeal of the advertising. For radio stations, competing media to evaluate include broadcast television, cable television, newspaper, outdoor, telephone directory, transit, Internet, and sometimes, other radio stations.

Television reaches virtually all audience demographic groups during some program time periods. All-news or -talk radio stations may reach their target audiences by advertising on local cable channels or on satellite-delivered cable newscasts. Country stations may reach their target audiences by advertising on a broadcast television station's country music special, while alternative stations might consider advertising late at night. Frequently newspapers, cable systems, and television stations will trade advertising time (on a dollar-for-dollar basis) with radio stations. The promotion manager, in conjunction with the sales manager, is responsible for developing these trade advertising sources and then making effective use of them.

Print media, such as newspapers and magazines, also are an advertising option for radio. Promotional inserts in newspapers, which can be inserted in only some copies of the paper, are especially useful for targeting specific geographic areas. Some larger markets also have local or regional magazines in which radio stations can advertise. Targeting potential advertisers sometimes is more consistent with the readership of the magazine than targeting potential listeners.

Figure 3–3 *A Painted Bulletin for KNBR. KNBR. Used with permission.*

Another form of print advertising, telephone directory advertising, may be especially important for stations desiring to reach newcomers to a market, such as young, upwardly mobile professionals. Directories of various types are particularly important in rapidly growing markets. Most markets now have competing telephone-directory companies, and advertising opportunities include not only the yellow pages but also the inside and back covers, as well as coupon pages. Web pages on the Internet are another popular way to promote radio stations. Listeners can provide feedback on their likes and dislikes. Contests and merchandise offers are easy to display. Depending on the user's connection, sound files with sample music can be downloaded or the station's music can be "streamed" live.

Outdoor advertising, generally available in medium to large markets, very seldom is offered on a trade basis. A radio station's outdoor advertising decisions will depend to a large degree on the importance of drive-time radio listening in the market. The much-repeated cardinal rule for billboards is to *keep the message short*; three to five words make the most effective message (eight is maximum). A second, but less repeated, rule is to *make the message provocative.* Just putting up pretty call letters and frequency is not enough to foster changes in behavior. By using information such as Arbitron's Fingerprint, stations can determine the most effective geographic areas for their outdoor advertising. Fingerprint will provide ratings information by Zip code. Stations then can target their outdoor placement to areas with good signal coverage but low listenership among the station's target demos. Figure 3–3 shows an example of an uncomplicated, painted bulletin that effectively positions the station.

There are two basic types of outdoor bulletins: poster panel and painted. The standard poster-panel billboard runs 12 feet, 3 inches high by 24 feet, 6 inches wide. Then, 10–15 sheets of printed poster paper are glued to it to create the large image. Painted bulletins are usually 14 feet high by 48 feet long. Each is custom designed and painted by hand. Because of different aspect ratios between painted and poster bulletins, the same graphic design cannot be used for both. Painted boards also may allow for some special effects (sometimes called *spectaculars*). Cutouts, for example, can be attached to the board to extend either its height or width. Because of the cost of repainting and moving, painted bulletins are less flexible than poster boards and usually are sold for a period of one year. Poster bulletins may be purchased for a few weeks or months, and they easily can be changed by repapering over the existing poster.

Transit advertising on subways, buses, taxis, and trains generally is available only in larger markets. Audience demographics vary depending on the geographic area and who rides or sees the vehicles. For example, the demographics of riders of buses and subways usually differ markedly from those of taxi or suburban commuter train riders, but the outside of all these vehicles may be viewed by the same inner-city population as they travel across town. In the largest markets, several types of transit advertising are available, including busboards (side, rear, and front), bus stop or station posters (including airports, subways, and train terminals), and taxi boards or cabtops. All these are traveling billboards and take only limited messages. Many transit vehicles also sell space inside the bus, cab, or subway for signs (cards), which is especially useful for advertising long-term contests and promoting news. In addition, the promotion manager probably has responsibility for the custom painting of station-owned remote vans, boom boxes, sales cars, and so on. The principles of emphasizing the message and stating a USP or benefit apply to all these media.

Cross-Promotion

One certain method for reaching light or nonlisteners to your station is to advertise on other radio stations. Many co-owned stations cross-promote each other's programming, especially in markets with five or more commonly owned stations. Less frequent are radio stations in the same market buying time on or trading time with their competitors. When it does occur, the trade usually involves a format change or a new station signing on the air. For example, a station that drops its hard rock format to go to all-talk may allow its former rock competitors to buy time promoting their rock formats (for example, "For all the Rock you used to get here on KXXX, tune to KYYY"). Sometimes two stations with complementary formats may choose to cross-promote each other's programming. For instance, an all-news station and a beautiful music station may trade time promoting each other's formats (using on-air lines like "When you want the news it's here, but when you're ready to relax, tune to WZZZ").

A less honest method for advertising on your competitor's stations is to do it without their knowledge. Some stations have created a fictitious product and, through an advertising agency or other mediator, purchased time on their competitors. Unbeknownst to the other stations, the product, in reality, was a promotional vehicle for the competing station. The message has to be rather obscure to deceive anyone for long. In one example, radio stations in Denver and Knoxville created a new "Morning Flakes" cereal. After advertisements for the "Morning Flakes" cereal had run on their competitors' air, the real Morning Flakes were revealed to be the station's new morning drive-time personalities. The "Morning Flakes" cereal (which was a generic corn flakes and actually sold through a local grocery store chain) was packaged with photos of the morning team and other station promotional copy.

The important point to remember in all external media buying is that the goal is to reach the largest number of nonlisteners in the desired demographics of your station. Thus, it might not make sense, from an audience acquisition perspective, for the all-news station to advertise in the newspaper or local television newscasts if a large percentage of those reached already are heavy listeners to the station. Information of this type can be gathered from station call-out, focus group, or survey research. Numerous consulting firms and outside research companies can be hired to assist you in determining the most effective media buying strategy.

MERCHANDISING

Merchandising involves the distribution of customized station products. Merchandising opportunities vary widely from the simple printing of station T-shirts and bumper stickers to the creation of a 40-foot, inflatable station mascot or hot-air balloon. Specialty merchandise firms inundate stations with offers of customized key chains, pens, paperweights, mouse pads, wind-chill charts, emergency-phone-number refrigerator magnets, coffee mugs, buttons, pocket knives, flashlights, clocks, rugs, umbrellas, clothing, luggage, and virtually anything else you can imagine—all, of course, emblazoned with the radio station's identifier.

Some stations have found that the merchandising of custom clothing and other items through local retail stores can be both profitable and effective promotion. KATT in Oklahoma City has met with great success selling its specialty merchandise through a chain of local truck-stops. Chicago's WLUP produced a flyer for selling its specialty merchandise via mail-order from the station. Many stations also use their web sites to offer merchandise.

Figure 3–4   *Bumper Sticker for WOWO and Two Advertisers. WOWO. Used with permission.*

Merchandising and specialty merchandise giveaways can be effective audience maintenance tools as well. Some stations (usually as part of a sales promotion) create coupon books or specialized plastic cards offering discounts at local retail outlets. The plastic card or coupon book appears to entitle the listener to special privileges as part of a "WXXX Club." This feeling of belonging and identification among listeners with membership or ownership in the station is central to promotional success. Coupons were offered in a B-97 sales promotion, part of a booklet paid for by dozens of sponsors. A plastic card carrier was used by KDES for touting discounts and cash prizes for listening.

Positive feelings for a station can be significantly enhanced by giving away specialty merchandise (often as simple as distributing bumper stickers) or manufacturing and selling clothing and other merchandise marked with the station's logo. For many AOR-oriented listeners (typically men 18–24 years old) and many country music station fans of all ages, the act of applying a bumper sticker from their favorite radio station to their first car represents a significant rite of passage. Wearing the name of a specialized radio station psychologically identifies many listeners with the lifestyle presented by the station. Wearing clothing or carrying useful items marked with their favorite station's logo can be a self-concept statement at least as significant as seeking out only Gerbeau jeans shirts or Nike footwear.

Figure 3–4 shows a bumper sticker for radio station WOWO. The sticker was sponsored by both Pepsi and Marathon Oil but successfully promotes the station by giving it top billing; the two sponsors receive only a small portion of the space but remain readable. Stations can also use a sticker's peel-off backing to promote programming. Many stations lose half of the value of their stickers by failing to utilize the reverse side and failing to put the station's identifier on the back. Figure 3–5 shows a bumper sticker's front with the station identifier and the back with the coupons.

Front

Back

Figure 3–5 *Bumper Sticker for ZPL-99½. WZPL. Used with permission.*

Publicity and Public Relations

The goal of a publicity strategy is to get free coverage for your station in competing media. This may be as simple as keeping the newspaper media critic informed of the week's sports broadcast schedule or as complex as creating a mystery character who randomly gives away $100 bills around town and later is revealed to be your station's new morning personality (but only after the newspapers, television stations, and other radio stations have covered the story). The $10,000 listening guarantee and ugly car contests mentioned earlier are excellent examples of promotions that also achieved publicity goals.

Press releases are written notices of newsworthy events. They generally are handled by the promotion manager and should be sent out for all station events, including internal station personnel promotions; the hiring of new personalities, sales, and managerial staff; and broadcast industry or local civic awards. Press releases should be sent to the local newspapers, television stations, broadcast trade magazines, and the employee's hometown newspaper. Press releases about publicity stunts should be sent to all the competing media in your station's coverage area. New station programming, call-letter changes, studio location shifts, and technical improvements also should be announced in press releases. Promotion managers routinely should maintain biographical data on all station management and air talent, because it can be needed in the next hour when a call comes from a newspaper editor seeking filler before deadline.

Remotes, Appearances, and Tours

The goal of a community-relations strategy is to develop one-on-one relationships with current or potential listeners. Word of mouth commonly is cited as the most effective form of advertising, and a public relations effort is one of the most effective methods for generating word-of-mouth advertising. PR strategies include live on-location broadcasts, station personality appearances, and station tours.

Remotes, broadcasts from locations other than the station's studio, often occur in conjunction with sales promotion activities, but they also may be used to generate higher visibility for the station's personalities. Broadcasting from the top of a flagpole, interstate billboard, underwater cabin, or other outrageous location may generate both free publicity for the station and greater listening among former light or nonlisteners. Some remote broadcasts may even originate from outside the station's coverage area. For example, some stations have sent their most popular personality on an around-the-world tour (usually part of a travel agency sales promotion) that included broadcasts from "30 countries in 30 days."

Personality appearances may involve speeches to local civic groups, a station softball or basketball team, interviews on local broadcast or cable television shows, and public participation in community events. As everyone learns the hard way, the station personality needs complete instructions regarding the exact time and location of the appearance and an ample quantity of station giveaway items (bumper stickers, photos, etc.). If the appearance is before a civic organization, the personality may want to show a brief videotape about the station, which needs to be provided, along with suitable projection equipment. The promotion manager should provide the organization's chairperson with the personality's biography, arrange for media coverage by the local newspaper and television stations if appropriate, and provide photographs and another copy of the personality's biography to the editor of the organization's newsletter. Better to have overkill than a wasted opportunity and annoyance all the way around.

Station tours commonly are conducted by the promotion manager. Various high school, civic, and even listener groups often want to see the studio facilities. Some stations have even sponsored vocational radio programs (for groups such as the Boy Scout Explorers or the local high school radio club). The promotion manager typically becomes the organization's advisor and in return gathers a nearly inexhaustible supply of energetic station interns.

Special remotes and personality appearances can have a strong impact on audience maintenance because they allow loyal listeners the opportunity to identify more closely with the station. At station-sponsored community events, loyal listeners should receive special consideration (such as priority seating, free tickets, or station giveaways). Such perks may be earned by random on-air invitations, direct mail, or telemarketing efforts.

Event Marketing

Stations often sponsor or cosponsor events large enough to attract attention from the community at large. Many radio stations have tackled coordinating the local

Figure 3–6 *Copromotion. WZYQ-AM. Used with permission.*

Fourth of July fireworks display or other holiday events. Accompanied by a custom music track, the event can be simultaneously broadcast by the station. Many music-oriented stations sponsor and broadcast a local charity's fund drive (such as Toys for Tots) as well as benefit concerts. Figure 3–6 shows a charity-based co-promotion by Z-104, two television stations, the Salvation Army, and several other agencies cooperating to produce a Christmas cash donation.

Promotion managers must use careful planning with large events. Without planning, the potential for attracting a great deal of positive attention can translate into the potential for negative results. The key to successful events is plenty of advance preparation, with several meetings with all station staff members to explain the goals of the event and how the goals will be met.

Direct Mail and Telemarketing

Direct mail, a rapidly growing area of broadcast promotion activity, refers to mass mailings, usually handled by commercial companies that specialize in them. By utilizing services such as Arbitron's Fingerprint, radio stations can target specific demographic groups (by Zip code) with direct mail campaigns. Most commonly, a station advertiser sponsors secret contests that only receivers of the direct mail piece know about. The mailer, for example, may inform the recipient that the first person to call the station after a specific song is played will receive a cash reward, although no mention of this is made on-air.

Telemarketing efforts, referring to telephone sales, are often directed at "in-office" listeners. At-work listening has become increasingly important to radio stations, especially during the midday, and raising midday listening can greatly influence afternoon drive-time ratings. Frequently at-work listening is *forced listening* (listening over which the radio consumer has no control). This occurs in carpools, shopping malls, retail outlets, and many workplaces. Forced listening has taken on a greater importance as a result of Arbitron's latest diary which asks diary-keepers to record all stations that they have "heard." The previous diary asked diary-keepers to record stations that they "listened to." Forced listening was apparently underestimated because diary-keepers felt that such listening didn't count unless they had chosen the station. Obviously, workplace listening can involve significant numbers of hours of exposure to a particular station.

Telemarketing efforts often reward those office and retail managers who control radio station selection at their workplace. Promotion managers (or their assistants) may randomly call businesses listed in the yellow pages and offer a cash reward and on-air business mention to the manager (as in "Thanks to Dan's Auto Repair for listening to Q95") if the station is tuned to. In a variation, after a mention, someone from Dan's would then have a limited period of time to call in and claim the prize. Telemarketing efforts also can be directed at households in problem Zip code areas (by matching telephone prefix numbers with geographic areas). Several outside marketing companies specialize in this type of promotion for radio stations and other businesses.

Some stations generate mailing and phone lists from contest entries and design specialized promotional appeals to these known listeners. For example, a direct mail piece may be sent, informing these current listeners of a secret contest that only they may enter. Telemarketing efforts may sample these listeners to generate feedback on station promotions or music selection. All such efforts give loyal listeners a special sense of belonging and identification with the station, and they ultimately increase TSLs.

On-Air Promotion

By far, the most important strategy for generating high levels of audience maintenance is effective use of your station's own air time. Arbitron counts someone as listening to a station if he or she reports hearing the station for at least five continuous minutes within a quarter hour. This ratings method affects the *formatting*—the scheduling of commercial breaks, news, and promotional announcements—at most stations. Some radio stations, for example, have designed their format clocks so that commercials appear between 6 and 9 minutes into a quarter hour (in other words, from :06 to :09, :21 to :24, and so on) under the theory that AQH ratings will be maximized by sweeping listeners across the quarter-hour breaks. Thus, a listener who tunes in at 10 minutes past the hour will not hear a commercial (and not have a reason to tune out) until 21 minutes past the hour. This listener then will be credited in diaries with two full quarter hours (one half hour) of listening, even though the listener might have tuned in for only 11 minutes.

Bumpers are another strategy for sweeping quarter hours. Stations place promotional announcements for station contests just before the commercial break ("Sometime in the next 20 minutes we'll have our next cash call contest") and preannounce the title and artist of the record coming after the commercial break ("After this break we'll have the latest from Mariah Carey"). All-news and talk stations often bump (preannounce) the local weather or another feature following the commercials. Also, many stations make a point of giving the time just before a commercial break, assuming that some diary-keepers will hear the time announcement and accurately record having listened for that full five-minute period within the quarter hour. A few stations have gotten a little carried away with this. One station in Chicago was caught giving incorrect time announcements. Although its time announcements were off by only a few minutes (for example, announcing that it was 20 minutes past the hour when it was only 17 minutes past), the fact that they were altering the time to influence ratings placed them in serious trouble with the ratings companies and the FCC.

While the term *cross-promotion* usually refers to promotion of the station on other media, it may be used to mean promoting the station's other dayparts on the air. Cross-promotions can be designed for vertical maintenance ("Later today on the Rollye James Show") or horizontal maintenance "Tomorrow at this time we'll be interviewing Mayor Delaurentis"). While this sounds simple, one of the most difficult tasks faced by a promotion manager is getting the on-air personalities to talk to or about each other (at least on the air). Many stations require on-air personalities to produce brief (10–20 second) promos for their next day's airshift. Often these are prerecorded by the personality for use throughout the day. Other generic promos may be produced by one personality promoting another personality's show. Remember the goal of cross-promotion is audience maintenance and recycling, giving the listener a reason to stay tuned or, when the listener must tune out (as is often the case following morning drive time), giving the listener a reason to tune in later (for example, a reason to listen to afternoon drive time).

Sales Promotion

Up to this point, we have focused on audience promotion. The goal of sales promotion is to give prospective advertisers an incentive to buy time on the station. Sales promotions that have an on-air component, such as a contest, actively involve the promotion manager. Sales promotions that interfere with audience acquisition and maintenance goals, however, should be avoided at all costs. Their short-term monetary gain may be attractive, but they are not worth the threat of long-term loss of audience. Sometimes, stations that are about to be sold to new owners will freely engage in such promotions in an effort to maximize the current cash flow of the station (and thus increase the station's sales price) without regard to the station's long-term best interests.

Client incentives that involve the promotion department usually are similar to the audience acquisition strategies outlined previously. For example, a station may offer free advertising (or discounted rates) to retailers who have the radio station turned on in their stores when an account executive comes to the store. Clients (or their children, friends, or relatives) often want station specialty merchandise or autographed photos of station personalities, and usually the sales department will expect the promotion manager to handle such requests.

Cosponsorship, the joint backing of events, often is the key to advertising sales and the promotion of big events. Stations need major national advertisers to cosponsor community events (for example, a "Miller Lite/KXXX Summer Tan

Contest" or a "Pepsi/WYYY Labor Day Fireworks Show"). Local and national advertisers commonly become involved in one of three ways: by serving as a registration location for a contest ("You can register at any Nite Owl Food Mart, Raven Records, or White Castle location"), by providing contest prizes ("Win a free computer from Data World"), or by jointly backing a sales promotion with the station (for example, paying the cost of bumper stickers when they have a coupon for a free Pepsi on the peel-off backing).

Such cosponsorship creates many promotional opportunities that otherwise would not be available to the station because of budget limitations. However, stations must be careful to limit the number of cosponsored promotions to avoid the listener perception that the station is merely an extension of its advertisers. Moreover, stations must limit the number of cosponsors for each contest or event; more is not necessarily better: Many station call letters have been completely lost when too many cosponsors were involved. For example, the "Cableworld, Daily Journal, WZZZ-TV-12, Burger World, KYYY-FM, Super Summer Sweepstakes" is of very little promotional value to the radio station.

Because some corporations now own as many as 200 stations, they have created corporate-level sales promotion management positions. The corporate sales promotion department is responsible for creating regional or companywide sales promotions for major advertisers. Revenue generated by these kinds of activities today is referred to as *nontraditional revenue* or *nonspot dollars*.

Station Morale

Station image campaigns are ineffective when they are inconsistent with the unwritten message the station's employees communicate. Personnel dissatisfaction and cynicism about the station easily circulate through networks of friends and business acquaintances, sometimes creating an identity at odds with the image management prefers. Promotion managers can help forestall image problems in several ways. The easiest is to encourage everyone to become involved in station promotions. Giveaway items should be readily available to station staff members (who may want them for their own use or to give to friends, relatives, or neighbors). More expensive items should be made available to station employees at reduced cost. Staff members should be kept informed of upcoming promotional events and station-sponsored community activities by distributing internal memos.

In addition, the promotion manager frequently will be responsible for an internal station newsletter, station business cards, station lobby or window displays, the outside building sign, the station van or car, and so on. All these items, of course, should reflect a consistent image of the station. Creating occasional in-house newsletters covering the personal achievements of staff members is especially effective for sharing management's pride in its people and their efforts, thus building morale. All employees should be reminded that they represent the station and what they say publicly is critical to its success. Hundreds of dollars in promotional effort can be irreparably damaged by something as simple, and avoidable, as a station staff member being rude to a listener or potential client on the telephone.

MORAL DILEMMAS

Radio promotion managers face complex ethical questions on a daily basis. Is it all right to target diary-keepers or potential telephone respondents with promotional activities, rather than everyday listeners? For example, is the on-air promotional tag "K109-Write it down" intended for all listeners or intended to influence diary-keepers? What about the tag line "Remember the time you've spent listening to Dr. Laura?"

Some stations design specialty merchandise products like refrigerator magnets and coffee mugs for use in the kitchen (where most Arbitron dairies are filled out). Are stations that alter their formats to sweep audiences across quarter-hour breaks acting ethically? Is it unethical to announce that the time is 20 minutes after the hour when it's only 19 after in an attempt to alter quarter-hour ratings?

Some stations purposefully attempt to sabotage their competitor's promotional efforts by stealing station slogans, by sending their station van to their competitor's remotes and community events, or by engaging in other efforts designed to confuse listeners as to which station is sponsoring which event. Competitive strategies, sometimes called *guerrilla marketing*, tempt some station managers during ratings periods. What would you do if you were asked to spearhead such activities?

What ethical issues are involved when a station announces plans to drop turkeys on a shopping mall just before the Thanksgiving holiday (copying a famous *WKRP in Cincinnati* episode)? The accompanying on-air promos (for an Indiana station) said "Turkeys will be hitting the sidewalk like bags of wet cement." Immediately, regional and local newspapers, local television stations, and even one national television network responded by covering the promotion; citizen groups formed to gather signatures protesting the event; local and national organizations of the Society for the Prevention of Cruelty to Animals became involved. All the while, the station had planned to drop only paper turkeys on the shopping mall. The paper turkeys contained coupons for a free Thanksgiving turkey (or a discount on a turkey) and were part of a sales promotion with a local grocery store chain. Is this an example of an effective publicity strategy or poor ethical judgment?

More clearly fraudulent are station contests that have been rigged so that current or potential clients (or client's friends or relatives) will win. Often contest prizes seem innocuous, and there are so many winners of something every week that who wins hardly seems to matter. What would you do if your general manager asked you to rig a circus promotion so the disabled six-year-old child of the station's largest client could be "Circus Queen for a Day"? If the station announces that the winner will be chosen randomly, the FCC will not look kindly on a sham.

SUMMARY

Listeners' perceptions of a station's image often are more important than actual listening behavior. Diary-keepers and telephone respondents seldom can record or remember accurately all their radio listening and often respond in ratings surveys with the name of the station that represents the image with which they most closely identify. Successful promotion managers research these listener perceptions and keep them in mind when creating and executing all station promotions. Radio audience promotion involves acquisition, maintenance, and recycling strategies. External media should be used to achieve acquisitive goals, while internal media (on-air) will achieve retentive goals. The kinds of contests, giveaways, and other promotions that will be most beneficial to the station depend on the station's format, AQH ratings, cume ratings, and TSLs. Merchandising, direct mail, and telemarketing are having increased importance as radio promotional tools. Sales promotions, often involving contests and giveaways, are crucial to the success of most music-format radio stations.

CHAPTER 4

Network Television Promotion

Douglas A. Ferguson

In 1987, the number-one program on television was *The Cosby Show*, watched by 44 percent of the viewers. By 1998, the number-one show was *Seinfeld* with only 34 percent of the audience. The decline occurred because the cable networks have slowly nibbled away viewers that once watched the big four broadcast networks. Just as the major Detroit automakers had to compete actively against foreign cars, the major broadcast networks now struggle to maintain dominance of television viewing against cable's challenge. The other minor broadcast networks, UPN and the WB, as well as PBS and Univision, vie for the same audiences, and a new broadcast-cable hybrid (Pax TV) is targeting families and seeking to join the battle. This chapter examines broadcast network promotion, although cable network promotion bears some similarity (see Chapter 6).

Promotion of a broadcast network involves nearly all the tools of contemporary mass communications, plus an assist from new interactive technologies like the Internet. The most visible tool is *on-air promotion*—that is, the body of commercial announcements that networks put on their own air to induce people to watch their programs. The secondary tools are advertising messages in magazines, newspapers, radio, outdoor, and web sites, as well as skywriting and any other imaginable form of paid communication. The other tools of promotion include sales promotion and presentations, art and design, and publicity.

Departmental structures vary from network to network. Moreover, the internal organizational structures continue to change, especially with regard to overall marketing and image branding. What does not change, however, is the basic goal of network advertising and promotion departments: *to maximize audience sampling*. The means for achieving this objective are on-air promotion and advertising incorporated in an annual cycle of network promotional events. A set of assumptions about audience behavior underlies this promotional calendar.

THE MARKETING APPROACH

With ever-increasing competition from new broadcast networks, cable, satellite, independent stations, home video, and web sites, the promotion of a network requires a total marketing approach. Building an audience starts with the first announcement that a new show will be going on the air. That very first announcement is the beginning of a campaign that reaches a climax with the premiere of the show and then continues in an ongoing competition for as long as the show remains on the air. The first phase, the publicity buildup, includes such events as the photo sessions for the picture service that publicity departments provide to newspapers and web publishers, talk show exposure, and plugs on radio—all the free things that announce new programs.

The next chronological phase is the on-air campaign that starts two, three, or four weeks in advance of the air date, depending on the project. Most start about ten days in advance of the premiere, although brief hints (in promos) of what is to come may be scattered throughout the summer. As discussed later in greater detail, on-air campaigns begin by introducing the concept of a program, establishing the identities of the characters or personalities, and indicating the time and place of the shows.

The uniqueness of television is that the four full-time networks (ABC, CBS, Fox, and NBC) and netlets like UPN and the WB compete with each other using very similar products. Therefore, the goal of each network is to make its programs more interesting to viewers than its competitors' programs, especially against the encroaching cable networks. Each network's objective is to be sure that the audience learns what programs are offered and to endow them with unique appeal. If the appeal coincides with what the viewers want, they will watch. If the appeal of the program does not relate to viewers' interests or needs, they have lots of other choices.

The function of advertising and promotion in television is to let audiences know what is on the air in an interesting, efficient, and memorable way. On-air campaigns should define the nature of individual programs, identify the casts of the programs, and make clear when the programs are on the air. Those are the three basic questions that need to be answered for viewers. Most people make an almost instantaneous judgment when exposed to a new program idea. Subconsciously viewers react emotionally and almost immediately to questions like "Does that appeal to me? Do I have an interest in it?" In that moment, most viewing decisions are made.

People also want to know who is in the program. People are attracted to certain actors or actresses. In television, however, the real persona must relate to the fictional character to be successful. Many "stars" have failed in television when the role they played did not match their personal appeal. For example, viewers rejected Tom Selleck in the role of a show-business agent. Conversely, television has the ability to make stars of performers who absorb the identity of a fictional character. Kathy Kinney, for example, transformed a one-episode appearance as Mimi on *The Drew Carey Show* into a popular recurring character throughout the series. Simply having performers appearing on a successful program will not automatically draw an audience. Exposure on network television is not equivalent to audience appeal. The appeal has to be quite clearly defined in viewers' minds before they tune to a program specifically to see a personality.

Overnight Ratings and Marketing

Overnight ratings measure the effects of promotion. When a show debuts on a Monday, the networks have a strong indication of its popularity by Tuesday morning. During the second week of a new program, there is an opportunity to increase the on-air, print, and radio promotion for a promising show. Program promotion is akin to refilling the empty shelves in a retail store. Merchants need to know which way to invest promotional dollars and how to rearrange the shelves to display products that are not moving.

With the advent of peoplemeters in 1987, audience measurement became more complex, not only for programmers but for promotion people. While the original metering system counted only heads, the peoplemeters also put demographic data at the industry's fingertips. Because this new information is available on a daily basis and used heavily by broadcast and multichannel competitors, promotional campaigns must be tailored to even more specific tastes and judgment than in the past and constantly revised and improved based on the peoplemeter ratings. It is no longer sufficient to be number-one in all households; networks need to reach the audiences targeted by advertisers.

Research and Marketing

Everyone in a network promotion department is aware of research. Promotion is discussed constantly with the research department, and research staff members sit in on a good deal of promotional planning. Because promotional research can focus on specific audiences, it can provide the information to schedule different spots for different time periods. Research also can suggest ideas for the appeal needed to produce the promos.

Print advertisements and on-air spots always are created to appeal to particular demographic segments of the audience. NBC's 1998 campaign for *Friends* targeted people who were less than 30 years old. ABC's 1998 campaign for *Two of a Kind* targeted TV viewers who were preteenagers.

Programs also are promoted by region when necessary. If a network's research department finds that a show is not doing well in a certain part of the country, promotional campaigns immediately can be directed specifically to that region through the use of radio, newspapers, and local on-air support from the network's affiliates. If, on the other hand, a show is not doing well with a specific audience segment on a national basis (if, for example, all of a sudden, fewer women watch because of something the competition is doing), nationwide on-air and print promotion can be redirected toward that audience segment. Research is the measuring device used to direct network advertising and promotion in terms of gross numbers of homes, demographics, and regional appeal.

Research is used in testing approaches to promotion as well. For example, research can be helpful in developing formats for print advertising. Networks' promotional staffs often consider 20 or 30 different design ideas and copy approaches for a single program. Five or six concepts eventually are field tested with focus groups in five, six, or seven different markets around the country. Finally, one is adopted for the upcoming fall (or midseason) campaign.

With demand approaching 7,000 spots a year per network, little time is left for testing daily on-air promotion. Certain basics come from experience, however. Finding something in a show that is promotable is relatively simple after talking with the people who make the show—mainly because one criterion for choosing prime-time shows is that they be easily promotable. Network promotion departments maintain day-to-day, hour-to-hour, minute-to-minute liaison with network entertainment divisions, news divisions, sports divisions, and the producers who make the programs. Liaison between producers and promoters is absolutely essential to the marketing of any product and certainly to the marketing of television programs.

How promotion departments tell the public about programs is where promotional creativity comes in. Do they show audiences a clip? Do they edit fast cuts of some kind? Do they use animation? Do they screen a show and elicit people's reactions to it? Do they have the stars talk about it? Do they treat the show like a product and create original commercials for it? All kinds of techniques are possible; and research, when available, will show which appeal to emphasize to different demographic groups.

NETWORK ON-AIR PROMOTION

Originally, the only type of television promotion that viewers saw on the air was a 30-second piece of video (a clip) with an announcer saying enticing things about the show (with voice-over). A few promos were more sophisticated in the 1960s and 1970s, and sometimes the dialogue in the clip came through so that viewers might hear a joke or a scream or the screeching of tires.

Increasingly in the 1980s, the networks began editing clips in the manner of movie trailers, snipping a piece from here and a piece from there and putting them together in such a way that they communicated the essence of the show in an entertaining or exciting way. Because of facilities and technical problems, however, production was limited to 300 or 400 spots per year for prime time and a few other dayparts.

While the traditional approach to promo making dictated the use of program clips, fully one third of networks spots now utilize original live shoots. In other words, prime-time promos are produced as commercials are, using specially produced original material and big budgets. Although about 80 percent of promos designed to introduce *new* programs continue to employ actual scenes, many key marketing points are now being made by means of specially scripted and taped spots.

The daily bread and butter of broadcast network episodic promotion for established programs, however, continues to draw on clips. Promos for situation comedies, for example, nearly always consist of a clip containing a joke within the dialogue, accompanied by a voice-over that identifies the show and time. All the broadcast and cable networks are seeking original ideas that push out the boundaries of both style and content. The creative challenge for promotion is to discover, write, and produce original promotional concepts. At the national level, a strong effort is being made to compete effectively with advertisers' commercials for the viewers' attention. When a promo succeeds in standing out from surrounding clutter, it is said to be a *breakthrough* and probably will win awards.

Another innovation of the early 1990s that has become commonplace now involves split-screen promos next to the closing credits of programs. Before this technique was developed, audiences were expected to sit through every show's closing credits with only a voice-over to announce the next show. The advent of *seamless programming* (no break in the action between adjacent shows) led to innovative uses of short, compelling promos to pass the viewers quickly from one show to the next, with minimal distractions from either closing or opening show titles.

Network promotion executives have recognized the need to reach out to creative resources outside their own departments for fresh ideas and new skills. Chuck Blore, head of his own creative services company and veteran writer-producer of television and radio promotion, explained the kind of innovation he thinks is required: "Promos that simply provide program information become part of the wallpaper of television messages. There needs to be an element of memorability built into the spots or ads to make them stand out. It is necessary

Before TV, two world wars. After TV, zero.

Figure 4–1   *Example from ABC's "TV Is Good" Campaign. ABC logo used with permission.*

to address the marketing problem from the perspective of the viewer rather than the advertiser." Effective television promotion seems to work on an emotional level through the devices of humor, warmth, or drama. Innovative promotion benefits the broadcaster through heightened viewer awareness of the advertising message. For the public, the rewards are promos with the values of entertainment.

For example, NBC developed a highly creative campaign for its summer reruns in the late 1990s, "If You Haven't Seen It, It's New To You." In these clever episodic promos, the announcer addressed the audience with specific questions about program clips: "Did you see Chandler and Joey's big secret about Ross and Monica? If you haven't seen it, it's new to you."

Another example involves ABC's 1997–1998 "TV Is Good" campaign in which tongue-in-cheek suggestions were made that television is a great way to spend time, in contrast to commonly held suspicions that it may be a waste of time. "Reading is overrated" and "Museums are boring" were some of the more memorable iconoclastic digs against high culture, with television as the time killer to be embraced, rather than shunned. Television is at the heart of popular culture, and ABC attracted a great deal of attention (albeit sometimes negative) by promoting the idea that no one should feel guilty about indulging in such an enjoyable way to spend free time. Figure 4–1 illustrates one of ABC's ironic messages.

BRANDING APPROACH

The most effective use of promos takes place when the network can organize a campaign around a theme. Must-See-TV ads, for example, provided NBC with a powerful *branding* tool that has enhanced all the programs on the network.

Catchy jingles and the use of a voice-over in the mode of a lounge singer helped NBC generate excitement in several "Must-See-TV" promos in the late-1990s.

Even upstart networks have achieved some success with themes that often go beyond their campaign slogans. For example, the WB network used a cartoon frog and the dubba-dubba song in the late-1990s to draw attention to its shows.

PROMO SCHEDULING

Television executives today have long recognized demographic differences in viewing patterns. The Saturday morning audience consists of mostly children; the Monday to Friday daytime audience is mostly women; prime-time audiences are whole families; ESPN attracts mostly men; MTV appeals mostly to teenagers. But certain shows have different types of appeal for different people within a demographic group.

In editing and producing spots for various time periods, both the content (appeal) and the scheduling of spots become critical functions. The networks produce an ever-increasing number of targeted spots for single programs, rather than continuing to run a few generic spots all over the schedule.

Cross-Plugs

A *cross-plug* is a specific promo for the next show inserted within the preceding show or a spot for the next episode of the same show inserted in the previous episode. A *vertical cross-plug* is for the next time period; a *horizontal cross-plug* is for the next night (or next week if scheduling is weekly). According to industry research, the highest number of sets-in-use is at 9:00 P.M. The strategy behind vertical network cross-plugging is to begin building toward that peak audience at the start of prime time. Thus, the goal of cross-plugging is to guarantee maximum audience flow from 8:00 to 8:30 to 9:00 P.M. and on through prime time. Cross-plugs to encourage audience flow have become common practice at all broadcast and cable networks and most stations. In 1998, one Hollywood producer made news by cross-promoting *The Practice* (on ABC) on *Ally McBeal* (on competing Fox). The technique was effective even if many Fox affiliates were upset with lost viewers following *McBeal*.

In cable, most networks are either *vertically formatted* (all the same type of program as in all weather, all sports, or all news) or *horizontally stripped* so that they can promote the same show or type of show every day in the same time period. A&E, for example, schedules documentaries at the same hour each night and improvisational comedy at another hour, thus the network can horizontally promote tomorrow's program in tonight's program. Ideally, the promotional spots play to captive audiences, those who already have shown an interest in that programming. USA Network takes the same approach, promoting stripped off-network "action" shows by using each episode as a vehicle for promoting the next show in sequence that night and the next episode the next night. It also cross-promotes different series within one another. These techniques were adapted directly from successful promotion practices by independent stations.

Multiple Spots

As explained in Chapter 2, *multiple spots* contain stacked promotion for more than one program, usually several scheduled sequentially on the same evening. Because promotional time always is limited, networks have to promote selectively. The more competitive the network television business becomes, the more important on-air promotion becomes, and every program acquires its own priority rank. The flexibility of tape makes it possible to fractionalize on-air spots; that is, instead of one 30-second spot advertising only one show, groups of shows can be promoted inside one spot.

In the early 1980s, this stacking practice was extended until, finally, an entire night's lineup was often included in a single spot. When the evening included many half-hour shows, multiples usually were poor promotion, because the audience can absorb only a limited amount of information in 30 seconds. A multiple spot works when dealing with a few easily identifiable programs in a stable schedule, but it can create overload on a night in which two or three shows out of five or six are new shows or specials. The mind cannot absorb sufficient information in 23 seconds (the usable amount in most 30-seconds promos). But because there are no reliable research findings on just how much information people can absorb about six television shows in 30 seconds, the subjects of the ideal and maximum numbers of how many shows to include in a multiple spot remain judgment calls. Typically, 30-second multiple spots (or their print counterparts, stack ads) promote from two to four or five shows today.

Fall Campaigns

Fall campaigns ostensibly are intended to achieve one primary goal—*to get the greatest number of people to sample as many of a network's prime-time shows as possible.* New shows have the highest priority for promotion; returning shows in new time periods have second priority in promotion. Movies also may have high priority at the broadcast networks because they represent "event" programming and occupy a large amount of an evening. Shows that return in their previous time slots have fourth priority. A show's time priority generally determines how many different promos are produced from it and how they are scheduled.

Fall campaigns involve certain tangibles for broadcast stations. Starting in the summer, the broadcast networks send their affiliates on-air promotional materials via closed circuit television for local use. All the fall promos, graphics, animation, and music go to the stations. They have to record them, edit them, and fit them into local needs. Stations get this at no charge. In addition, the broadcast and cable networks send money for joint *cooperative advertising* between the network and the station, and co-ops usually promote network prime-time programs. Figure 4–2 illustrates the type of co-op print promotion ABC used in the late-1990s.

The networks also send slicks (named for the glossy paper on which they are printed), generic print ads for adaptation into local stacked ads or tune-in ads in newspapers and program guides. Networks also supply slides and videotape for use in shared IDs. Stations insert their own identifiers in promos and ads that promote network programs to show local viewers where to find the programs.

Networks also produce radio spots, prerecorded and supplemented with scripts for local live tag copy. They send posters featuring new shows and photographs of personalities starring in network shows. Moreover, promotion experts are available to help individual stations. During the summer, a 30-minute videotape dealing with the network's programs is distributed free to affiliates to use in local sales promotion. The thematic opening and closing of those tapes serve as the basis for station spots to tie in with the network's generic approach to the fall campaign.

Promotion is a 52-week-a-year operation. National television ratings occur year round, and marketing and promotion budgets must be continuous. Even so, promotion peaks in the third and fourth quarters (fall and Christmas) and peaks again in the first quarter (February) with the promotion of new programs. But frequent preemptions of the regular schedule for specials and movies, and introductions of new programs all year, mean there is no such thing as a slack time. Every period is measured by research companies and examined under a microscope by the industry. Nevertheless, the broadcast networks continue to create their glitzy fall campaigns, aimed as much at exciting the affiliates at their annual meetings and attracting advertisers as at building audiences.

Co-Op Advertising

All commercial broadcast and cable networks offer co-op advertising programs to their affiliates in which the network supplies the materials and pays half the cost of the ad. The networks want affiliated stations to advertise network programming in any measured local media at specified times (such as in the fall). Stations decide what media serve their needs best in their own markets.

Co-op advertising typically is a 50-50 arrangement wherein the networks return 50 cents per dollar spent by affiliated stations. A fixed amount is generally

Figure 4–2 *ABC Co-Op Ad. ABC Sports. Used with permission.*

allotted to each of the 211 markets, and each affiliate is in charge of that budget. Affiliates usually can spend it at any time of the year and for any program within the prime-time schedule, but priority recommendations are supplied by the networks. The rule of thumb is that the most popular shows don't need the affiliates' help, and the weakest shows won't benefit from help, so most co-op dollars are spent promoting the "almost hits" in the prime-time schedule. The networks occasionally pick up even more than half the cost of co-op promotion for pivotal programs, in hopes of having additional promotion boost audiences during ratings periods.

A B C D E F G H I J K L M N O P Q R S T U V W X Y Z
1 2 3 4 5 6 7 8 9 0 -TV ℗

Figure 4–3   *CBS Newspaper Co-op Ad. CBS. Used with permission.*

Although network co-ops are primarily for prime-time programs, occasionally the networks offer news co-ops, as discussed in Chapter 5, and frequently encourage advertising that jointly promotes local shows adjacent to network programs (see Figure 4–3). The networks, of course, want the strongest possible lead-ins to prime time and their newscasts. For example, early-evening local and network news sometimes are promoted in the same stack ad or multiple spot; the station's 7:30 P.M. access show and the first show in the network schedule usually can be effectively promoted as a unit; the last prime-time show, ending at 10:59 P.M., sometimes can be effectively promoted with the local late newscast. The networks usually pay only half the cost of the network portion of the ad, however, not half the total cost of the ad. Co-op strategy is becoming even more important as the television marketplace becomes more competitive. Network strategy is to maximize advertising support even in the smaller markets.

Some broadcast networks even pay affiliates in larger markets to run network promotion during their high-rated early fringe, news, and access programs. ABC began this practice in 1989, and other networks followed, but it is practiced only sporadically and only for particular programs.

Web Sites

Networks maintain sophisticated web sites to promote their programs and market tie-in merchandise. The CBS site (www.cbs.com) begins with a page that requests Zip code information to determine where the user lives, before going to the main page. Subsequent pages are tied to the local affiliate for that Zip code area. NBC (www.nbc.com) also requests Zip code information but asks the user after the main page is shown. Fox (www.foxnetwork.com) and ABC (www.abc.com) provide a "go to" box on their main pages so that the user can visit the local affiliate. Regardless of the method, each network is interested in connecting the potential viewer to the local affiliate.

The content on network sites is similar but laid out differently. Moreover, the page layout undergoes continual revision. The common thread among the network web sites is an effort to promote "tonight's" program lineup. Various buttons and click boxes also allow the user to obtain more information about a favorite show, enter a contest, download the new-season schedule, or participate in chat groups and forums. Some networks have special sites dedicated to particular shows and personalities. NBC promotes Jay Leno and Conan O'Brien, for example; Fox displays banners for its top prime-time shows like *King of the Hill*; CBS reruns the latest Top 10 list from David Letterman; and ABC links users to its popular daytime soap operas.

Banner advertising exists on some network web sites to cross-promote other web sites. For example, NBC advertises Microsoft, with whom it co-owns the MSNBC cable channel. The "Foxworld" site links its users to other Fox sites: Fox Kids, Fox News, Fox Sports, fx cable channel, and the main 20th Century Fox movie studio site (www.fox.com).

In addition, some television web sites promote television in general, with web banner ads placed by the broadcast and cable networks. The premier web site for this material is www.ultimatetv.com and its sister site www.promolounge.com, which provides video clips of network promos over the Internet. The networks seek additional venues for their multimedia promotion and marketing by linking to such general television sites as www.ultimatetv.com.

Network web sites serve to acquire and retain viewers, but the most important function is to obtain immediate feedback. Most promotion and marketing discussed in this book is "one-way" communication. Web sites combine high-impact graphics and information with the ability to connect with viewers, providing them with information and entertainment, and providing the network with responses to their programming.

OTHER MEDIA

Print, radio, web sites, and other special promotions are secondary in importance to network on-air promos. Still, benefits are to be derived from the judicious use of outside advertising in at least some of the 211 television markets. The growth of independent stations, the development of programming from newer networks like UPN and the WB, the rise of cable viewing, and time lost to web surfing have dramatically reduced the size of the total network audience, making it necessary for the networks to seek additional means to reach potential viewers.

In television promotion's infancy, newspaper and magazine advertising enabled the stations and networks to reach an audience eager to learn about the medium. Experts quickly discovered that such advertising of television programs served a dual function: First, it promoted the programs, and second, it unexpectedly created a general interest in the medium among viewers and potential advertisers. But as television's reach grew across the country and newspaper's reach shrank, the television networks turned more and more to their own medium, to radio, to cable, and to a greater use of such listing publications as *TV Guide*, because they provide more intense reader involvement. Radio's immediacy provides an invaluable reinforcement of printed ads. Moreover, broadcast networks have added cable to their promotional media mix, and at the same time, cable networks advertise on the commercial broadcast networks, at least in a generic sense. *TV Guide*'s readership tends to be older and female, and like newspaper TV supplements, it stays near the TV set and thus is handy when the viewer is not already committed to watching a particular program. The listings for broadcast services once were dominant in guides, but coverage of an increasing number of cable networks has made their programs more salient. Nonetheless, *TV Guide* and similar publications are valued for their feature stories, and the issues dealing with the new fall season are particularly well-read.

The networks also seek promotional tie-ins with other mass marketers. Reaching out, with the help of Sears, K-Mart, Coca Cola, and others, became the hallmark of 1990s broadcasting promotion. CBS was the first to announce national tie-ins with TWA and American Airlines for in-flight advertising programs and with the K-Mart Corporation for a national contest. The joint television–retailer promotion was built around a viewers' contest on the network, backed by multimedia promotions inside the huge string of 2,200 K-Mart stores and in print advertising. It was estimated that the 1994 fall program schedule for CBS received monthly exposure to more than 76 million K-Mart customers within the stores and even more through the chain's own advertising efforts (see Figure 4–4). In 1998, CBS offered a free videocassette that promoted its fall lineup to Target customers. The program featured Ray Romano introducing the 1998 season, and the show included commercials for Target stores. Declining overall network shares coupled with the growing popularity of alternative entertainment sources also motivated NBC and ABC to seek new promotional opportunities in conjunction with nonmedia businesses.

Each network is on the lookout for new domestic distribution systems for its marketing messages. The aim of these efforts is to increase sampling of new and returning prime-time programs. External promotion has become necessary because the effectiveness of traditional network on-air declines as audience size decreases. The impact of TV–retailer campaigns will come down to how well the media are used. All promotional things being equal, creativity, that most un-

Figure 4–4   *CBS/K-Mart Ad. CBS. Used with permission.*

measurable of dimensions, probably will determine the success of future tie-in campaigns.

Radio

As readership flattens or declines for major daily newspapers, the networks have begun to move a good deal of their national advertising to radio, especially for co-op buys on stations in the local affiliate's market. The networks recognize that promotional information is best delivered in the late afternoon, when the audience may be deciding what to watch that evening on television. The demise of afternoon newspapers has led to more reliance on afternoon drive-time spot announcements on the radio to remind listeners about the evening's prime-time lineup.

Radio is particularly useful in attracting attention to new programs targeted at specific audiences. Radio is a medium where the advertising target easily is decided by a music format that appeals to a particular group. Networks and their affiliates can enhance the audience sampling of appropriate programs with well-placed promos on radio stations that reach the same target audience.

Network News Promotion

News viewers change their attitudes and therefore their viewing habits very slowly and sometimes reluctantly. News ratings on a national level change through the course of years rather than in weeks as with entertainment programs. The messages, both verbal and graphic, in news promotion make lasting impressions that strongly influence viewers' choice of newscasts. Every ad or television spot should be designed to assure the public that a news organization and its personalities are reliable, competent, and knowledgeable. How that impression is transmitted is the result of creative imagination.

The means used to promote entertainment shows also are available for news promotion: on-air, newspaper and magazine advertising, radio, billboard. But specialized magazines, news-oriented radio stations, and sections of the newspaper other than the television listing page may be particularly useful for reaching news viewers. The far-in-advance closing dates for national magazines (*TV Guide* needs its ad materials three weeks before publication) force the networks to use radio and newspapers to achieve national exposure for topical news promotions.

In on-air promotion of news, tying the national and local newscasts into a unified campaign can be useful to both the network and affiliates. In addition to the spots they produce for their own programs, the networks make special promos that show local news personalities with network news personalities. In print advertising, cooperative ventures that join the local and national news programs have become the norm. In some cases, the network provides special advertising materials free to stations for local integration. More commonly, the network pays half the media costs for ads that feature a combination of local and network news (news co-ops).

In general, network news campaigns tend to be less than memorable. There is so much risk of offending regular viewers that few imaginative campaign ideas get realized. In any event, the percentage of viewers who tune in the network nightly newscasts has plummeted over the years, with only about 38 percent regularly watching what nearly everyone watched in 1980. The advent of CNN and the more-recent proliferation of similar 24-hour news channels has had a devastating effect on the size of network news audiences, but the newscasts remain flagships of each major network, and the absence of an evening newscast condemns a network to less than equal status.

PROMOTIONAL TECHNIQUES AND STRATEGIES

All kinds of promotional techniques are available: comedy, documentary, cartoon and graphic animation, demonstration, star and public endorsements, and others. Advertisers use them all on the air every night in commercials. The question is whether the techniques of television advertising are applicable to program promotion. Few people, even in the television industry, traditionally have thought of promos in the same terms as television commercials. The advertising industry tends to denigrate TV promos by comparison with TV commercials. Commercials seem to have an environment and prestige of their own.

However, the pressure of competition (and the advent of the remote control) have pushed network television promotion operations to become as sophisticated as commercial production houses. Network practice requires dealing 24 hours a day with pictures that move and with sound. It is necessary to make images entertaining because boredom easily sets in. Constant innovation is required. Yet there have been classic exceptions to the transience of promotional work. Certain film graphic images have emerged from promotion's changing patterns and become permanent: the CBS eye; the ABC circle; the NBC peacock (see Figure 4–5).

Techniques that compress energy, excitement, and color into 2 or 3 memorable seconds are valuable tools indeed. Promotional impact has to be instantaneous, and immediate memorability is the key to tune-in promotion because it leads to an ephemeral moment in time. Once the program goes by, there is no second shot. A network's image is the sum of all its parts—the promotion as well as the programming. And the technical and aesthetic qualities of on-air promotion are central to the creation of image.

Figure 4–5   *NBC Peacock. NBC. Used with permission.*

However, an inherent conflict exists between network and affiliate strategies. For networks, the overriding strategic objective in promotion is to increase prime-time tune-in. For affiliates, on the other hand, the overriding goal is to increase local early and late evening news viewing. It is extraordinary in marketing for a national manufacturer and the local distributor to have differing marketing priorities. In television, this issue largely has been swept under the table—the networks making the improbable assumption that their traditional promotional approaches can apply equally to prime-time entertainment and local news. However, the problem offers the potential for a significant promotional breakthrough. The following chapter continues this examination of the relationship between networks and affiliates, this time with the emphasis on the latter.

CHAPTER 5

Local Station Television Promotion

Douglas A. Ferguson and Bradley A. Moses

This chapter addresses promotion and marketing for two types of local commercial television stations: the network *affiliate* and the *independent*. With the advent of digital television and increased options for video delivery from the Internet, VCRs, and direct broadcast satellite, the continued reliance of stations on major television networks is tenuous. To a greater extent than in the past, the local station must place its own priorities ahead of the network, especially as the financial relationship between them changes.

The only way a local station can truly differentiate itself from the rest of the multichannel universe is to focus on *local programming*, which for most stations means its local news product. Although not all stations have local news, this chapter includes a good deal of attention to this critical area. First, however, it is important to examine promotion devoted to network, syndicated, public service, and nonnews local programs carried by affiliates and independent stations.

NETWORK AFFILIATES

A two-way relationship exists between the four major television networks and their affiliated stations, which affects programming, news, and promotion as well as the related departments of public affairs, traffic, and business affairs. Changes in network affiliation alter the identity of stations, something that must be explained to viewers via promotion. Furthermore, changes in television standards and delivery systems affect the underlying audience perception of local television service. The switchover from analog to digital channels is creating huge challenges for local stations (and their networks). Promotion will help explain the new digital video landscape to the viewer as the various new services unfold.

Understanding Affiliate–Network Relations

A *network* is a group of stations interconnected through a single programming source so that all affiliated stations are able to broadcast the same program material simultaneously. Occasionally, the network is temporary or geographical, as in the case of regional sports networks. Networks can also be part time but permanent, as in the case of UPN and the WB networks, which began with less than a full prime-time schedule of weekly programming to their affiliates, as did Fox in 1987. In addition, many cable services such as the USA Network, Lifetime, and MTV also are networks because they distribute programming nationally by satellite to thousands of cable systems. Traditionally, however, when we think of networks we think of the four major commercial broadcast networks: CBS, NBC, ABC, and Fox.

Networks exist because expensive, high-quality programming requires wide distribution and daily promotion to build an audience large enough to offset their production or purchase cost. Because the four major commercial networks continue to capture the largest portion of the national viewing audience (except occasionally during summers), they can afford to engage in the expensive process of advertising their schedules. More and more, however, the larger cable networks are investing in innovative on-air promotion comparable to the best of network promotion. The promotional practices of the 150 or so cable networks and their 12,000 cable system affiliates are discussed in Chapter 6.

The affiliate–network relationship is built on the principle that the network supplies programming and the affiliate is its outlet. By contractual agreement, one station is the primary distribution outlet for one broadcast network in a particular market. For this service, the station usually receives compensation in the form of cash payments from the network, although the expense of high-cost sports programming increasingly is shared between the network and the affiliate. The network has sold its air time using audience projections based on the number of affiliates agreeing to air a program (*clearances*). The networks also have rules pertaining to the promotional ads they air. The most important of these rules is that local affiliates cannot preempt any of the network's time to promote their own local and syndicated shows.

Promotional Priorities and the Programming Mix

How does local program promotion fit with network programming? Does the local affiliate seek audience flow into or out of network shows, or should it concentrate on its dayparts without considering the impact of the local lead-in effects on network programs? How promotion managers treat the affiliate–network programming mix promotionally establishes their relationship with the network, and this relationship differs among the more than 800 affiliates of the Big Four. Most stations develop a formalized strategy regarding the programming and promotion mix.

One of the first principles is that a promotion department cannot promote everything. There just isn't enough time to produce and schedule on-air promotional material for all of a station's programming. Affiliates therefore focus their promotional efforts on those dayparts that bring in the most revenue—local news, early fringe, prime access, and late news. Most affiliates' local images are tied to their evening news performance. About 75 percent of a station's promotional effort goes to promoting its local news, mostly on the radio but also in newspapers and *TV Guide*. The typical affiliate allocates most of its syndicated program budget to early fringe and access, acquiring such expensive off-network and first-run shows as *Seinfeld* or *Entertainment Tonight* to anchor these important time periods. Because of the program expense involved, 20 percent or so of a station's promotional effort goes to attracting an audience for the programs that fill these two key time periods. Only about 5 percent of an affiliate's promotional effort is left for promoting other nonnetwork or network programs.

On-air promotion is key to any station's promotional effort, network affiliate or independent, and there often is more dollar value in all on-air promotion than in the outside media discussed in this section. On-air promos also provide a unique opportunity to target viewers who may be tempted to switch to another channel.

Network Support Material

Summer is the time when stations get ready for the premiere of the new fall network season. During summers, stations have to collect material on new and changed network prime-time and daytime shows. The networks provide their affiliates with information in the form of such material as prime-time promos, advertising and promotion kits, tie-in packages (shared theme graphics and music), web page graphics, and information about co-op promotion to support network shows. In addition, most syndicated shows turn over in the fall, too, so summers are a busy time for affiliate marketing managers.

During midsummer the networks send the stations completed episodes of new fall programs via closed circuit. Promotion managers record them for later use in on-air promotions and for sales department use as sales aids. The networks also send tapes of the new fall promotion campaigns first shown to managers earlier in the year at the annual network affiliates' meetings and often discussed at the annual June PROMAX (Promotion and Marketing Executives in the Electronic

Media) meetings. PROMAX has its home site at www.promax.org on the World Wide Web.

The networks also send the affiliates completed promos for new and returning shows with new campaign animation and music. Some networks produce *combination promos* with an open space at the beginning for insertion of material about local access shows. These combination promos are designed to stimulate audience flow, not only from local to network programs, but also in reverse because a strong network lead-off at 8 P.M. aids local prime-access shows. Advance tune-in occurs when the audience recognizes that adjacent programs are a combination, especially if they are similar in appeal.

Network promos, unedited footage from new programs, and other video materials are scheduled at predetermined times throughout each week and then sent to stations via satellite. Color photos and radio spots are delivered over a private internet. The networks also send much of their advance promotional material directly to local newspapers. Included with press information are black-and-white pictures, outlines of specific episodes, and names of guest stars.

Two other network services are star weekends and star junkets. Star weekends take place at various times during the year but most often prior to the new-season premieres in late summer. Stations are invited to bring their local talent to a central location where the network tries to assemble a cross-section of stars to do promos, interviews, and material for the fall preview parties. Satellite interviews, where stars are interviewed on closed-circuit feeds by local talent, are another means of localizing the appeal of national shows.

Star junkets are promotional trips around the country made by network stars, usually performers in daytime programs. Junkets are scattered throughout the year. The network arranges stops at participating affiliated stations in the top-25 markets; the affiliate arranges visits in smaller markets. While a star is in town, the affiliate's promotion manager can arrange television and radio interviews, news conferences, shopping center appearances, publicity in other local media, and of course, promo taping at the station.

Local news talent junkets are arranged throughout the year. The star network journalists do not travel, however. Instead, the affiliates send their anchor teams to New York for joint promo taping sessions with network anchor people and key reporters. If the affiliate's network has a popular and well-regarded newscast, tying the local and network personalities together can be an effective promotional strategy.

Co-ops

As explained in Chapter 4, co-ops are offered only during periods prescribed by the networks, such as the fall premiere weeks and the ratings periods in November, May, and February. Co-op funding is restricted to the amounts set by the network for each station. Some networks also require that the advertising be limited to designated network programs on designated days. A variation on this practice occurs when a network buys ad space in the 100+ versions of *TV Guide* and then customizes each ad with the local affiliate's channel number. The typical co-op print ad is a stack ad containing an evening's lineup of programming (see Figure 4–3 in Chapter 4). Space is provided in the stack ad for the station's news or prime access programs. The network reimburses the station for only half the ad, the network programming portion. Affiliated stations must pay for the space they use to advertise local programs (usually local news). Co-op is a great vehicle for promoting local news.

An affiliate's participation in a co-op plan depends on the value the station places on outside media promotion for network programs. Some stations tie their success closely to the fortunes of the network. In the case of an affiliate with a struggling network, the focus on network promotion is somewhat less critical. For participating stations, a stream of day-to-day promotional aids arrives, often far more than any promotion director can use. At best, co-op is offered 20 weeks a year, compared to the 52-week schedule for on-air promotion.

INDEPENDENTS AND DISTRIBUTORS

The promotion manager at an independent television station functions with little outside support in advertising, press relations, or on-air and general promotion. Unlike network-affiliated stations, independents have no preexisting network concepts, promotional spots, graphics, press releases, or built-ins. Independents were largely on their own until the emergence of the Fox Broadcasting in 1986 (now a major network) and two newer networks (UPN and the WB) in 1994. Independents affiliated with these two new "netlets" have become *hybrid* independents. Some *true* independents remain, especially those "affiliated" with religious or ethnic groups.

While the promotional needs of network-owned and -affiliated stations are similar to the needs of independently operated outlets, their promotional practices are different. Network affiliates receive promotional packages that accompany daytime and prime-time programming provided by the network. Independent television stations traditionally purchase most of their programming from program distributors that strive to compete with the marketing prowess of the big networks. Station promotion directors now can expect promos for high-priced syndicated shows to resemble in quality those received by their network-affiliated brethren.

Distributors of both first-run and off-network syndicated programs make videocassettes of on-air promotion materials (*electronic kits*) available. These include episodic promos in various lengths, generic promos featuring the series' stars, open-ended interviews with the stars, and wild lines for stations to utilize in multipromos covering blocks of programs. Stations are at the mercy of the syndicators. If promotion managers want to promote the local news, they need only arrange it with local talent. Getting the national talent to perform in a promo is more difficult to control.

Promoters of many syndicated weekly programs (because they get so little attention from stations) bypass the local station altogether by using web sites to market directly to viewers. In the case of low-rated or small-niche programs, such as the *U.S. Farm Report*, advertiser and audience tie-ins are possible as never before.

Despite such support, hybrid independents and true independents face the perplexing problem of promoting 18–24 hours of programming daily with no national promotional support. Although syndicators purchase large quantities of advertising space to promote their programs, it is almost exclusively in the trade press and directed toward selling their programs to stations; it is seldom in the consumer press and directed toward audiences. This pattern prevails because syndicated programs are picked up by scattered stations and aired at different times of day and on different dates (in contrast to simultaneous network-affiliate programming).

The promotional challenge at independents is to create what is not always supplied: attractive newspaper ads, innovative merchandising, engaging on-air promos, and effective publicity. Promotional materials on independent stations must have the same professional look and quality that viewers, the press, advertisers, and agencies have come to expect on the broadcast networks—at a fraction of network budgets. In many cases, the independent station is *less* focused on on-air promos because it has a smaller audience. Hence, the value of indies' on-air time is less valuable than that of an affiliate, which has a larger available audience.

The Independent Station's Image

The only identity that a nonhybrid independent station has is the one it creates for itself. The more successful an independent is in promoting its image, the more impact it creates for every program promoted. And gone are the days when the networks and their affiliates misrepresented the audience demographics of their independent competition. The independent's image changed when management began to outbid network-affiliated stations for high-priced reruns like *Seinfeld* and *Home Improvement*. These popular syndicated programs are now scheduled against the heart of affiliate schedules: evening news, early fringe, and access programs.

Just One Of The Highlights From Last Season's Number One Show.

The Cubs On

See all-new exciting episodes this season.

Figure 5–1   *The Cubs on 9WGN-TV. WGN-TV. Used with permission.*

Many independent stations have successfully competed with network affiliates by promoting themselves as movie or sports stations (see Figures 5–1 and 5–2). Not all independents, however, can afford to purchase an extended schedule of sports events or build a film library. Moreover, usually only one station in a market can credibly adopt a movie image or a sports image, although large markets often have several independent stations.

One alternative for these remaining "indies" is to promote off-network series. Since the four major network affiliates usually hold the top four ratings positions in a market, competing independent stations vie for fifth place—the "top indie" spot. If an independent station does not feature sports or movies, it must rely on strong off-network series (or sometimes its part-time network affiliation) to beat the competition.

Independent Promotional Priorities

Independents have many more programs per day to promote than affiliates. Affiliates program about 6½ hours on weekdays (between 7 A.M. and midnight); "true" independents program all 18–24 hours of their broadcast days. Therefore, independents must set promotional priorities favoring the entertainment programs that cost the most and have the greatest audience potential (such as off-network reruns of *Friends* or *The Drew Carey Show* during access time).

Whereas affiliates focus on news promotion, independents emphasize movies or sports and comedy blocks. Programs that fill large amounts of time (movies and sports) have the highest priority in promotion when the station carries them. Among series, new off-network and new first-run shows take priority because they usually are the most expensive. Another high priority for independent promotion is original prestige programming once provided by *ad hoc* (temporary, single-purpose) networks, now supplanted by the newer networks. WB affiliates and their network give WB programs large amounts of on-air and print promotion, a crucial element in the rising ratings for prime-time series like *Dawson's Creek*.

Programs that are habit forming (older stripped series after they are established or moved to low-priority time periods) and programs that change guests and features daily (topical talk and magazine shows) occupy the lower rungs of the promotional ladder because viewers come and go depending on the show's daily content. These priorities can shift temporarily as new programs come into the schedule and as others become firmly established in their time periods.

Press Relations

Independent station promotion strategies involve an entirely different approach to press relations than those of network-owned or -affiliated stations. Because in-

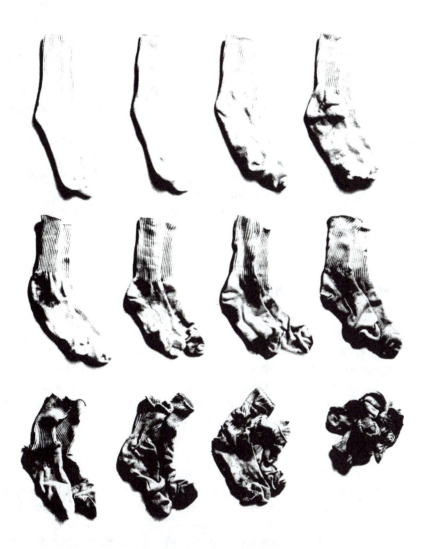

FOLLOW THE WHITE SOX ALL SEASON LONG.

WFLD is carrying seventy White Sox games this year. We suggest you tune in as **32** often as possible. After all, you should never go too long without watching your Sox. WFLD

Figure 5–2   *Generic White Sox Promotion. WFLD-TV. Used with permission.*

dependents promote programming that is not seen in 100 percent of the country, they do not benefit from the national coverage that network programming often garners. Local newspaper editors may be less familiar with the titles of independent station programs and the names of their stars, so the newsworthiness of items about them at first seems less salient.

Consequently, promotion managers, who generally supervise press relations at independent stations, need to create publicity materials and make strong personal contacts with local editors, writers, and critics as part of the station's overall promotional strategy. The pragmatics of getting publicity in print or on the air basically are the same for all broadcasters. There are three essential elements: telephone interviews with stars, feature stories about a star appearing in a program, and promotion kits. All need to be distributed by a persistent publicist (promotion manager) who recognizes the value of personal communication with the press.

THE IMPORTANCE OF ON-AIR SCHEDULING

For *all* local stations, scheduling on-air promotion is certainly as important as creating it. A well-produced spot needs to be seen—and it needs to be seen by the right audience. Effective promotional scheduling is vital to a competitive station. The station must schedule promos in the same way it handles commercial spots for its best client, by targeting a key demographic or psychographic group in advance of a promoted program's air time. Leftover available air time generally is not good enough to sell a program effectively, and when the station and the economy are strong, there are few leftovers.

Most stations recognize the importance of selling their shows, so they work out systems for clearing promotion spots during all time periods, regardless of the sales climate. This system commonly is called *fixed-position promotion*, because the promotion department actually contracts with the sales department for fixed times throughout the day. These times cannot be sold to commercial clients except on rare occasions. The times may be specific (30 seconds at the 3:00 P.M. break) or for specific dayparts (90 seconds between noon and 3:00 P.M.). A billing system usually is established for these spots for internal accounting purposes. Therefore, the promotion and the sales departments must reach an agreement that strikes a balance between the need for creating commercial inventory to sell and the need for building an audience to sell.

Combo spots, shared IDs, and audio tags are three ways to maximize leftover positions and create other on-air promotion opportunities at stations with only a limited number of fixed positions or no fixed positions at all. Combo spots, mentioning more than one program, maximize the effectiveness of the positions that are available. Combo spots also can be useful for promoting a programming block with a theme of some kind, such as "The Afternoon Funnies," if the station is running a block of situation comedies. Used in this way, combo spots can help create audience flow between programs.

It is important to know what availability exists before producing on-air promotion materials. Commercial breaks usually are divided into 30-second multiples: 30, 60, or 90 seconds. Ten- and 15-second spots also have become increasingly popular. When the sales department sells a heavy schedule of 10-second spots to clients, 20-second available spots are created. Few advertisers, however, produce 20-second commercials. The marketing manager who knows this in advance can produce 20-second promos especially to fill these spots. Marketing managers should have access to sales availability reports so that promo production plans can be tailored to a possible overabundance of abnormal lengths such as 10- or 20-second spots.

Another on-air promotional opportunity is the *shared ID* (explained in Chapter 2 and illustrated in Figure 2–8), where the legally required station identifier shares the position with a program's promotional announcement. Because the FCC requires a legal ID only to identify a station's call letters and city of license with either audio or video, there are many ways to construct a promo-identifier mix. For example, topical video of a special guest can be pulled from a talk show and combined with a topical audio announcement. The networks also have adopted shared IDs. Not only do they add opportunities for promoting network programs during network dayparts, shared IDs also encourage promotion of network programs during local programming. Affiliates are more willing to share IDs with their network (as opposed to reserving them for local shows) than give up 30-second available spots in local programming for network promos.

Another effective method is the *over-credits* promotional announcement. The copy usually is mixed with the last few seconds of the program's theme music while the credits are rolling but squeezed smaller. Squeezing the credits into a smaller portion of the screen to present video clips is a technique borrowed from the networks. Many prime-time network programs now provide a vertical split-screen for the local news anchor to tease the upcoming late local newscast.

Because promotion time is scarce and very valuable to local program promotion, strong justification is needed for a local station to air a network promo in local time. Generally, highly successful affiliates sell most of their advertising time and are able to use network filler promos only very late at night, if at all. If the programming mix is such that network programs are important to local programs as lead-ins, however, the station may decide to air some network promos to help itself. For some stations, large audiences for the last network prime-time show (at 10:00 P.M. EST) are crucial to the ratings for the late local news at 11:00. Therefore, the station may choose to promote the last network show earlier in the evening to bolster its ratings and its value as a lead-in. The networks also experiment with trading network spots for local spots in key markets.

For any local station, despite all the talk of "appointment TV" from some of the networks, the promotion of programs is tied very much to what is being shown today or tonight, not "this Wednesday" or "next Saturday." This is especially true for stations whose focus is on local news, but less so for stations whose central theme is a local sports franchise or high-demand syndicated programs. For example, promoting today's local news story or tonight's network lineup creates a greater sense of immediacy and makes the promotion more appealing.

Promotion Guidelines

To ensure the effectiveness of well-produced promos, seven guidelines should be followed in scheduling on-air promos at television stations:

1. *Establish promotional priorities.* Promotional priorities are the product of three-way communication between the programming (or news), sales, and promotion departments. Clear priorities are especially crucial during ratings periods. Since the station cannot promote all its programs, it should establish which ones are important for sales. Some marketing managers use a gross ratings point (GRP) system with weekly goals. Gross ratings points are sums of all the ratings points in a week's available spots. Here, the quarter-hour ratings for programs on either side of a break containing a promo are averaged to get a "break rating," and all the break ratings for the week are totaled.

2. *Use topicals before generics.* Unless a show is a newcomer and needs thematic promotion, topical (specific) promotion of daily episode content is always preferred. Topical promos should also be run more often than generic promos. Frequent exposure of topical promos is needed because the content changes every day.

3. *Target on-air promotion.* Schedule promotional material in programs that reach the audience desired for the program. A promo for the late movie may be wasted in the late local newscast if the audiences are not compatible.

4. *Give news promotion priority.* Local newscasts often dominate a local station's image. A highly-rated early local newscast aids network news ratings, which in turn lead into the station's access-time programs. Because of the importance of news, a base should be established for the early and late newscasts with good generic image promotion. The base then should be reinforced with daily topical promotion. The anchors' personalities are the vital, promotable elements of local newscasts. Generic spots for top personalities should be produced and scheduled in addition to image promos for the entire newscast and topical promos for daily news features.

5. *Keep a good rotation.* Separate promos for the same program by at least half an hour. This separation allows for sufficiently frequent exposure without excessive repetition.
6. *Keep informed of network on-air promotion.* Keeping an eye on network promo schedules helps in evaluating the network's promotional efforts for individual programs. Spot matching (keeping the episode and temporal sequences correct) is essential when the affiliate is supporting network programs. The station also must try to avoid promo duplication (both airing the same spot) when switching between network and local feeds during breaks.
7. *Focus on the chronology of the program schedule.* Audiences are less likely to memorize the time of shows than they are to learn *what* program comes after *what* program. Promos that teach the temporal sequencing of the program schedule often are effective in promoting audience loyalty.

NEWS

News is the arena in which most network affiliates (and many major market independents) choose to compete for ratings supremacy in a marketplace. At virtually all the 800+ affiliated television stations in the United States, including Fox affiliates, promotion of news has the highest priority. At approximately 300 independent stations, counterprogramming affiliate news and promoting an "early" late newscast in prime-time are typical strategies, along with promoting prime-time movies, sports, and off-network sitcoms. However, the station that is number one in news ratings usually is number one in overall ratings and in total dollar revenue in the market (even though, paradoxically, the number-two news station can be the most profitable station if its news expenses are lower).

Stations label programs "news" when in fact they range from local headline services to daily information capsules to in-depth magazine features. Newscasts, of course, generally have all three components. Most affiliate news promotion consists of delivering basic information about an early evening or late evening newscast to the largest possible audience. Adding showmanship to the presentation enhances the effort, but the content is the key ingredient, particularly in *tease* promos (discussed later in the chapter). News promotion messages fit into two broad categories: long-term *campaigns* (using generic spots) and short-term *topical* promotion (using specific spots).

Long-term campaigns can competitively position anchors and reporters or upcoming programs, such as a revamped noon, early evening, or late evening newscast. They also can be used to mount competitive assaults on the ratings leader in the marketplace or to demonstrate bragging rights by the station leading in the ratings. The second type of news promotion is the daily topical that re-

Figure 5–3   *Topical Local News Promotion. WTVG 13ABC. Used with permission.*

quires no more than one or two days of lead time. The subjects of these promotions are local story exclusives, special features on current issues (see Figure 5–3), or timely reactions to such public events as a court decision relating to a local issue. Whatever the category, every promotion should have a goal that is both achievable and measurable.

Early fringe programming provides a good opportunity for some stations to steal viewers from competitors' newscasts. Custom research can tell a station running an afternoon talk show how many viewers in a particular demographic group watch but then switch to a competing station for news. A well-placed promo can encourage these viewers *not* to switch. For example, a station that learns its *Rosie O'Donnell* program attracts older women (who watch another station's news) can give heavy on-air promotion to an upcoming story or series on the needs of the elderly.

Defining News Goals

The three common objectives of news promotion are to gain ratings supremacy, personality acceptance, and newsgathering credibility. Everyday promotional tactics are as direct as simple announcements of news features or new program times or the acquisition of major newsgathering equipment such as weather radar, news helicopters, or satellite newsgathering gear. More precise acquisitional goals include altering the demographic mix of the audience by capturing the 18–49-year-old women currently viewing the competition or attracting viewers from an ethnic group that makes up a significant portion of the demographics in a market. In large cities with diverse ethnic populations, such as Chicago or Detroit, targeting local audience subgroups is an important strategy. In practice, news promotion mixes acquisitive and retentive goals, but the most effective campaigns usually give primacy to a single goal.

The Importance of Research

Ratings reports show the times when a market's HUT (homes using television) level goes up. The typical causes are bad weather, a major news happening, or some other factor that causes more viewers to watch television news. Ratings analysis will spot which station gets most of the viewers during these increases. The station perceived as the most credible generally gathers the largest news audience during major news happenings where visual content is secondary. Stations with exploitative news reporting do better with coverage of weather disasters, family tragedies, and dangerous accidents, where the lurid pictures grab attention.

Successful promotion also causes the HUT level to rise. Analysis of a series of rating books will tell how much audience increase came from new "turn-ons" as opposed to "switches from competitors." When poor weather or some other outside factor causes the HUT level to increase for all stations in a market, the amount of increase at one station by comparison to competitors suggests the part promotion played.

In highly competitive situations, stealing a rating point from competitors really amounts to a difference of two points: one the station gained and one the competitor lost. And two rating points, as any research director will say, is a substantial success story.

News Consultants

Virtually all news departments at network affiliates in the top hundred markets subscribe to outside research companies for periodic analysis of their newscast content, their news delivery, and the professional and personal appeal of their news personalities. This information is available to the promotion manager, who should participate in meetings between the station's news staff and research team.

Two important agenda items in discussions with news consultants are how to make the news product more promotable and how to use the station's news personalities for promotion. Research indicates that some anchor personalities are perceived by audiences as especially credible and consequently they appear to deliver headlines in news promotion better than others. Some anchor personalities appeal to younger audiences; others are more popular with women. Whatever the strength, such features should be exploited by promotion.

Equally as important as data gathered from outside research firms is information compiled internally from ratings books. Careful study of program audience demographics often suggests more efficient scheduling of on-air news promos. For example, if the goal is to attract more male viewers to the newscast, clearly promos for news should then be scheduled in programs that attract a larger audience of men. The difficulty is to get the sales department to give up the commercial time in local sporting events.

Mini-Docs, Features, and Projects

Promotionally-oriented news operations schedule news mini-documentaries, magazine features, and special news series to take advantage of their promotional potential. Promos are placed well in advance of air dates in major rating periods. In some markets the major rating periods are so competitive that choosing and promoting nonheadline news features has been polished into an art form. Since most of the headline news is common to all stations, rating battles are won and lost on these extra features.

Depending on the length of newscasts and the size of feature reporter staffs, news directors may schedule anywhere from one feature per rating period to two or three per week. If the news contains a sizable number of promotable features, the news promotion budget should take into consideration the cost and facilities needed to inform the viewers about when and where the features will appear. It is not uncommon for local news stations to be running different promotable features at the same time. The promotional advantage usually goes to the station that ties together all media with a consistent, unified, creative design approach.

Media Advertising to Support News

A station's own air time is the most flexible kind of advertising since commercial availability can be used when unexpected news stories occur. Radio time is especially flexible because it is relatively inexpensive and requires little lead time for production. Most of the larger radio and television stations in a market have similar coverage areas. Talk radio and all-news radio have the ideal demographics for reaching potential viewers of evening television newscasts. Advertising on these stations has exceptional promotional value because of information radio's timeliness.

The largest type of out-of-home radio listening generally is conceded to be via car radio. In cities with little or no mass transit, the car radio is a distinct medium in its own right. The timing of drive-home traffic has significant carryover effects for evening television news promotion. It usually is the television station's last chance to promote its latest headline story or remind the "arriving-home/turn-on-the-news" crowd of special features planned for that day's early newscast.

In many markets, the competing television stations employ last-minute radio promotion by means of special telephone lines from their news facilities through the central telephone switching facilities directly to the radio stations. Produced and executed well, this last-minute news promotion via radio stations can achieve extra rating points, drive down the competition, and actually steal audiences from other media and outside activities.

Advertising on radio allows more content in promotions than either transit or billboard messages. For both campaigns and daily announcements, radio adds depth to the promotion effort. And because spot radio advertising has some flexibility in length (30 or 60 seconds), more than one message can be stacked on another. Stacking is of special value for news because stations that have 60-, 90-, and 120-minute newscasts accommodate larger numbers of magazine and nonheadline news features than stations doing half-hour newscasts. Since news directors choose these features not just for their informational and credibility value but to attract larger audiences, the station's on-air promotion producers can billboard several news topics within each 30-second spot and can run them back-to-back within a 60-second spot for individual newscasts, features, or a combination of early fringe, news, and access programming.

Print Space

Because major news features and mini-documentaries generally are scheduled for major rating periods, the number and size of print ads to support them usually can be estimated accurately in the annual budget. Major newspapers have a Sunday television supplement, similar to *TV Guide*, that lists the entire week of television fare (sometimes included in the Saturday or Sunday paper). These supplements generally have greater staying power near home television sets and, in many cases, higher readership than the newspaper's daily television section. Because of the supplement's longer ad deadline, it usually carries generic station ads, as well as specific promotion for preplanned news features. Mini-docs intended for known ratings periods often require a lengthy period of preparatory research and writing. Therefore, annual amounts of news print promotion should be the easiest to plan for in promotion budgets.

News Graphics and Animation

The typography in news promo signatures (usually an animated logo with a soundbed) and the titles for news features should be coordinated with the station's overall look. These are significant elements in establishing station identity and an important strategic tool.

News art should be selected with long-term use in mind. Corporate and news program logos often are retained for years (and then modernized rather than discarded). An effective station concept, embodied in news art as well as the other elements of station identity, should have longevity. Capturing the desired image in high-quality logo art and good animation is worth the extra cost and can be justified by amortization over the life span of their use.

Media Advertising Options

In large, spread-out cities with little or no mass transit, billboards along highways and main streets have greater value for news promotion than in cities where train, bus, and subway advertising reaches millions of people daily. Because of the lead time for printing the messages and the very limited number of words that will be effective, billboard and transit advertising usually are restricted to generic reminders to watch a newscast. Sometimes they introduce new personalities or features or changes in program times. If a news promotion budget can afford reminders to "Watch the news when you get home," train, bus, and subway posters are a good buy. Occasionally, these media can be bartered, partially or entirely. Paper and production costs for outdoor advertising vary substantially from market to market, however.

Whatever the medium, the length of the advertising message must be measured against the cost per thousand people reached (cost per hundred for smaller-market radio) and the speed of delivery. The history of both transit and billboard sales suggests that these forms of advertising can be traded for television air time. Other elements in media advertising strategy are the timing and size of buys. For certain times in the year, it is wise to overbuy in anticipation of major news events. In particular, planning up to a year in advance for a last-minute need to advertise unknown news features during the rating sweeps is sophisticated strategy and money well spent.

News Promotion Campaigns

Good news campaigns sell something. They sell news personalities to the viewing public; they sell special features and special ideas; and they sell positioning in a marketplace. Like every commercial product ad, every promotional advertisement should "ask for the sale"; that is, ask the viewing public to buy this newscast because of the benefit the viewer will get from watching this newscast or this news feature. Viewer benefits can be stated explicitly (as in "your most reliable news source") or by implication (as in "a professional news team, on your side," and so on).

However creative a campaign, the promotional theme comes first, and it should be embodied in a simple statement. A campaign concept that uses wordy messages can be broken into stages and taken one step at a time in separate pieces of promotion. The most successful advertising campaigns in television news have evolved from a simple statement or concept and continued to build in scope and reach. News teams seldom attain leadership position overnight; they take months or years to build momentum.

News Promotion Themes

Beneath the gimmickry and flash of most news promotion, creative brilliance reflects a dozen basic themes used alone or in combination in a promotional campaign. When deciding which theme to use, it is important to decide in advance whether the campaign should strive to retain current viewers or acquire new viewers. Some campaigns focus on the attributes of news personnel, others on the attributes of the newscast or station:

1. *The leading newscast.* If a station can lay claim to the highest ratings in its market, it can use this achievement as a promotional tool. Slogans such as "Number One in News," "The News Leader," or "Colorado's News Channel" can appeal to viewers and advertisers, as well as motivating the station staff. This campaign usually serves a retentive function for the station by reassuring its viewers that they have chosen the best channel for news coverage.

2. *The professional newscast.* This type of campaign tries to communicate the high standard of professionalism practiced by a news anchor or team. This positive message focuses on the expertise or dedication of the newscaster, touting the person's credentials or experience or the serious way in which the news team approaches their work, as in "The Professionals," "The Specialists,"

or "The Newsbreakers." A professional campaign serves a retentive function. When a station has suffered from a ratings drop or has introduced a new anchorperson, however, such a campaign becomes acquisitive.

3. *The folksy anchor.* News anchors are highly visible and serve an important role in their communities. It sometimes becomes useful to portray them as ordinary citizens with everyday concerns in a "people like you" campaign. This campaign works especially well if the audience can be convinced to identify with the anchor. When used primarily in small markets, ready identification breeds long-term loyalty.

4. *The hardware newscast.* When a station acquires a new piece of newsgathering equipment, it can use the equipment as the basis for a short-term promotional campaign. Many stations have produced promos touting their fancy helicopters, microwave news vehicles, sophisticated weather graphics, or satellite newsgathering gear. This promotional strategy primarily serves an acquisitive function by impressing potential viewers with the newsgathering capabilities of the station.

5. *The live-on-the-scene newscast.* This type of promotion concentrates on promoting the station's live, on-the-spot coverage. The increased availability of remote equipment and satellite delivery gives stations the opportunity to dominate competitors by providing a constant stream of live coverage from distant places, including the hot news spots in other countries. Research usually shows that live-on-the spot coverage is a significant determinant in newscast preference, demonstrating its acquisitive role in middle and larger markets.

6. *The feature newscast.* Some stations find it profitable to air lots of news specials and mini-documentaries (short news series included within evening newscasts) to foster audience interest (see Figure 5–4). This strategy works acquisitively, but only with about 5 percent of the audience. It also can be a maintenance device in that multipart mini-docs encourage the newscast's regular audience to watch more often.

7. *The deep newscast.* This refers to the newscast with the most in-depth coverage among stations in the market (see Figure 5–5). The more competitors step up their pace and story count, the greater is the opportunity to stress depth of coverage and attract more mature, upscale viewers. Such campaigns usually are most effective as long-term retentive campaigns, but function acquisitively for the target demographic group.

8. *The new newscast.* When a station adds news programs, expands into hourly headlines, or revamps its newscast by changing anchors or remodeling its news set, the change can be made the basis for a promotional campaign. Generally, news expansion themes, such as "Your 24-Hour News," have positive audience appeal. An effective "new newscast" campaign will serve to acquire

YOU'RE LOOKING AT
THE SUBJECT OF OUR MOST
DISGUSTING NEWS EXTRA...EVER!

 It can live up to three weeks without food or water.
It eats virtually anything from food to glue to hair
to paint chips. It's a notorious spreader of food
poisoning and carries 100 different types of bacteria.
If a nuclear holocaust were to occur, it is likely to be
the sole survivor. It may be in *your* modest apartment or palatial
estate. How do you know? And how do you defend against it?
Tom Hooper reports.

COCKROACH • STARTS TUESDAY
ONLY ON NEWS AT TEN, ⑥
(WHEN YOU'RE NOT EATING)

Figure 5–4   *New Mini-Doc. WITI-TV. Used with permission.*

new viewers curious to see the changes announced by the station, but then
the station needs other means to hold them.

9. *The best newscast.* The claim of being the "best" newscast (as in "the one and
    only") can be made in conjunction with the claim of being number one, or
    it may be made separately and accomplished either through promoting sta-
    tion or system awards or viewer testimonials. The image of a newscast can be
    strengthened by testimonials. Community leaders, celebrities, and news an-
    chors from an affiliate station's parent network can effectively laud a station's
    newscast in promos. The person giving the testimonial must be carefully se-
    lected, however, and the copy carefully written. The speaker must be some-
    one who is esteemed in the eyes of the community, and the copy cannot be
    overblown and lacking in credibility. The station's own news talent also can
    be used effectively to sell the newscast to viewers. Since the newsperson does-
    n't know the content of stories that will air in the future, a campaign of this
    sort must sell the concept of the newscast as a whole, rather than the content

Figure 5–5   *News Team Billboard. KSL-TV. Used with permission.*

of specific newscasts. Some network affiliates utilize network anchors for this purpose, such as having NBC anchorman Tom Brokaw add a spot endorsing a local affiliate's newscast.

10. *The community newscast.* Promos and ads that stress the ways the newscast represents the needs and interests of viewers can create a "community-minded" image for a station or cable system. The value of promoting community involvement is exemplified by the success of KARE in Minneapolis in the 1980s. Its newscasts and promotion were oriented almost entirely toward community and viewer needs. The station soon overcame the market's two traditional news leaders and took control of the race for local news ratings, demonstrating the long-term acquisitive potential of promoting community involvement.

11. *The constant newscast.* Another news strategy emphasizes the ongoing and continuous nature of coverage and wakefulness of the news team. WISH, Channel 8 in Indy, brings viewers the "24-Hour News," promoting the idea that the station is there, all day, every day, aware of what's going on, reporting the biggest headlines hourly and ready to interrupt with any important breaking news events. Such a strategy is largely retentive.

12. *The convenient newscast.* This strategy plays on the availability of Headline and CNN by local stations. Stations use the claim "We're there when you are," which definitely is acquisitive.

Daily News Promotion

Everyday news promotion, whether on air or in print, is more direct than campaign promotion. In most cases, the goal is to gain a viewer within 24–48 hours.

The information a promo sells may be that day's headlines, a special feature, or a one-time-only live appearance of a nationally known personality. Most stations promote their mini-documentaries, one item to a promo. And if the mini-doc has segments lasting through an entire week of newscasts, it warrants an ad all its own.

Billboard copy has only six to eight words to cover the topic; print ads are much the same because less than half the people who see ads read beyond the headlines. One 30-second promo, however, can combine promotion for three news features and hold attention because the ad unfolds out of the viewer's control. It is important to sell everything salable about news features in the spot or ad while keeping the words to a minimum. Daily promotion is quick selling; and a promotion manager has only a limited number of print, television, and radio spots to do the job.

News Teases

News headlines and teases sometimes are shorter in length than shared on-air promos lasting 15–30 seconds. Many stations take advantage of their 3- or 4-second station identifications to promote their news with a headline. The size of the audience for these brief messages is much larger than it is for longer on-air promotion scheduled outside of prime time, so the potential impact is far greater.

Writing the headline itself goes one step beyond writing billboard copy. There is a big difference between saying "The Cubs win the big game" and "See the final highlights of the Cubs game at 11." News headlines on television and radio should not be miniature newscasts but should whet the viewers appetite for watching the news. As often as possible, billboard-type headlines should refer to an exclusive feature in the next newscast.

Almost-Free Promos

Cross-plugging news features is almost like getting a free promo. Cross-plugs are not charged to commercial time and do not show on the programming log. Their only costs come from the time for a newswriter or program producer to insert the plug somewhere in the program. Within the news itself, many newscasts tease the features coming up right after each commercial break with copy that reads, "Stay tuned for . . . right after these messages." This type of tease also is called a *bumper*.

Stations that have two early newscasts—5 P.M. and 6 P.M., for example—can take advantage of the earlier newscast by having the 6 P.M. anchor appear about 45–50 minutes into the first hour with a tease for the 6 P.M. feature stories. The networks' morning shows all have local minutes blocked out, in which stations can insert a mini-newscast. Such miniature headlines also may contain a plug for exclusive news features in the early or late evening newscasts.

Weather breaks always should contain the name of the program, the channel number or call letters, or the name of the weather personality—as in, for example, "Channel Seven's Herb Brooks says we can expect rain later today." When people talk about the weather, they have a tendency to repeat the entire statement they heard and create their own word-of-mouth promos for a station's name or weather personality.

Network Cross-Plugs

Network news shows frequently make their personalities available to affiliates to cross-plug local and network newscasts. Prerecorded tapes, whether full length or tag lines, can ensure smooth transitions between network and affiliate news, thereby linking the two newscasts. Should network news personalities be visiting locally, it is ideal to prepare on-air promotion showing both the local and network anchor people seated on the local news set. Taping several promos will allow frequent airing without wearing out the same promo in night-after-night display. The local news anchors, however, carry the news burden in a market; seeing that they come off well in a tandem production with network news is the promotion managers' first priority.

Public Service Cross-Plugs

Since every station runs a large number of public service announcements daily, it often becomes possible to have news personalities prepare charity or community-oriented spots. Every free mention on the air is a personal promo for the station as well as for the news personality, generating goodwill and a sense of community involvement. Some of a station's personalities may have time for only one big project a year (such as requesting toys for a local children's hospital at Christmas), but they also can be asked to do on-air public service spots for the station. Outside press organizations frequently rally behind public service efforts, thus creating more news with rewards that go beyond personality promotion.

Press Relations for the News

Facts about a station's news personalities and daily news features should not be overlooked in everyday press bundles. Most newspaper columnists shy away from reviewing mini-documentaries and news features, primarily because the newspaper competes against the local broadcasters for news coverage, but at times special features can be telephoned to the newspapers. Uncommon timeliness or an outrageous fact uncovered may stimulate interest. When columnists have a slow day, they may be eager for that extra information.

A promotion staff member should make daily runs through the newsroom to inquire if the news anchors intend to make appearances on their own (not arranged by the promotion department). If so, the promotion department should furnish biographical materials, a photographer, or other useful assistance. In the larger markets, news personalities are celebrities of such magnitude that they frequently have agents or business managers to handle their public appearances. When this is the case, coordination is required to bring about the maximum amount of goodwill.

Promotion departments occasionally set up a speakers' bureau to assist station personalities (and often management and production staff as well) in public appearances. Before initiating such a project, the station's news personalities should be polled to assure their interest in participating. A speakers' bureau requires brochures to mail to community service and industrial organizations that regularly use speakers, parade personalities, contest judges, and grand marshals. The brochures need periodic updating and at least two mailings a year. Obviously some of a station's news personalities will welcome a speakers' bureau more than others, but the more a station's talent meets the public in functions, the easier it is for the promotion department to expand its viewing audience and create station goodwill.

PUBLIC SERVICE

Public service promotion allows a network, station, or cable operator to position itself as the friend and ally of its audience and, at the same time, draw new audiences to its programs. While other media in a market use their advertising, promotion, and public relations resources to tell their audiences how important they are, stations (and cable systems) using public service promotion actually can perform invaluable services on behalf of their audiences or subscribers. These services can enhance a radio or television station's image and improve its ratings and build audience loyalty for cable operators. Most of all, public service is an opportunity to give more exposure to its local on-air personalities.

The two major elements of on-air public service are public service announcements and public affairs programming. *Public service announcements* (PSAs) are announcements for which no charge is made to promote activities of federal, state, or local governments (such as anticrime efforts, see Figure 5–6, or Partnership for a Drug-Free America), the activities of nonprofit organizations (such as the United Way or Red Cross), or any other announcement serving community interests (such as messages urging listeners or viewers to vote). PSAs can be highly produced spots using actors or station personalities at remote locations. Most radio and television stations and many cable systems also air a simple audio-over-slide "community calendar" listing upcoming local activities.

Most stations are inundated with local and national PSAs, often to the point where demand exceeds the supply of air time. Stations or local broadcast associations usually organize rotation plans that manage the flow of spots. These rotation plans generally work against the impact of any individual spot, delivering the reach but seldom the frequency required for impact. Because public service announcements are a large part of a station's community outreach, they need to reflect current public issues and needs.

Public affairs programs deal with local, state, regional, national, or international issues. They include, but are not limited to, talk programs, commentaries, discussions, speeches, editorials, political programs, documentaries, mini-documentaries, panels, round tables, vignettes, and extended coverage (whether live or recorded) of public proceedings (such as local council meetings, congressional hearings, or political conventions). Production quality for local programs ranges from "talking heads" to sophisticated, goal-directed series aimed at specific ascertained com-

HANDS UP

A NATIONAL
VOLUNTEER EFFORT
TO HALT CRIME

Figure 5–6 *Hands Up Logo. Used with permission.*

munity problems, highlighted by a prime-time special. They often include a news series, PSAs, editorials, and segments in all locally produced programming.

As with public service announcements, many broadcast stations feel obligated to air their public affairs programming in the time periods with smallest audiences. And yet, public service announcements and public service programming can contribute to a station or system's total marketing strategy. Instead of placing this material in time periods with small audiences or allowing the spots and programs to lose their impact by covering a wide range of social issues, many stations harness a significant part of this material under the umbrella of a specific goal-oriented campaign. The spots and programming then not only fulfill promises to serve the audience but can be used to promote the station's own community image.

Strategies of Public Service Promotion

The strategies of public service can be divided into three broad categories: passive, active, and interventionist. Stations and, increasingly, cable systems commonly are classified by community groups and business organizations according to their public service policies and practices. The *passive* stations and systems present no more than the required share of public service announcements and rotate them in accordance with their license commitments. These stations run PSAs sent to them by national or local organizations. Infrequently, they produce some of their own but see little need to showcase them in highly visible time periods, give them high production quality, gear them to overall promotional needs, or carry out campaigns with flair or a sense of commitment.

Active stations and systems involve their staffs and air time in advancing local causes. They typically associate themselves with established community projects and charities, furnishing enormous amounts of support to ongoing local institutions such as hospitals, rape crisis centers, and mental health facilities. They participate actively in services such as United Way campaigns, Muscular Dystrophy telethons, or Red Cross emergency drives. These stations typically provide service that takes advantage of promotional opportunities.

Stations and systems active in public service commonly take local fund drives and turn them into annual crusades. They use local personalities, tie in local sponsors, coordinate with dozens of community organizations, and powerfully persuade their audiences to participate. By allying efforts with other media, stations can get printed flyers and radio announcements provided "in kind." A station in Toledo, Ohio, for example, got behind a community effort to create awareness of Metroparks, a citywide system of outdoor parks.

Interventionist public service promotion is not just fund-raising or appealing for assistance on behalf of local charities. The strategy requires that the broadcaster or cable operator identify specific social problems and, in alliance with such partners as business, government, and organized volunteers, intervene in those problems on behalf of the audience while meeting a number of the station's or system's public service, ascertainment, and promotional needs. The basic idea is to use the airwaves to allow *others* to find solutions to problems, not for the station to tell the community what to do.

If it is properly tied to a station's or system's general advertising approach, public service promotion leaves the public with a strong image of a substantial force in the community. Interventionist public service promotion brings a wide variety of benefits. Although no single campaign should be expected to achieve all the benefits summarized here, different campaigns can aim at clusters of goals. Some can be targeted to enhance the station's or system's image and garner accolades; others can serve as rating boosters and a means for creating teamwork. Among the benefits of interventionist public service promotion are these:

1. Performance of meaningful, measurable service on behalf of the station's or system's audience.
2. Intense, highly dramatic, relevant programming.
3. Short-term programming and promotions that increase ratings.
4. Long-term positioning of the station or system as a community leader and "friend" having a positive influence on all on-air and off-air efforts.
5. Positive local and national public relations.
6. Tools for merchandising for the sales department.
7. Opportunities to advertise the station's or system's identity legitimately as community friend and ally.
8. Provision of a management tool to encourage teamwork and morale among staff members.
9. Attraction for local and national service awards.

The strategies for achieving these benefits are identifying and intervening in social problems while coordinating public service, promotional, and advertising efforts. Public service departments at stations usually are separate from promotion, but opportunities to benefit both create close ties. Stations adapt generic campaigns to their own promotional needs. As mentioned earlier, stations frequently use local news personalities to deliver PSAs.

Organizing a Campaign

Ascertainment and community outreach are the best ways of identifying local issues. One should look for an issue that

1. Is important to a large segment of the local audience.
2. Can be explored in a fresh and exciting way.
3. Actually can show measurable change for the better in the community.
4. Has natural allies in the community who can take on much of the work.
5. Takes advantage of the station's or system's strengths.

The judicious selection of a problem is crucial to whether or not a campaign will work. Obviously, a local television station or cable system is not going to solve the issues of world peace and nuclear disarmament. It might help mediate a school board problem, however, or encourage a dramatic increase in volunteers to alleviate specific local problems.

Management should be wary of taking on a campaign topic that its audience might regard as dull or depressing. Unless handled properly or carried on-air for just short periods of time, some topics may cause the audience to tune out. This does not mean that a station or system should ignore these topics, only that it should be aware of the pitfalls. Moreover, those designing public service campaigns should be sure that their efforts are truly constructive. A health campaign that gives people faulty medical information can only tarnish the station's or system's image.

Intervention is at the very heart of public service promotion. Unless a campaign finds an imaginative way to deal with a problem, it does not meet the criteria for interventionist public service. A basic outline for such a campaign follows:

1. Isolate a community problem.
2. Talk to those in the community who are trying to deal with the issue. Ask them what they would do if they had a broadcast facility at their disposal.
3. Make a list of those who actually can work on the campaign and resources they might be able to commit.
4. Determine what the staff can hope to achieve.
5. Allows the community to make use of the airwaves to "solve" the problem.

Resources

The major difference between large-market and small-market participation in interventionist public service is a matter of scale. Social problems are as easy to find in small cities as in large ones. The key challenge faced in conceiving and mounting the public service or promotional approach in small markets is securing staffing and dollars. One is advised to select only projects that realistically can be implemented and to take advantage of the close community ties usually found in smaller cities by leaning heavily on local resources.

A station can produce its public service promotional campaigns for little or no out-of-pocket expense if it is creative and resourceful. A community group or business that wishes to sponsor costs, provide staffing, or supply services (such as distribution) usually can receive on-air credit—a form of institutional advertising that may well bring them business. Spots crediting local service groups and businesses with support often can be counted by the station as part of its PSA commitment. Since each case is different, it is prudent to check station (and group) policy. If these obstacles are surmounted, a campaign has a powerful way to fuel itself with money and personnel.

Another approach is to sell a campaign to one or more clients, thereby increasing the station's revenue during slow sales periods. In this case, the on-air material must be logged in as commercial matter. A third approach—split logging—allows the station to log a campaign spot as "other" except for the sponsor's tag, generally logged as "commercial matter."

Most broadcasters and cable operators engage in some public service activity. Many, however, complain that they do not receive full credit for these activities. The best way to maximize the value of community involvement is by ensuring that the public service activities are fully integrated into the station's or system's overall identity umbrella. Management can gain credit in the public's mind through consistent promotion. When the station's or system's overall promotional strategy, including theme and IDs, reflect public service commitment, the message will get to the public. Remember, "If you keep it to yourself, don't expect the public to know about it."

SUMMARY

Local station promotion encompasses many types of stations, from full-network affiliates to true independents, focusing on entertainment service, local programs (primarily news), and image promotion via on-air programming and print promos and public service. The promotion director at a local station cannot afford to specialize in any one area because a station serves a diverse group of constituents: entertainment viewers, news viewers, and local groups associated with business, government, and community. To the extent that it can be the "voice" of a community, the station is valued by the public. In large part, the public's image of the station is influenced by the efforts of the promotion department.

CHAPTER 6

Cable Marketing and Promotion

Randy D. Jacobs and Robert A. Klein

This chapter focuses on the cable television industry, although many of the strategies and tactics are equally applicable to other technologies, such as direct-to-home satellite (DBS), MMDS, and open video systems. Indeed, there has been a trend toward calling all such delivery systems *multichannel television*. Still, the word *cable* communicates quite well the idea of multichannel service, at least in the minds of viewers, advertisers, regulators, and investors.

As of the turn of the century, the cable industry was solidly established with more than two thirds of all U.S. television households subscribing to nearly 12,000 systems, many of which had installed advanced digital converter boxes. Cable network viewership was continuing to grow at the expense of traditional broadcast networks and their affiliates, with up to 160 channels collectively attracting more than half the total viewing audience. By 1998, for example, the combined audience share of the cable networks occasionally was greater than the combined share of the four biggest broadcast networks in prime time. Cable advertising revenue was increasing as advertisers acknowledge the impact of the medium. Competition from direct broadcast satellite services and telephone companies is now a dynamic cable industry with changing marketing and promotion needs.

Government regulation supposedly aimed at restricting cable business practices actually opened the door to new opportunities for cable growth and profitability. Technology is advancing with fiber optics, digital compression and transmission, and other innovations fueling the expansion. Industry concentration has also grown as companies like Time Warner and Viacom expand their network offerings and multiple system operators (MSOs) merge, sell off, and swap systems to achieve greater regional concentration and operational efficiency. But, with over 160 national cable networks and pay-per-view services competing for system carriage and more on the way, it has become more difficult than ever to launch new channels and almost impossible to launch on a basic tier. And with the MSOs controlling primary access to the audience, no network can survive without substantial MSO commitment or, more commonly, an MSO ownership position ("equity").

Nationally, close to 100 percent of all homes are passed by cable so operators no longer are preoccupied with initial cable construction. Now, they are concerned with upgrading existing systems and installing advanced digital boxes to allow the creation of broadband networks that, in addition to enabling traditional cable service (basic, premium, and pay-per-view), also will deliver digital TV and radio, voice and data telephony, and high-speed modem service. Cable is in such a strong position that telephone giant AT&T merged with cable giant TCI in 1998.

Marketing is the engine behind cable's growth and ability to adapt in this era of extraordinary change. The focus is on strategically manipulating the "4Ps" of marketing—pricing, product, placement (distribution), and promotion. Promotion is a primary concern and consists of network and national trade sales promotion and advertising, system acquisition and retention advertising, direct sales and public relations, as well as a heavy emphasis on program tune-in promotion at both the network and system levels. Promotional tie-ins also bring together the networks and systems.

CABLE SYSTEM CONSUMER MARKETING AND PROMOTION

Most local cable systems are owned by MSOs, which control dozens, even hundreds of systems from a central headquarters. To achieve economies of scale in purchasing and production, marketing materials from central or regional offices often minimize local identification. For example, many promotional materials for AT&T-owned (formerly TCI) systems show the parent corporation's name and an 800 number but do not identify the local system. Other MSOs take a more bottom-up approach to their marketing. In general, companies like Time Warner and Cox Communications handle their cable marketing in a decentralized fashion with local systems taking responsibility for much of their own marketing efforts. Still, even these parent companies provide local systems with corporate image campaigns and customized cross-channel, tune-in promotion.

Cable system operators' marketing goals include acquiring and retaining subscribers (by keeping them satisfied), rolling out new services, and establishing a brand image. To accomplish these goals system operators must persuade nonsubscribers to take service, encourage upgrades, reduce *churn* (turnover among subscribers), build brand image, manage subscriber perceptions, introduce new services, and encourage viewing of cable-only channels.

Acquiring Subscribers and Upgrades

Given the high percentage of homes passed and rate of subscribership, attracting new subscribers is not the marketing focus it once was. Nevertheless, paid television, radio, newspaper, magazine, and outdoor advertising are used to reach potential subscribers. Personal selling by representatives going door to door is used for launch of a system in some newly constructed residential areas (*new builds*) and for marketing new product tiers and advanced telecommunications services such as digital TV and Internet access. Direct mail and telemarketing also are used, primarily for remarketing basic service—reselling to households that chose not to subscribe during previous marketing efforts—and for gaining upgrades to expanded basic and premium channel packages.

By the late 1990s, cable operators had developed cross-marketing and promotion programs with long-distance telephone services that offered discounts to subscribers in select markets. Cooperative ventures give the long distance companies the opportunity to maintain or gain market share. For example, leading operators Comcast and Cox have begun partnerships with Sprint, the number three long-distance company. At times, Comcast subscribers who take Sprint's long-distance service get a discount on a premium movie channel package or their basic or basic-plus cable bill. Cox customers have been offered reductions in their overall monthly cable bills equal to 10 percent of their long-distance bill. And AT&T and MediaOne have employed a similar cross-promotion that allows subscribers to receive discounts on either their cable or long-distance telephone bill. The merger of AT&T with TCI is expected to set the pace for cross-promotion within the future, and telephone eventually may come via cable lines into the home, ending any meaningful distinction.

Many MSOs are moving away from mass-market advertising on television, radio, and newspapers to a targeted approach. The key is *database marketing*— using an enhanced, in-house database to reach potential customers through direct mail and telemarketing. Some system operators are supplementing their own database enhancement efforts with the PRIZM cluster system. It identifies blocks in their subscriber areas by demographics, and permits tailored direct-mail appeals to their likely viewing interests. This reduces costs and increases response rates. To a large extent, precision targeting is driven by the roll-out of digital television and advanced telecommunications services in existing service areas. When Time Warner Cable of New York City began its late 1990s roll-out of MetroChoice, a system upgrade with a lineup of many new channels, much of the direct mail and telemarketing to upgraded areas was database driven and highly targeted.

For marketing purposes, nonsubscribers are commonly divided into two groups: former subscribers (*formers*) and those who have never subscribed (*nevers*). Formers often are easy to convince to resubscribe when they have moved to a new location, and many, in fact, will telephone the cable company to subscribe without prompting.

Former pays are basic subscribers who downgraded (i.e., canceled one or more pay channels). Cable system direct mail and telemarketing can be effective at persuading them once again to upgrade, perhaps to a different pay channel. The offer made to former pays typically is at a discounted rate or for a multi-pay channel package.

Nevers, those people who have not previously subscribed to cable television, also can be divided into two groups. The first consists of young people just starting their own households. Their families may have had cable or they may have had cable in a college setting, and they are ready to subscribe if they can afford the monthly payments. In fact, young people often view cable service as an indispensable utility like power, telephone, and gas services. The second group consists of those people who, for a variety of reasons, consistently have refused cable service. Although this group is shrinking in number, some people still refuse cable because the off-air broadcasts in their area are reasonably plentiful and signal reception is of good quality. Others, especially those in rural areas, may have purchased satellite dishes before their communities were wired for cable. And still others may look unfavorably on television in general or simply are unable to afford cable service. Even the most skillful marketers will find these consumers' objections difficult to overcome.

Marketing plans that target just one subgroup of formers, nevers, or downgraders (for upgrades) have a greater likelihood of success than broad, multipurpose advertising. Cable operators should be cautious, however, not to overmarket by persuading consumers to subscribe to more than they can afford or really want. Overmarketing usually results in unwanted churn, discussed next.

Subscriber Retention and Churn

These days, subscriber retention is more of a priority to cable operators than subscriber acquisition. Appeals from competing local telephone companies and national DBS (direct broadcast satellite) services resonate with cable subscribers long frustrated by their lack of choice of a multichannel video provider. About 10 percent of multichannel subscribers presently take DBS services, and projections point to continued growth. Of concern to system operators is the outward migration of their subscribers. Research shows that over one third of DBS subscribers switched to DBS from cable. And these lost subscribers apparently are partial to highly profitable premium services like pay-per-view movies; about 68 percent of

The Comcast Cable Channel Line-up

2 ESPN	**11** WXIN – 59 Fox Broadcasting	**20** WFYI – 20 Indianapolis (PBS)	**29** CNN Headline News
3 The Discovery Channel	**12** WTHR – 13 Indianapolis (NBC)	**21** MTV – Music Television	**30** TNT – Turner Network Television
4 WTTV – 4 Indianapolis (IND.)	**13** The Weather Channel	**22** FAM – The Family Channel	**31** Cinemax
5 WRTV – 6 Indianapolis (ABC)	**14** Showtime	**23** Lifetime	**32** The Disney Channel
6 Beech Grove: Municipal/School *	**15** Cable News Network	**24** Weather Radar	**33** QVC – Home Shopping
7 WISH – 8 Indianapolis (CBS)	**16** Government	**25** Home Box Office	**34** VH-1/Video Hits One
8 School Channel	**17** WTBS – Atlanta Superstation	**26** USA Network	**35** C-SPAN
9 WGN – 9 Chicago	**18** Arts & Entertainment	**27** BET	**36** Comcast Indpls. FNN/SCORE Movie Time Community Ch.
10 Nickelodeon & Nick-At-Nite	**19** Nashville Network	**28** Real Estate Channel	**37** Preview
■ Premium Channels * Available only in Beech Grove & Southport areas.	ⓒ **COMCAST®**		**38** Pay Per View

Figure 6–1 *Comcast Lineup Card. Comcast. Used with permission.*

DBS subscribers purchase pay-per-view movies compared to under 10 percent of cable subscribers generally.

To minimize churn (turnover among subscribers) and build loyalty, cable marketers use several basic marketing and promotion techniques. Customization of print, broadcast, cross-channel promotion, and specialty advertising materials with the name of the local system helps to establish an image. Channel lineup cards, as in Figure 6–1, make using the system more convenient and encourage sampling of cable-only channels. They help subscribers recognize the value of their cable service. Cable-only program guides further enable subscribers to maximize and efficiently use their cable service. Guides may be printed or electronic, generic or customized.

Some systems mail program guides to all subscribers each month without charge, others offer guides for a monthly charge. Printed guides typically provide channel-by-channel listings of programs, feature stories, and photographs. Guides also may contain local advertising for businesses in the community. Generic guides list the programs of only the most widely distributed cable networks (e.g., Discovery Channel, ESPN, TBS, CNN—see Figure 6–2), while customized guides are tailored for a single cable system listing all or most of the channels that system offers. Electronic guides are common, especially on larger systems, but, as the number of channels has grown, the slow scroll has become more cumbersome for subscribers to use. Preview channels and built-in program guides also are an important means of assisting subscribers to learn about new premium channels and pay-per-view movies. In 1998 *TV Guide* acquired the best-known electronic cable guide, the Prevue Channel, in an attempt to sort out the often confusing compe-

Figure 6–2   *ESPN and Discovery Channel Logos. Used with permission.*

tition among listings. Another advanced service is a program guide built into the cable box with program information available at the touch of a remote-control button: An "info" request shows a program's running time, elapsed time, and show synopsis.

Building Brand Image

Before the mid-1990s, most MSOs did little to brand their systems and rarely put effort into developing a positive image in subscribers' minds. Changes in the marketplace—negative subscriber attitudes, government pressure, and emerging competition—convinced operators that traditional efforts to build name recognition and reduce churn were inadequate.

As described in Chapter 10, brand-building has emerged as a significant strategy to retain subscribers by increasing satisfaction and loyalty. In cable, brand-building programs articulate an image based on the communication of one or more messages about customer service, reliability, and technological leadership. Nowadays, brand-image efforts typically are full-blown multimedia campaigns that may include a name change, logo development or facelift, new creative message and slogan, print and broadcast advertising, outdoor billboards, direct mail, coupons, and joint promotions.

Cox Communications, formerly known as Cox Cable, has unfolded several brand-image campaigns in recent years. Cox's current focus is on strengthening customer relationships and leveraging its strong company image across new product launches, such as Internet connection. TV spots that run on cable channels promote Cox as a leader in technology, customer service, and reliability with the slogan "Expect the best."

Image marketing by TCI aims to foster loyalty among its current base of analog customers. TCI's efforts include television and direct response advertising, coupons in statement stuffers, joint promotions, and a frequent-buyer continuity program. Subscribers receive coupons good for discounts at chains such as Red Lobster, Holiday Inn, and Circuit City. The frequent-buyer plan rewards subscribers, based on the amount of programming they buy, with points good for the purchase of airline mileage and phone card minutes. The underlying strategy is to add value to TCI service.

MediaOne, formerly Continental Cablevision, changed its name and budgeted $20 million for an image campaign designed to position the company as a leader in interactive broadband services. TV, radio, and print advertising were used to deliver the theme "This is Broadband. This is the way." As follow-ups, MediaOne launched campaigns specifically promoting its high-speed Internet service and challenging DBS competitors.

Sponsorships also are used in cable operators' brand-building efforts. For instance, Comcast sponsored *The Cable Guy*, starring Jim Carrey, despite the film's negative take on the cable industry. Comcast was the title sponsor of the film's Hollywood premiere and showed the party live on its systems. Comcast also hosted local premieres in 45 markets.

Managing Subscriber Perceptions

The cable industry and its operators are extending their marketing efforts with the goal of managing consumer perceptions and addressing negative perceptions already held by subscribers. The industry has made several unsuccessful industry-wide attempts to build a positive national image. But, when the National Cable Television Association developed its "The Future is on Cable" marketing effort and its on-time service guarantee to address negative consumer sentiment about cable service, many system operators created tailored marketing campaigns of their own. Time Warner of New York created advertising with the tagline "We just might surprise you" to exploit the ingrained cynicism of New Yorkers. Ads depicted locals barely reacting to dramatic occurrences but being astonished by the timely delivery of cable service. Cox Communications ran a six-month campaign with the tagline "First in reliability, service, and technology."

Consumers are highly rate sensitive, and some system operators have attempted to strategically market rate hikes to avoid tarnishing their developing, yet vulnerable brand images. To cushion rate increases, TCI has used a marketing packet with news releases, Q&A sheets, letters to franchise authorities, and point-of-purchase brochures. The packets were sent to TCI systems months in advance of the increases. Adopting a different tact, in its notification letters, Jones Intercable (now Comcast) included literature comparing cost and program advantages of Jones' service versus DBS and, to soften the impact of the rate hike, included promotional incentives for discounts on premium services.

Marketing New Services

Increasingly, cable systems offer subscribers cable modem service that provides high-speed Internet access. The roll-out of these services presents operators with interesting new marketing challenges. The two most prominent services are Time Warner's Road Runner, named after the speedy Warner Brothers cartoon character, and @Home, a TCI venture also involving MSOs Cox Communications and Comcast. Before cable operators can introduce modem service, they must upgrade their systems for two-way capability. Relatively high installation costs and monthly rates also present barriers to adoption. With the development of Internet-ready PCs (with built-in modem and network card), installation cost should all but be eliminated. It is estimated that 7–10 million households will subscribe to cable modem within the first few years of the twenty-first century.

Cable operators have proceeded cautiously with their roll-outs, working out bugs in the service and building customer-service infrastructures. Marketing, therefore, has been slow. Promotion for @Home has used the tagline "The High Velocity Internet Service" in television advertising. Free demonstrations and discounts on installation also have been offered to new subscribers.

Initial promotion for Road Runner included simple education and awareness ads, promotional spots and infomercials, and strategically placed demonstration kiosks. To build their customer base early on, Road Runner offered cable operators two integrated marketing campaigns. Both themes position Road Runner competitively against other access providers and exploit customer frustration with slow service and long download times. The "It's a Crime to Waste Time" campaign included TV, radio, and print advertising. The "You Don't Have to Take It Anymore" effort launched with an outdoor teaser campaign followed by cable TV, radio, print, and collateral materials. Road Runner also inserts topical promotions of its features and content in its local cable ad available spots and makes extensive use of web site promotion to target computer users with up-to-the-minute information. In the world of high-speed modem services, both interface design and web sites are very much a part of marketing and promotion strategy and tactics. Time Warner, for example, has wired every school in its high-speed markets and is providing a free computer to each in order to educate the next generation of high-speed Internet users.

Tune-In and Cross-Channel Promotion

Tune-in and cross-channel promotion refer to both self- and cross-channel on-air promotion by cable systems and networks. *Tune-in* promotion by cable networks refers to self-promotion, in which promos encourage viewers of a cable channel to stay tuned or come back later for a particular program. *Cross-channel* promo-

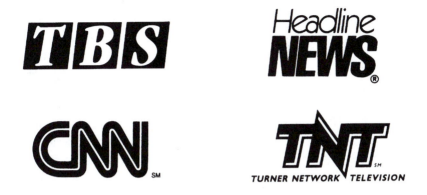

Figure 6–3   *CNN, TBS, Headline News, and TNT Logos. Used with permission.*

tion refers to scheduling promos for cable-only channels in unsold or dedicated spots on a variety of channels. Time Warner, for example, cross-promotes its own channels as well as all the former-Turner channels: Promos for TBS, Headline News, and CNN regularly appear on TNT and vice versa (see Figure 6–3). This practice enhances subscribers' perceptions of cable service value, a vital element of retention, and boosts cable network ratings making them more desirable as carriers of spot advertising.

There is widespread acceptance among cable marketers that 20–25 percent of local system spots should be devoted to system promotion, which includes tune-in as well as ads showcasing improved customer service, system upgrades, repair and maintenance service, and local public service. And with increasing channel capacity, the commercial inventory available for promotional spots increases.

Effectively promoting dozens of cable channels is a logistically complex task, requiring adequate budgets and dedicated promotion staff or outside suppliers. *Insertion capability*, the technical equipment to place local spots in the positions intended for them on the major basic cable networks, is necessary to cover up cable channels' network promos and other filler with the local promo. Systems with insertion equipment either take network promos directly from the satellite feed or rely entirely on independent suppliers like NuStar and The :30 Airborne. Network promos taken from the satellite feed are run with or without local identification and tagged with day, time, and channel information. NuStar syndicates highlight spots for insertion, and The :30 Airborne customizes and localizes network promotions to package them with local system branding. Although most local cable systems insert cross-promotional spots in unsold local time, that arrangement is haphazard, and the networks do not know when, where, or how much cross-promotion they are getting. Of the nearly 12,000 cable systems, an estimated 5,000 have insertion equipment, and all of them cover up different times on different channels. Accountability virtually does not exist.

Cable operators have moved beyond traditional cross-channel promotion, adopting other marketing practices to draw viewers to their program lineups. Comcast implemented one of the more aggressive efforts with daily spots promoting "What's on Comcast Tonight" airing nationally on all Comcast systems. The spots promote two different shows a day and run on the eight highest-rated basic networks from midafternoon to about 10 P.M. The promos are oriented toward program genres featuring, for example, sports one day and movies the next. The spots, inserted by Customized NuStar, include clips from the shows. By contrast, the telco-Disney partnership, Americast, promotes only newer networks to its customers to differentiate the service from conventional cable.

CABLE SYSTEM ADVERTISING SALES

Cable systems compete with radio, television, and newspapers for precious local and national spot advertising dollars. Operators typically handle the sale of advertising in one of four ways. Some of the largest systems employ a regional or national sales representative firm (a rep) to sell their spot time. Some systems have their own sales staffs to sell time. Some, mostly in middle-sized markets, use a local advertising agency (a *turnkey arrangement*) to sell their time in the local market. The arrangement that has emerged as most important for the growth of local cable sales, especially to national advertisers, is the *interconnect*, a cable, microwave relay, or satellite connection of two or a dozen or more systems in one geographic area to simultaneously distribute the same commercial signals. This allows cable systems to sell ads on a multisystem or marketwide basis and requires negotiation of just a single contract. Hence, the audiences of the collection of systems are about equal to that of a broadcast station, and thus the time is much more salable to advertisers than before interconnects came along. Interconnects now exist in hundreds of cable markets across the United States and represent systems that reach subscriber audiences numbering from the tens-of-thousands in smaller markets to millions in the largest designated market areas. Interconnect ad sales may be handled cooperatively or by a dominant system or an MSO in a market.

Regardless of how cable systems sell their local advertising time, professionally produced sales promotion materials are needed to convince advertisers to buy time. As described in Chapter 9, geographic coverage maps, displays of demographics for the system's subscriber base, lists of audience ratings and demographics for cable networks, and colorful information on key programs commonly are used in sales presentations to cable advertisers. In some cases, the MSO supplies such promotional information to the system, sales rep, or interconnect, which prepares the final printed materials and slick presentations and then makes sales calls. Some local systems generate the related information themselves.

Among the emerging marketing practices that help local operators sell advertising are promotional tie-ins, event promotions, and cobranding efforts. These marketing tactics leverage the success of cable networks on behalf of their affiliates. System operators exploit network programming to target specific ad client categories with promotional tie-ins. For example, Adlink, the Los Angeles interconnect, worked with the Food Network to create a series called "Food Bites" to capture the interest of a major food advertiser. Food Bites is a short vignette series offering food preparation tips such as how to make vegetables attractive to kids. The advertiser became the exclusive sponsor of the series and the distributor since has made its first significant national spot cable buys. Similar strategies have been executed successfully elsewhere. For instance, CNBC has produced a series on tax tips that can be sponsored by local financial advertisers. The New York Interconnect has sold these tie-ins to Chase Manhattan Bank.

Operators and interconnects have increased their use of event promotions to sell ad time. For example, Comcast Cable of Philadelphia boosted its sales on Nickelodeon by partnering with the network to create Nick at Nite at the 76ers, a promotion designed to draw families to a professional basketball game and turn the spotlight on Nick characters such as Ren and Stimpy. Comcast also participates in mall promotions with Nick's animated characters and has seen sales of its cable ad time to children's advertisers climb steadily.

Another benefit of mall promotions and special events to system operators is the opportunity to generate advertising revenue beyond the air time sold. Some events allow operators to extend the credit they receive from carrying a marquee event. Affiliates associated with the MTV Music Awards generated $3.5 million in extra revenue through a localized merchandising program. And E! Entertainment Television provided affiliates with Hollywood Party-in-a-Bag kits, enabling them to tie into its coverage of major award ceremonies.

Cobranded events also are effective at raising an operator's local profile. Some cable operators have cobranded their systems with the Food Network's Cooking Across America tour. One-day tour events feature well-known chefs offering cooking tips to consumers. System operators sell tickets to the events, offer advertisers sponsorships, and enjoy the positive publicity that association with the events generates. Examples of other cobranding programs include A&E's effort surrounding *Biography*'s tenth anniversary, History Channel's plan for its signature program *In Search of History*, Lifetime's cause marketing campaign for breast cancer awareness, and USA's cause marketing campaign to "Erase the Hate." The exposure that operators, advertisers, and networks gain from cobranding extends

Figure 6–4 *USA Network Logo. Used with permission.*

beyond event signage, cross-channel, and on-air spots. Operators get extensive off-channel promotional exposure from statement stuffers, retail point-of-sale displays, cable office displays, and sweepstakes entry forms, all showing their names and logos (see Figure 6–4) as well as those of the advertiser.

CABLE NETWORK MARKETING AND PROMOTION

Cable networks' marketing expenditures grew dramatically throughout the 1990s. Basic networks' expanded marketing activity reflects the realization that substantial ratings gains are achievable and that competition extends beyond cable to vie with the broadcast networks. Pay networks spend an even larger percentage of their revenues on marketing to viewers because they rely entirely on subscription revenues.

There are two types of cable networks: basic and pay services. Basic services, including superstations, are supported by advertisers as well as monthly per-subscriber fees paid by system operators. Pay services include premium channels, supported only by subscriber per-channel fees, and pay-per-view networks, also supported only by subscriber per-program fees. Basic cable networks can further subdivide into services with broad and narrow appeal and broad and narrow content (see Figure 6–5). The Weather Channel carries a very narrow range of content, but its appeal is broad; almost everyone is interested in the weather sometimes. Nickelodeon and Lifetime carry a broad range of programs, but they appeal mainly to children and women, respectively. TNT and USA Network are examples of cable networks carrying a broad range of programming with broad appeal; ESPN2 and MTV carry programming content that is restricted and has relatively narrow appeal.

At one time, basic and pay services carried recognizably divergent program content. Increasingly, basic channels have diversified into movies and variety specials while pay channels now schedule sports and entertainment series. Both pay and basic services have moved aggressively into original series and movies. Therefore, cable networks share the marketing challenge of competing against each other and broadcasters for viewers and against each other for cable system affiliates.

Developing a Niche in Basic Cable: Brand Building

In a highly competitive programming environment, building a brand image is fundamental to the success of all cable networks. The key to building a cable network's brand is identifying a viable niche and developing a distinct, positive image based on programming and promotion. Indeed, strategies created to compete effectively against other networks depend on differentiating a network from its competitors. To develop a niche and achieve differentiation, cable networks create sophisticated, brand-building, integrated marketing programs.

As explained in Chapter 10, integrated marketing calls for consistent communication of a message across promotional vehicles and media over time. The goal is to establish, then reinforce, an image for the network among already established channels. The niche is developed by attempting either to reach a demographically, psychographically, or behaviorally defined audience that established networks do not serve or, more commonly today, to challenge existing services for their audiences.

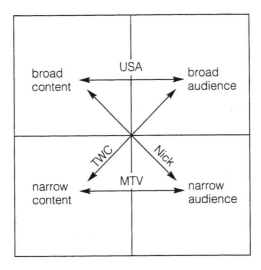

Figure 6–5 *Broad versus Narrow Appeal.*

The foundation of cable networks' branding efforts is the creation of distinctive logos or signatures and advertising with identifiable themes or taglines. As explained in Chapter 2, logos are distinctive marks that identify a network, and *signatures* are the name of the network written in a distinctive type style (also called *wordmarks*). Cable network logos often are acronyms of their full name such as TNT, QVC, and HBO. Several cable networks, especially relative latecomers, rely on signatures placed inside or underneath their acronyms. The History Channel and the Sci-Fi Channel exemplify this and make apparent the nature of their highly differentiated content. Some network acronyms take advantage of the recognizability of their parent company's logo such as CNBC and MSNBC and the ever-present NBC peacock.

As the result of long-term consistent use, some logos such as CNN and MTV have become instantly recognizable. MTV and its associated basic cable networks VH-1, Nickelodeon, and Nick at Nite have deliberately broken the usual consistency rules by varying the treatment and colors of their logos and, in on-air IDs, altering the animated motion to give their identifiers a nontraditional slant that appeals to younger audiences.

As the digital age dawns, cable networks are creating many line extensions, positioning themselves for a future of abundance as opposed to the scarcity of the past. *Line extensions* are the creation of new networks under the existing brand and logo. For example, the ESPN brand is one of the strongest among cable networks; line extensions of the brand now include ESPN2 and ESPNEWS on cable and ESPNET Sports Zone on the Internet. CNN and its sister networks CNNfn, CNN/SI and CNNI clearly represent this trend as does the Disney Channel's Toon Disney.

Over time, logos and taglines may be updated to reflect programming changes. For its first-ever advertising campaign aimed at promoting the USA brand, USA Network (whose emphasis at launch was more on sports) reworked its logo to better reflect its later focus on originally produced entertainment programming. Later, the slogan for USA became "The Cure for the Common Show." The Disney Channel also underwent a makeover. With more original productions blended into its programming lineup and a new logo, the idea is now to brand the Disney Channel as a place families feel connected with information and entertainment.

Many services have adopted a campaign theme or tagline and paired it with their logo or signature in their promotional materials. The tagline is intended to better define a network's offerings and clarify its positioning relative to competitors (Figure 6–6). For example, the VH-1 logo has been paired with "Music First." The A&E tagline "Time Well Spent" was later combined with "Escape the Ordinary." Lifetime's signature has been underscored by "Television for Women." Other networks combine a logo, signature, and tagline. The Discovery Channel's

Figure 6–6   *Cable Channel Logos. Used with permission of MTV Networks.*

signature and picture of planet Earth are combined with "Explore Your World." The Animal Planet signature and profile of an elephant reaching for planet Earth are linked with the tag "All Animals. All the Time." The History Channel's "H" logo and signature are underscored by "Where the Past Comes Alive."

Cable networks' integrated marketing now typically extends beyond logos and taglines in advertising. Innovative marketing tactics in use include in-store merchandising, sport and event sponsorships, program guides, newsletters, network seals of approval, CD-ROMs, and web sites. To mold its brand image, The Fox Family Channel uses the slogan, "A Pinch of Fox, A Whole Lot of Family . . . and Movies Every Night."

Comedy Central has utilized an integrated marketing program aimed at distinguishing the network from competitors that target the 18–49-year-old male audience. Adapted from its affiliate campaign "Save World Sanity," the consumer effort included spot cable buys in 11 markets, and print and radio ads for image and tune-in messages. A series of stunts in six suburban markets by "Jackson," the central character of the campaign, who visited these markets in a Comedy Central customized 1972 Chevrolet El Camino, and a three-market "wild posting" spree, applying posters to blank walls like urban construction sites, were among the more innovative aspects of the campaign.

Many other examples of the creativity and sophistication of cable network branding efforts exist. Lifetime sponsors a woman Indy race car driver, and its web site is designed to support the network's brand with content that includes related, practical information on women's health, parenting, sports, and fitness. The Discovery Channel owns a chain of retail stores (including the former Nature Company outlets), where merchandise such as dinosaur fossil kits and telescopes is sold. The stores' environment and merchandise supports interest in Discovery programming, while the channel's programs create interest in the merchandise. The Discovery Channel also heightened its profile when it partnered with Coca-Cola in a pavilion at the 1996 Summer Olympics in Atlanta. MTV has its MTV Video and Movie Awards and theatrical motion pictures based on its programming. The Sci-Fi Channel markets image-consistent merchandise like computer trivia games and has boutiques in Spencer Gifts stores. Nickelodeon publishes *Nickelodeon Magazine*, with a circulation of 500,000-plus. And product licensing agreements with Mattel further extend the Nickelodeon brand into viewers' lives. Even upscale toy retailer F. A. O. Schwarz features a Nickelodeon boutique at its flagship New York store.

Brand Building Among Pay Services

Brand-building campaigns for pay services differ somewhat from those developed by basic networks but not significantly. Logos, signatures, and taglines anchor the brand identities with widespread, consistent use in advertising. But, since pay services are not dependent on advertisers for revenues, much of the merchandising and cobranding activity is unnecessary. For example, Home Box Office has built widespread recognition of its HBO logo with taglines like, "It's Not TV. It's HBO."

Figure 6–7   *Showtime Ad. Used with permission of Showtime Networks Inc.*

This theme, capitalizing on HBO's critically acclaimed original programming, is designed to set HBO apart as a programmer that adds value to the viewing experience. Even so, to maintain its competitive edge HBO changed its on-air IDs, which supplement the brand-identity campaign, for the first time in 25 years. In that campaign the letters *HBO* appeared as the stars of brief action or comedy vignettes.

In an attempt to emerge from HBO's shadow, Showtime has employed an ambitious plan to intensify its brand marketing (Figure 6–7). A new lineup of original movies and series provided fodder for a new brand-identity message. The campaign featured Showtime's redesigned logo that emphasizes the letters *Sho* by placing them inside a spotlight. *Sho* is how Showtime is listed in program guides across the country. The theme for the campaign, "No limits," appealed to television enthusiasts looking for programming that pushes the boundaries of traditional television. The ads were scheduled on broadcast and cable networks, on radio, and in consumer magazines and trade publications. Posters, direct mail, and telemarketing also were planned for the campaign.

Pay per view (PPV) has evolved beyond the days when subscribers had to be taught a complex ordering process. Still, pay per view offered by national services like Viewer's Choice has never reached its potential on cable, while DBS, with many more choices to offer such as "Season Pass" sports, achieves a much higher buy rate. DBS offers so many more pay-per-view channels, while cable systems, until now, have had only a handful. Marketing efforts largely are restricted to constant tune-in promotion to attract viewers. Movie clips, schedules, and descriptions typically are included on preview channels; some systems have dedicated a channel to pay-per-view ordering, start times, and cost information. Depending on the resources of the local system, local newspaper, radio, and television ads may be used to promote the daily schedule or special events. In 1998, the two main PPV services (Request Television and Viewer's Choice) merged, which will likely bring forth further changes in promotion.

Network Launch: Affiliate Sales and Growing an Audience

The strategies employed to launch basic and pay cable services have been changing. Once, new pay networks concentrated primarily on "pull" audience promotion tactics, and basic networks focused on "push" trade promotion, convincing cable operators to provide carriage for the new channel. Today, most service launches employ elements of both push and pull strategies to sell operators on carriage and spur viewer interest in and requests for the channel.

Few truly new premium network launches have been attempted in the past decade. In fact, the number of premium channels has declined somewhat. Instead, existing premium services such as HBO and Encore have multiplexed their programming (e.g., HBO Plus and HBO Signature) for high-capacity digital systems and DBS services. When new premium networks are launched, national umbrella campaigns typically are rolled out. These campaigns include a high level of nationwide consumer and trade advertising to create awareness of and interest in the programming. Sneak previews and telethons are used to provide cable viewers an opportunity to sample the programming. Discounts and multi-pay channel packages routinely are offered to stimulate acceptance of the premium channel (see Figure 6–8).

Basic network launches have become more challenging as the number of new channel concepts has grown, and channel capacity remains scarce. Competition for carriage now is intense, and acquiring cable affiliates is by far the greatest marketing priority at launch. Without a significant number of cable subscribers to reach, a network is in no position to attract advertisers. The carriage challenge is especially great for the few remaining independent networks not owned by the leading MSOs or such entertainment conglomerates as Disney or Viacom. But well-known brand names, logos, and generous incentives for affiliates can carry a

Turn on cable. And turn on a smile!

Free Installation with $5.00 donation to MDA!

We'll install your choice of cable services FREE when you donate $5.00 or more to fight Muscular Dystrophy. We'll even give you a receipt for a tax deduction.

Save even more! HBO, Showtime or Disney just $5.00 a month!

Sign up now! And get any of TCI's great premium channels for just $5.00 a month. Order any two for just $11.95 a month! You'll see blockbuster movies. Exclusive sporting events. And exciting concerts by your favorite stars—only on TCI's premium channels.
- 24 hour in-depth news and weather coverage.
- Classic movies and family entertainment.
- Exclusive made-for-cable specials.
- Sharp, clear reception on dozens of channels.

Help Jerry's Kids!
Call Today!

Toll free 1-800/888-0445 ext. 70 or call your local TCI office.

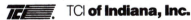 TCI **of Indiana, Inc.**

Limited time offer. Costs for premium services are in addition to regular basic charges. Offer restricted to existing service areas only. Disconnected accounts with past-due balances are not eligible.

Figure 6–8 *Pay Channel Promotion. TCI. Used with permission.*

network only so far; high-quality programming with appeal supported by strong marketing and promotion is needed to sustain interest.

The most fundamental marketing tool for any new network is the product itself. The programming must be *brandable*, compelling to viewers, and system operators must perceive that subscriber interest exists. For many networks such as Home & Garden Television (HGTV) and Outdoor Life, that means lots of original programming. For Fox's fx that means off-network reruns seasoned with a sprinkling of original shows and sports. And for the Classic Sports Network, that means highlights and entire rebroadcasts of classic and recent sporting events. In the ever-expanding universe of cable networks, the channel's niche must be apparent.

To "pull" a new network onto cable systems, networks advertise in the trade and consumer press to increase distribution and viewership. The first classic cable network campaign, "I Want My MTV," was pure "pull." M2, a line extension of the MTV brand, uses advertising on MTV to spur viewer requests to cable operators to pick up the new channel. Nick at Nite's TV Land has targeted consumers with cross-promotions on Nickelodeon and other MTV networks sister channels. Since its launch, The History Channel has advertised to viewers on its sister channel A&E and other cable networks.

Network launch "push" efforts target potential affiliates with trade advertising, personal selling, partnerships with MSOs, and equity offerings (ownership shares). Affiliate incentives such as upfront carriage fees, discounts or waivers of the subscriber fee, and expanded local ads are used more aggressively than ever.

Trade advertising designed to interest affiliates in carrying a network runs in publications such as *Broadcasting & Cable* and *Multichannel News*. One campaign created by ZDTV, a fledgling network dedicated to programming about computers, introduces the ZDTV logo and tagline "Your Computer Channel," teases readers with references to "Wireheads. Geeks. Techies. Jillionaires." and invites inquiries from potential affiliates.

Partnerships with MSOs and equity offerings continue to be used by cable networks to gain carriage by affiliates. In fact, many networks are owned, in part, by MSOs TCI, Time Warner, and Comcast. When launching the Fox News Channel, Rupert Murdoch gave an option to buy 20 percent of Fox News to TCI as an inducement to carry the channel.

The use of affiliate incentives, especially upfront carriage fees, has escalated to exorbitant levels. The turning point was when News Corp. launched Fox News Channel to compete against CNN and MSNBC. News Corp. began paying cable operators $10 for each subscriber they delivered to Fox! Now it is extremely difficult for a network to gain widespread carriage without offering generous incentives. For example, TV Land has given operators $1.25–1.50 per subscriber in upfront carriage fees and 3 minutes of local spots per hour (compared to the industry average of 2 minutes), and it allows cable operators to carry the network

Figure 6–9 *Pay Channel Logos. Used with permission.*

for 5 years with no monthly subscriber fees. HGTV incentives have included payment of $3–5 for each new subscriber that operators contribute to the HGTV subscriber base and has a unique arrangement whereby cable operators are provided three separate half-hour blocks of time for local programming.

Remarketing

Remarketing is the reselling of basic or pay services to subscribers. Called *upgrading* when households already take a basic service package, the pay networks and local operators want to persuade subscribing households to take one or more pay channels (becoming a *one-pay* or *multi-pay* channel subscriber). Both the networks and operators have an incentive to market pay channels extensively because the monthly revenue from pay subscribers is shared between the local system and network. The pay networks (see Figure 6–9) commonly sponsor telephone sales campaigns offering package deals; for example, "two pays for the price of one" (for a limited time) for HBO and Cinemax or Showtime and The Movie Channel.

The major basic and pay networks also supply large amounts of free camera-ready advertising to their affiliates for insertion in local newspapers and magazines, enclosures in monthly bills (*statement stuffers*), and inclusion in plastic bags left on the doorsteps of nonsubscriber homes (*door hangers*). In addition, they supply customized direct mailers and "last chance" postcards targeting nonsubscribers to large cable systems. Small systems receive noncustomized materials. The pay services such as HBO and Showtime also supply cable operators with point-of-purchase displays for free or a low charge. Generic *advertising slicks* (camera-ready pictures and copy) for print media and billboards leave space for

Figure 6–10   *CNN Slick. CNN Used with permission.*

tagging with the local system's name and telephone number (see Figure 6–10). Many small, ready-for-distribution pamphlets and threefolds for statement stuffers, however, promote a network without leaving space for local system customization, thus they do nothing to brand the operators as the suppliers of this "network programming." Nowadays, most cable networks also supply generic and some topical TV and radio spots for local system insertion, as well as spots for co-operative advertising or tradeouts with broadcast stations.

As operators try to interest subscribers in paying for new channels, they rely mostly on marketing packages of basic and premium services. One MSO, Falcon Cable in California, markets three different SATPAC packages, featuring new channels with existing services.

Boosting Ratings

Basic and pay cable networks must encourage viewers to watch their programs through daily tune-in advertising on the air and in program guides. Cable networks have adopted many of the strategies of their broadcast counterparts, including network IDs and on-screen billboards of upcoming programs during program breaks. They also utilize high-quality 30- and 60-second topical promos (specifics) for episodes of stripped series, for guests on daily talk programs, and for specials, as well as generic spots to reinforce their identities and viewing of long-running popular programs. To more effectively direct viewers to their shows, pay networks and some basic networks supply consumers with program guides listing only their programs. For example, HBO distributes statement stuffer-sized guides for HBO and Cinemax. When permitted, cable networks also purchase advertising time on the national broadcast networks to reach as wide an audience as possible in an effort to bolster ratings. However, the big networks increasingly are refusing ads from direct competitors.

Marketing to Advertisers

Virtually all basic cable networks (except C-SPAN), at least in part, are advertiser supported. Consequently, selling the network to advertisers is an important marketing activity and has become even more so as new networks relinquish per-month subscriber revenues as a condition of MSO carriage. The most commonly used promotional tactics are trade advertising, personal selling, and multimedia package deals.

Advertising in industry publications like *Advertising Age* is one way to reach advertisers and agency decision makers such as media planners and buyers. However, the most important point of contact is the sales pitch. As the major cable networks have matured, often into a line of several branded networks, they revamped their approach to advertising sales. Multimedia sales presentations that communicate demographic and programming information are becoming the norm.

CNN's laptop computer–driven sales presentation incorporates full-motion video to present CNN's whole portfolio of network offerings such as CNN, Headline News, CNN International, CNN Airport, CNNfn, and CNN/SI. Sales staff can tailor a presentation by moving with a mouse click between their offerings and other sections such as lifestyle and features and sponsorships. Comedy Central has used a novel technique, an interactive trivia quiz on demographic details of the network that plays up the strengths of the network's programming and audience. For each correct answer, a piece of the Comedy Central logo, which appears to cover a naked couple, falls away. The disk has been sent to media buyers and planners and also is used in sales presentations.

Bundling advertising opportunities is an effective, product-based strategy for boosting advertising sales. Cable brands with multiple networks (e.g., MTV, Discovery, Nickelodeon, CNN) can offer advertisers package deals for buys across their networks. This strategy can be extended into multimedia buys by including the networks' web sites, magazines, cobranded sponsorships, and so on. Cable networks also can offer attractive multimedia packages by partnering with other media such as network radio, major market newspapers, national magazines, and syndicated television. All this is aggressively supported by cable's national sales promotion organization CAB, Cable Advertising Bureau, which tirelessly promotes cable as an advertising medium and sponsors an annual national conference (CTAM) to showcase industry progress for advertisers and agencies.

DIRECT BROADCAST SATELLITE MARKETING

Direct broadcast satellite (DBS) services such as DirecTV (which purchased USSB in 1998), Echostar, and Primestar are significant competitors to cable system operators. Initially, these services attracted primarily rural households where cable service was not available, but research suggests DBS is luring existing and former cable subscribers, especially highly desirable multi-pay channel subscribers. The marketing demands of a DBS differ somewhat from that of cable system operators. DBS service is available nationwide, requiring national promotional efforts. The dishes and set-top receivers are sold through consumer electronic retailers such as Radio Shack. Therefore, trade promotion and incentive programs are necessary.

DBS services use big budget advertising campaigns to create consumer awareness and interest and to acquire subscribers. But the DBS services have adopted different message strategies. DirecTV, Echostar, and Primestar all have used advertising to sell crystal-clear digital video and audio, a large selection of programming, and special sports and movie packages. But DirecTV has been especially aggressive at positioning itself as superior to cable.

As with cable, incentives in the form of discounts, allowances for pay-per-view movies, and free programming packages are offered to consumers who subscribe to services within a given time period or take premium program packages. In-store demonstrations also are used to interest consumers. Some services even are employing standard public relations techniques to create a positive public image. For example, Primestar participated in the American Red Cross 1996 Community Campaign. To raise community awareness, specially created Red Cross commercials tagged with the Primestar logo were aired on broadcast and cable networks. Primestar also donated over $1 million to the effort.

Cable operators have responded to the DBS threat with anti-DBS commercials. TCI has produced commercials that draw consumers' attention to a major weakness of DBS—in most markets subscribers cannot receive local televisions stations unless they switch out of DBS to a regular antenna. Other spots depict DBS as too complicated for consumers to install and offering merely the same programming as cable.

CABLE MARKETING AND PROMOTION IN THE TWENTY-FIRST CENTURY

The cable industry has successfully addressed many of the marketing demands of the past decade. Just ahead lies the digital age, which will allow for the further proliferation of channels and advanced telecommunication services, technological convergence of TV and the computer, and the new dynamic of electronic (e-)commerce. These changes, plus the ongoing threat of competition, will continue to challenge the industry's marketing prowess and elevate the importance of promotion.

As the marketplace and competitive landscape changed, cable marketing and promotion have grown in scope, sophistication, and importance. At the annual National Cable Television Association (NCTA) conference and the Western Cable Show, cable promotes itself within the industry: A bevy of star appearances, merchandise giveaways, and extravagant multiscreen product promotion all are aimed at maintaining momentum for the established networks, creating an irresistible buzz for new ones, or promoting new technology.

Defining and differentiating the cable industry's mass of programming and service choices will preoccupy cable marketers as the new century begins. And as information society consumers become more sophisticated, so must cable's promotional strategies and tactics. Further use of the Internet, beginning with the application of web sites as promotional vehicles for cable channels and system operators, will provide new opportunities to interact with subscribers and prospects. E-commerce also will provide a huge, but not yet realized, potential for promotional and merchandising innovation. Whether for use as promotional tools or as products to be marketed, new technology will place fresh demands on cable marketers. The opportunities ahead in cable marketing and promotion remain numerous and attractive for people coming into the field.

CHAPTER 7

Promotion in Public Television and Radio

Robert K. Avery and Suzann Mitten Owen

The public television membership organization (the Public Broadcasting Service) and the public radio counterpart (National Public Radio) developed their promotional strategies with the central purpose of protecting their audience share in the multichannel television world of specialized cable and direct-broadcast channels and format-specific radio. Increasing emphasis on sophisticated marketing and promotional strategies during the 1990s laid the groundwork to secure not just its audience but, eventually, its funding. When a systematic approach to marketing added strong value-based, institutional promotion to existing tune-in program promotion, some members of the U.S. Congress threatened to end federal funding, but the general public was sufficiently aware of public broadcasting's value in their own lives to rise up and insist that federal support continue. The marshaling of advocates for public television was an unexpected benefit that illustrated the value of shaping viewers' attitudes about a media service through building and reinforcing its brand.

PTV PROGRAM AND IMAGE PROMOTION

Public television (PTV) was born as a creation of the Federal Communication Commission's historic Sixth Report and Order in 1952. The class of license "noncommercial educational" had been created for the medium of radio when FM (frequency modulated) broadcasting was authorized in 1945.

To meet their programming needs, individual television licensees joined in 1969 to form the Public Broadcasting Service, PBS. The PBS staff would direct program acquisition and scheduling, education services, advertising and promotion, audience research, broadcast and technical operations, and engineering and technology development. The stations, based on their size, would pay for the services they received. This was in contrast to commercial networks, which were paying stations to carry their programming and the advertising embedded in it.

Through the 1950s, 1960s, and 1970s, public television focused on developing its programming product, maintaining its educational role through instructional programming for classroom use, and keeping its schedule full. Neither PBS nor the individual stations considered promotional activities an essential part of routine performance.

Although there are four basic types of stations—state, university, school, and community—some of the community-licensed stations achieved national status as regional production centers. Such stations as WGBH, Boston; WNET, New York; WQED, Pittsburgh; WETA, Washington; WTTW, Chicago; and KCET, Los Angeles attracted underwriters to produce major program series such as *Nova, Evening at Pops, The French Chef, National Geographic Specials,* and *Great Performances.* Series such as those gave a national identity to public television during the 1970s and demonstrated the importance of building program-promotion costs into production budgets. Major underwriters such as General Motors, Mobil, Exxon, and Gulf understood that if the programs they made possible were never viewed, the funds that enabled production were a lost investment.

Despite a clear understanding of the rules of the commercial marketplace by these major production houses, most of the 300 or so public-television stations generally limited their promotion to the traditional tune-in tactics, using occasional newspaper advertisements and 30- and 60-second on-air promos. Few developed institutional or image promotion campaigns.

A new era in PTV promotional efforts began in the 1980s, after Lawrence Grossman became PBS president. Grossman came from the competitive ranks of commercial television, where fighting for a market share was critical. Grossman initiated steps at both the network and station levels to devise strategies to counterprogram commercial television stations to maintain and build loyal audiences for public television.

An important element in Grossman's plan was to institute a common carriage schedule, or *core schedule,* during prime time from Sundays to Wednesdays. Public broadcasters had been a very independent lot who committed more than lip service to the concept of localism. Contrasting them to commercial network affiliates, communications scholar Thomas McCain once observed, "When you've seen one public television station, you've seen *one* public television station!" The PBS-imposed requirement that stations carry the core schedule intact was resisted by some who believed that only the station's program director knew what was best for the local market. But Grossman was successful in pushing his idea through with the 1979 fall season, and the results were immediate. With a consistent evening program schedule, extensive national advertising and promotional campaigns could support the core programs in the major markets where they could get high visibility and garner press attention. Grossman's concept continued to evolve, with PBS enticing stations to participate in same-day common carriage by funding advertising in their local markets.[1]

Increasingly refined and systematic approaches to promoting both programming and the PBS image continued over the next 20 years. Much of the success of PBS in positioning itself against specialized cable channels like The History Channel, Discovery, and A&E resulted from PBS's adopting commercial network marketing philosophies. In the early 1990s, PBS Advertising and Promotion vice president Carole Feld enhanced that approach in public television, drawing on her background as director of promotion and retention marketing for Home Box Office.

Signaling Value

When Feld arrived, at least two facts were abundantly clear. First, as Bill McCarter, president of WTTW-TV in Chicago observed, "For public television, the era of assumed virtue is over, and it must now focus its assets where it can compete and excel." The days when public television stood alone as the provider of high-quality cultural and educational programming were gone forever. And second, the unique niche that public television once owned was being threatened by cable channels that were not only PTV look-alikes but commercial entities with the financial resources to beat PBS at its own game. If this were not enough, the hostile congressional environment created by promises of tax relief and a balanced budget made the prospects of letting the commercial marketplace take over the mission of public television look very appealing. Both PBS and the local stations needed to start *signaling value*—bringing attention to what was already in place and making viewers think about the services they were receiving from PBS stations in a new way. It was a time to think about the benefits rather than simply the product.

While the concept of institutional positioning was hardly new, it was close to revolutionary for a system that was built on notions of "assumed virtue." PBS provided professional development materials and workshops for station staffs and put together instructional kits to help them identify the institutional position they wanted to attain and own. Stations were instructed to develop message points as the basic tools for communicating their value as essential community institutions. These were positioning statements, not slogans or taglines. For example, KERA in Dallas adopted the following statement: "KERA Channel 13 plays a vital role in the education and development of children in our community."

Once station management articulated its position, it could use PBS's specific guidelines for integrating the station's positioning message into all public communications—press releases, on-air announcements, brochures, speeches, advertising, and the station's program guide. The key to this strategy was to create a boilerplate statement in one or two sentences that would signal the value of the station to the community served. In promoting specific programs, such as KERA's two-hour special, *A Better Childhood Quiz*, the station would include statements like "part of KERA's continuing commitment to children."

By integrating value statements into all public communications, a station could speak with a single voice, regardless of the message form or the target audience. Successful implementation depended on a shared vision by everyone on the station staff, so internal communication was of particular importance. Staff heads could lead their respective staffs in developing "proof of performance" objectives, along with identifying specific projects in programming, education, membership, underwriting, or outreach that could be leveraged to deliver the station's institutional message. And staff members learned to recognize and celebrate all station efforts that signaled value successfully.

At the national level, PBS continued to supply stations with print ads and on-air promos, but added message points for local stations to use, especially in pledge drives. The messages were designed to reinforce core messages and were drawn from research on why people give to public television. Stations could develop pledge scripts and on-air and print campaigns to stress voluntary viewer involvement that underscored the value people placed on the institution of public television:

> Public television is made possible by the financial support of viewers like you. Viewer contributions represent public television's single greatest source of funding. In partnership with government, corporations, and foundations, viewers have made public television an essential educational institution within their communities.
>
> When you join WXXX, you are joining more than 5 million families nationwide in saying that public television makes a difference in your life.

Branding

PBS's "signaling value" initiative created a whole new awareness of the distinct value of public television in the minds of the viewing public. That sense of value among viewers, combined with blockbuster pledge-drive programs that attracted large audiences, raised the record dollar amounts of viewer contributions at stations across the country. The groundwork was in place to move to the next phase in promotion.

In the mid-1990s, PBS mounted a new national branding campaign using Hal Riney & Partners agency for on-air spots and a major national public-relations firm for staff training and development of station materials. The positioning platform emphasized that public television is a valued national and local community resource. Its brand was built on its high quality and related multimedia activities—not just television—dedicated to serving the public in the digital age. News releases included closing statements like

> The Public Broadcasting Service, a longtime leader in advancing communications technology for public service, is a private, nonprofit media enterprise owned and operated by the nation's 349 public television stations. A trusted community resource, PBS uses the power of noncommercial television, the Internet, and other media to enrich the lives of all Americans through high-quality programs and education services that inform, inspire, and delight. Available to 99 percent of American homes with televisions and to an increasing number of digital multimedia households, PBS serves nearly 100 million people each week.

Building a brand had started with the earlier station commitment to common carriage that elevated the consistency of the public television product. That in turn laid the ground for creating trust among the viewers and building their sense of value for the programming available to them. Once the viewers consciously or subconsciously appreciated the greater benefits from public television, they would use it more and, it was hoped, be satisfied.

PBS encouraged stations to develop promotion campaigns to direct the existing and potential viewers' attention to public television's distinctive characteristics that produce satisfaction. The national slogan, "If PBS doesn't do it, who will?" was adaptable by local stations to highlight their own unique, locally produced programs. In Bloomington, Indiana, for example, it became "If WTIU doesn't do it, who will?" The campaign effectively *branded* public television as an educational and cultural institution, in contrast to the host of other program services available on the television dial.

Over less than 20 years, using a unified national promotional strategy, public television repositioned itself in the minds of viewers who were faced with an average of 54 off-air and cable channels, but still watched only 13 channels a week. By the late 1990s, the job of building audience numbers by pulling viewers away from the commercial—and, in some markets, other public—stations had become the paramount goal. The quality of the full program schedule offered by the local station drove station image and position within the market. Local promotion directors understood that they must preserve their own individual and *local* brand in the minds of their viewers.

By contrast, the PBS Advertising and Promotion staff saw genre channels such as Discovery, A&E, The History Channel, and The Learning Channel as direct competitors. The challenge shifted to getting local stations to recognize that these specialized cable channels posed the greatest threat to public television, not local commercial competitors. While viewers *do* give their financial support to the local stations and not PBS, most viewers think of the local station as a PBS outlet. Audience research in the majority of markets supports that claim. Further, cable niche services competing with public television have so successfully branded themselves that PBS viewers get confused and think some PBS programs are aired on a cable competitor.

To reduce the likelihood of such confusion, PBS follows the industry practice of placing its translucent PBS logo "bug" on most programs. It encourages stations to cobrand by placing their own logos alongside the PBS "P-head" logo on air in station IDs, prime-time spots, kids' spots, on-air bug, pledge, positioning spots, in print, signage, web sites, educational materials, special events, and all station efforts (see Figure 7–1, before the bug was added). The use of the PBS logo alone as a bug is limited to PBS-distributed programs and materials.

Some stations attach their channel number to PBS, an idea originated by NBC stations. Thus, a local station identifier might read PBS-32, for example.

Program Promotion Strategies

Since PBS introduced its KEY program promotion strategy, the system and the stations have moved into a more cooperative and mutually beneficial arrangement. For the local stations the new strategy has meant a rather effortless turnkey promotional package, while for PBS it means a consistent promotional thrust from market to market. The central element in the KEY promotion strategy is to give priority to programs fed to the stations each month and to identify two or three programs that are to receive high viewer and press attention as well as common carriage. A formula has been developed for generating gross rating points (GRPs) for each station to ensure the appropriate audience impression it needs to achieve (based on a requirement of three exposures per viewer). PBS then provides each station with a suggested promotional spot schedule.

Research for KEY programs suggests that promotion needs to begin one month in advance of the air date for stations to achieve their GRP levels. In addition to the package of 10-second teasers and 30-second spots that often take the viewer behind the scenes to meet the director and program principals, the materials for each KEY program include press releases, 30-second radio spots, feature stories, talent bios, photos, and ad slicks that can be tailored to the station's advertising needs.

Figure 7–1 *Tote Bag Design for WTIU Indiana University Television. Graphic by Milton Hamburger. Used with permission.*

PBS buys ads for selected common carriage programs in *TV Guide* magazine and *TV Week* newspaper inserts that incorporate the stations' logos for each market (*cobranding*). The ads mention PBS air date, but not air time to allow for variations in scheduling by multiple stations in the region the publication serves. After gaining 100 percent participation among the stations eligible for the cobranding advertising in 1996, PBS reported overnight ratings for the programs advertised in *TV Guide*, on average, were 38 percent higher than the PBS prime-time average.

Advance copies of the KEY programs are fed to stations for press parties or local TV writers. PBS negotiated a discount contract with *TV Guide* to enable the local stations to have a near weekly presence with ads for specials and series beyond the targeted KEY programs of the month.

This systematic promotional strategy pays major dividends for PBS. During its first full season of operation in 1997, the KEY program promotional strategy generated increases in KEY program ratings of nearly 60 percent higher than PBS's previous prime-time average. Perhaps of equal importance in resolving the tension between the local stations and PBS, 89 percent of the stations reported to PBS through an internal survey that the KEY program promotion campaigns were effective.

Another strategy devised to compliment the promotion of KEY programs is what the network advertising and promotion department terms *pop-outs*. The pop-out promotional strategy identifies one or two programs over the entire season to receive a heightened promotional push, including augmented paid media, ad grants to local stations, special events, and features via PBS Online, the network's highly acclaimed web site. The pop-out initiative is part of PBS's strategic goal to increase time spent viewing PBS prime-time programs and hence an integral element in the overall tune-in strategy designed to maintain current viewers primarily through on-air promotion, publicity efforts, and station program guides and to attract new and occasional viewers through paid advertising. Like the KEY program promotion, the pop-outs have been judged highly successful.

Able to move faster with new media technology than the commercial networks, public television has led the way with such new technological developments as the creation of a satellite delivery system, use of closed captioning and descriptive video service (DVS), and the production of high-definition (HDTV) programming. PBS uses a completely digital information system for distributing promotional materials to local stations electronically. The monthly press kits developed for the KEY program promotion strategy and pop-outs that formerly were hard copy materials have been available on-line since 1997. Three separate but interrelated digital transmissions—PBS Express, PBS Inline, and the Electronic Graphics Service—provide for delivery of text and graphic support materials, interactive discussions and response to station questions, and auxiliary promotion information.

PROMOTION PRACTICES AT PBS

Faced with increased competition for viewers, PBS ratcheted up its promotional and advertising campaigns in the late 1990s. Based on data derived from audience testing at four pilot stations (KUAT in Tucson, Maine Public Television, WNET in New York, and WVIZ in Cleveland), PBS was determined to beat cable channels seeking the educational niche at their own branding game. The principal focus of the competitive strategy was directed against The History Channel and The Discovery Channel, where research indicated the greatest amount of audience confusion exists regarding what channel viewers actually were watching.

A PBS tracking study (1996) had previously revealed that some 56 percent of the study's respondents rated Discovery as their first choice for nature programs, compared to 14 percent for PBS. Discovery also got top marks for science programs, and The History Channel beat out PBS in the history program category. Yet these results failed to match standard television ratings data that suggests public TV has a much higher regular viewership across all three of these programming genres. The problem, according to a PBS promotion executive, was that since cable channels have been so aggressive in their own promotion, viewers tend to think they are watching one of the competitors when they actually are tuned to their local PBS station. PBS responded first by bundling its history programs so they could be labeled with a "History's Best on PBS" promotion campaign and consistently scheduling them on Monday nights. It then worked through the other genres in an effort to take the competition head on. Underlying its promotion was the message that PBS had the "best" of each genre, whereas the cable channels that had to keep their respective genre programs on the air 24 hours a day had lower quality overall.

The problem of keeping viewers on track about their programming sources worsened as programs that once were the exclusive province of public television were syndicated to the cable competition by the program producers. For example, such popular children's shows as *Sesame Street* and *The Magic School Bus* began to appear on both cable and independent broadcast television channels. In 1998, Nickelodeon bought the rights to the entire Children's Television Workshop programs (e.g., *Sesame Street*) for its new commercial-free network The Noggin.

The success of the cable channels in inflating audience perceptions of their dependence on cable for their favorite programs is explained in terms of the massive promotion budgets of the commercially supported competition. According to figures released by Competitive Media Reporting, promotion budgets for 1997–1998 were estimated at $14.2 million for A&E, $12.6 million for Discovery, and $8.2 million for The History Channel. To go head-to-head with these competitors, PBS upped its promotion budget to $15 million for 1998–1999, about 8 percent of its total budget, to $20 million (about 10 percent) by 2000, and planned to reach higher, if necessary, by 2005.

The central thrust of recent PBS campaigns is that PBS, in partnership with the local PTV stations, is the exclusive service providing noncommercial educational multimedia. Tune-in and institutional promotion of public TV programs claim a qualitative difference between what viewers find on public television and on the commercial competition. They argue that PBS programs have a far greater impact because of educational and other associated materials provided via PBS Online and the member stations. In other words, the PBS brand is the best, and hence member stations deserve viewers' financial support. Figure 7–2 illustrates one way stations acknowledge their viewers' support.

Continuing Campaigns

The two major objectives for continuing campaigns are to increase use of PBS programs and related services and to build philosophical and financial support for the public television enterprise. These goals are key to promotional philosophy and practice at PBS.

WE COULDN'T DO IT WITHOUT YOU!

Figure 7–2 *Localized Campaign. WTIU. Used with permission.*

PBS Objective 1. Increase Program Usage

To increase the use of PBS programs and related services, the PBS communications plan emphasizes both image and awareness of prime-time and children's programming, and it promotes an awareness and understanding of public television's new digital channels and the premiere of HDTV programs. To close the perception gap between actual PTV viewing and audience members' perceptions about their own viewing behaviors, prime-time information is targeted to adults 35 and over (but with a special emphasis on the baby boomers aged 35–50) and to preschool and school-age children, along with their parents and care givers watching with them. Although more than 56 percent of America's nearly 100 million TV households tune in to PBS at least once a week, the average viewing household watches just under 3 hours of public television weekly. Increasing time spent watching PBS is an obvious challenge.

In addition to KEY program and pop-out program promotion, PBS also gives help to stations to promote their on-air pledge drive programs and TOOPs (targets of opportunity, single-event pledge programs, such as live music events) to maximize viewer contributions. Producer deliverables—new producer promotion guidelines for addressing delivery issues, production values, and program priorities—developed in concert with representatives from each station ensure appropriateness of fit for each market.

PBS Objective 2. Build Support

PBS's on-air positioning materials clearly differentiate the PBS member stations from the competition by emphasizing the benefits the viewer derives from watching and supporting public TV. To focus viewer attention on the three-part mission of high-quality programs, education, and community service, PBS offers members a turnkey local positioning campaign that includes packaged on-air spots as well as accompanying institutional print ads. Extensive use of the cobranding concept is encouraged in virtually all promotional materials.

PBS takes advantage of its award-winning web site by using on-air promotion, publicity, and paid advertising to tout its on-line services and show hot links to local stations and other educational outlets. In assessing PBS Online, author Brooke Shelby Biggs wrote: "What PBS [understands] is that the Web isn't the place for ads for the television content the network is known for. It is about providing additional resources and content to extend and enhance the broadcast product. The result is the closest thing to really interactive TV we'll probably see in the next 20 years."[2]

LOCAL PUBLIC TELEVISION PROMOTION INITIATIVES

With all the leadership and guidance provided by PBS to the local stations, the advertising and promotion department at each station operates with sophistication often comparable to commercial stations. Budgets still vary greatly from one station to another, but several local promotion strategies exist at virtually all local stations, regardless of market size.

On-Air Breaks

Although PBS actually provides a satellite program service (Schedule X) that includes 24 hours of continuous programming with station breaks, almost all stations build their own breaks between programs, which usually are about 2½ minutes long. If they use the PBS continuous feed at all, it usually is for an overnight service (midnight to 6 A.M.) or for blocks of children's programs.

The amount of time that can be used for on-air promotion is a major difference between commercial and public television. Commercial network affiliates usually get only 30 seconds per half-hour during network programs. During local programs, a commercial station may have only one 30-second spot during a commercial pod for tune-in or station promotion, although it usually does have two internal pods within every 30-minute program, plus pods between nonprime-time programs, which the station can use part of to promote itself. A public station may have three to five 30-second spots (or 2½ minutes) for promotion in each break, depending on whether the preceding or following program requires a local underwriting credit. Those breaks, however, occur only between programs, which may be at 30-minute, 60-minute, 90-minute, or even 2-hour intervals. Fortunately, PBS often breaks such long-format programs as the 3-hour *Live from Lincoln Center* performances into segments and includes time for positioning spots and local promos in the feeds.

An on-air producer at the local station produces promos by combining local elements with PBS video. The breaks may consist of several spots scheduled individually or may be one package lasting an entire break. Digital technology that stores the promos on computers rather than on videotape has reduced the amount of work because on-air control operators can integrate the elements seamlessly at playback.

Although the break technically may be only 2½ minutes, viewers perceive public television breaks as longer. In a study for the Corporation for Public Broadcasting, the Norman Hecht Research Company determined that when the local station break is combined with the nonprogramming material within the PBS feed, the actual "perceived" break time may seem longer than the comparable break on commercial television. A public television break with closing production credits, book offers, national underwriting credits, local underwriting credits, and a few promotions makes the viewers feel the environment is as cluttered as the commercial television landscape.

Before it repackaged its program endings, WGBH in Boston, a major producer of PBS programs, learned, for example, that four fifths of the viewers of both *Mystery!* and *The American Experience* tuned away as soon as the credits started to roll. In comparison, end credits for commercial TV shows, often combining program content on screen with text, were twice as effective at holding the audience.

Based on research that closing credits with simply a voice-over are far less likely to signal viewer departure than text-only credits, stations often begin their local breaks with voice-overs that reach targeted audiences before the actual break begins. These placements are valuable for promotion of items that are not program related but similar in content or audience to the program just presented. They also build audience flow through "Coming up next . . ." messages.

Because public TV breaks do not have to include elements that sell products, they are devoted to

- Selling shows—horizontally, vertically, by genre, and for appointment viewing.
- Increasing viewer and corporate funding.
- Building the brand.
- Keeping viewers.

Public TV breaks usually start with a program tune-in promo that is attractive to the viewers of the previous program. They then may move to a promo of contrasting tone and content. This may promote a genre (like "History's Best on PBS") or may be a station or PBS positioning spot. Preferably, it will not be another tune-in spot because that might confuse the viewer by adding an air date and time to the one to be remembered from the previous promo. The next element may be a longer program promo, perhaps bundling several programs like the next night's lineup, which can be remembered as a group with no need for specific recall. Along the way, there may be a membership promotion for something like planned giving (e.g., for donors to bequeath their estates) or even a program guide promo. The final element often is combined with the station identifier.

The average commercial prime-time break has eight or nine elements, including both commercials and promos, but the average PBS station break has seven to ten elements—all promotional in one way or another—of varying lengths. With 70 percent of all programming choices being made by surfing the channels, public TV stations seek to capture viewers who are avoiding commercials and who pause at video that most resembles actual programming.

Program Guide

Since the founding of public television in the early 1950s, stations have promoted their own unique identity and program services by offering monthly *program* or *viewing guides* to members who contribute financially to the station. The guides are a staple for attracting viewers to become members ("friends") of the station through a basic membership gift usually in the range of $35–50. A guide normally contains the regular program listings for the month, an alphabetical listing of programs, weekday schedule, and feature stories about the special programs and series, both national and local. It also may include station highlights, articles on and photos of special events, donor salutes, underwriter lists, advertising, and a general manager's letter. Consistently, viewing guide surveys have indicated that readers want to receive the program information the guide delivers—what is on and when—and all else is peripheral. But television schedules in most newspapers provide too little information beyond program titles, so viewers rely on their station guides for program content information. Still, the guide can be a major outlet for delivering the station's "message points," through the regular features on its broadcast and nonbroadcast services to its community. Both public radio and television stations create local guides for their members (see Figure 7–3).

Stations that trade out advertising with local businesses and cultural organizations (symphony, theater guild, opera company, art museum, etc.) frequently offer a member card in conjunction with the program guide subscription. In return for on-air underwriting announcements and mention in the program guide,

Figure 7–3   *WFIU Program Guide. WFIU. Used with permission.*

these businesses and organizations will provide free tickets, meals, or services during the station's pledge drives and also two-for-the-price-of-one benefits to member cardholders. Beyond the promotional advantages for emphasizing educational, cultural, and corporate partnerships with the community, the program guides have enormous value to regular public broadcasting viewers for planning their own television viewing. Listings often employ graphic layouts that emphasize locally produced programs, major program genres, and repeat program schedules, plus tie-ins to other station services.

Web Sites and Internet Promotion

Just as PBS pioneered the use of the Internet to extend its value, local public television stations have embraced web sites for a variety of reasons: providing program and station information to viewers, supplementing program content with resource materials, and promoting station services. The one third of public TV stations licensed to colleges and universities paved the way when the technology first became available, but the stations that had to buy the services of local Internet service providers (ISPs) soon also found ways to get on-line, often establishing tradeouts for web site design and server space. By 1998, stations were able to apply for grants to develop web sites specifically to promote their local initiatives and provide voter education on-line for the PBS Democracy Project. Some added audio and video streaming of their local programs, and many included chat rooms and guest books to add an interactive element for their viewers.

Local stations also regularly employ electronic mail for targeted program promotion, replacing the distribution of news releases by postal services. Station promotion staff maintain distribution lists for special interest groups, media outlets, and individual viewers. Some provide e-mail notification service to their contributors who want to know about program schedule changes or program repeats. Promoters also may develop e-mail lists using user names they acquire from "cookies" (miniature computer programs that capture the identity of visitors to their web sites).

The local station's promotion staff is usually the recipient of e-mail addressed to the station's account. It is the staff's responsibility to answer viewer inquiries or pass the messages on to appropriate departments for handling. The timely handling of incoming e-mail is as important to a station's public relations efforts as prompt and efficient handling of a telephone call.

Direct Mail

Public stations have been using direct mail to solicit contributions for many years, but targeting community organizations and demographic groups to receive special mailings to announce upcoming programs has become an important promotional strategy for many local stations. A wide variety of up-to-date mailing lists, electronic or postal, keyed to specific program genres is an extremely effective way of utilizing community opinion leaders to help the station promote upcoming programs and series. Just as the monthly program guide serves as a periodic reminder of the station's appreciation of the member's support, an announcement letter in the mail serves to signal the special bond that exists between a public TV station and the audience it serves. It reinforces the concept that viewers are the "public" in public television.

Advertising Trades

Regardless of its size, a local station's promotion budget is never enough. Increasingly, promotion and development directors work hand in hand to prepare proposals that include a mix of cash and in-kind support or complimentary advertising in return for on-air exposure in the form of underwriting credits. Interpretations as to what constitutes appropriate underwriting recognition varies widely from station to station, but even the most conservative guidelines now include use of corporate logos, slogans, and product lines. Critics of this trend toward *enhanced underwriting* claim the crediting of sponsors is making public television look more and more like its commercial counterparts, but many promotion directors argue this is a fair exchange for the rates charged for underwriting, which now approach the level used by commercial stations with the same size audience.

PUBLIC RADIO PROMOTION[3]

From the standpoint of the public television promotion director, the task of promoting public radio is far less complex. Indeed, it has been suggested that the promotional strategies used by public radio are more parallel to those of commercial radio than those of public television. First, the radio medium is used differently than television, thus dictating different acquisitive and retentive strategies. Second, the programming strategies differ considerably: Public radio stations tend to be dominated more by local programs as opposed to national or syndicated offerings, and public radio stations generally have a strong local presence *within* national programs. For example, public radio stations commonly insert local newscasts and features in National Public Radio's *Morning Edition,* sometimes occupying as much as one third of the total program. These differences in audience consumption patterns and program forms influence the style and content of public radio on-air promos, publicity, and advertising.

While many of the rules that apply to commercial radio apply equally to public radio, contrasting missions and means of support add a unique dimension to promoting public radio programs. Simply put, the role of commercial radio is to deliver an audience to advertisers. By contrast, for public radio to survive, each station must develop an audience so loyal that it will send money to keep the station on the air and so distinctive that it will attract businesses that will pay to reach these listeners with their program underwriting message. Its strategy must include the usual goals of acquiring and retaining listeners, with the added goal of converting some of those listeners into paying members. Ads such as in Figure 7–4 point out some of the benefits of "listening" to public radio.

**PUBLIC RADIO
IS FUN TO WATCH.**

Public radio doesn't stop with your ears.
In fact its uniquely colorful sounds can make
you giggle. Shout. Shudder. Or boil.
The range of commercial-free music, news,
classic literature and ideas is awesome—with
everything from Brahms to Brubeck.
So look into Public Radio. It's a clear, crisp
cut above what you've been hearing. And it's
changing the face of   **WAMU-FM 88.5**
America, every
minute of every day.   **WETA-FM 90.9**
WPFW-FM 89.3
YOU CAN SEE THE DIFFERENCE ON PUBLIC RADIO.

Figure 7–4   *Public Radio Newspaper Ad. WAMU-FM. Used with permission.*

Listeners become members because they believe the station, or more accurately the programming, is *personally* important. One promotion objective, therefore, is to get the listener to use the station more often. But, unlike commercial
stations, public stations cannot buy loyalty with forced-listening promotions such
as contests and giveaways. Indeed, the process of turning a listener into a member can take years. Although increasing the number of people who listen (*cume
audience*) and time spent listening (*TSL*) are both important, the critical objective
is to attract listeners and lead them to that family of friends who are paying
members.

Actual listening, as opposed to *reported* listening, becomes crucial to promoting public radio. The spectrum of listeners includes those who are not aware of

public radio and those who are shareholders in their local public radio station. Promotion and advertising must speak to both groups, and those people aware but not donors, often at the same time because of small budgets. Meanwhile, staff at public radio stations must keep in mind that the *20/80 rule* applies to public radio. This informal marketing rule refers to the common research finding that a small portion of listeners (about 20 percent) do most of the listening (about 80 percent) and an even smaller portion of listeners contribute the bulk of the pledges. Therefore, concentrating on upgrading membership levels and maintaining large donors usually results in more revenue for the station than focusing on small donors.

Public stations also differ from their commercial counterparts in programming strategy. While most commercial stations air the same formats throughout the broadcast day, most public stations air two or more formats, such as public affairs and music (usually classical and jazz), with blocks of diverse programming. *Multiple formats* tend to give public stations an inconsistent on-air sound, making it hard for listeners to know when to tune in to hear their favorite format or causing some listeners to tune out when the program format changes. Public radio program directors in markets with competing public stations sometimes attempt to pull listeners away from the competition by staggering their move to another format. For example, if WXXX shifts from its public affairs block to classical at 9:00 A.M. on weekdays, station WYYY might continue its public affairs programming for another hour or two in hopes that public affairs enthusiasts will change stations to stay with their favorite format.

Setting Goals

Whether public television or radio, a promotional strategy requires *measurable goals*. One standard might be the station's cume or average quarter-hour (AQH) audience; another might be the level of listener contributions. Either of these measures can be influenced by effective promotion. The precise goal will determine how messages are crafted and which media are used.

If the station's goal is to increase the audience for a certain program or in a certain daypart, the promotion director must first decide from where the audience should come. As a general rule, most promotion and advertising affects *which* station a person listens to at a particular time, not *whether* a person listens. Hence, the promotion director's objective is to get people to listen to a specific public station when they would otherwise be listening to a competitor. The audience targeted for the station's promotional appeals consists of two groups: people who already listen to the station but not at the desired time, and people who never listen to the public station. The former can be reached through on-air and off-air (external) promotion strategies, while the latter can be reached only off air and are much more difficult to influence.

It seems only natural that the audience-building process would start with acquiring then retaining listeners. But in public radio, the process usually works in reverse. Many stations have established firm program schedules and try only to increase listening by existing audiences. Retaining listeners for longer periods of time is especially important given public radio's reliance on listener contributions. *The promotion director's main objective, then, is to get current listeners to use the station more often and to listen for longer periods.* This strategy builds TSL and AQH, leading indicators of whether a listener is likely to become a contributor.

Public radio stations commonly use tactics of *forward, cross,* and *horizontal* promotion to change or reinforce listener behavior. *Forward promotion* is a variant of the teaser. It attempts to increase the duration of each tune-in. It gives the current listener a reason to stay tuned for what is to follow. Copy that begins "Stay tuned for . . ." is forward promotion. Always program-specific, forward promotion touts the immediately upcoming program. *Cross-promotion,* on the other hand, attempts to increase how often an individual tunes in. Cross-promotion encourages the listener to sample similar programs at another time of the day. Generic or specific, it should promote programs having demographics or psychographics matching those of the program in which the promo is inserted. *Horizontal promotion,* the third tactic, attempts to increase the number of tune-ins by an individual. It encourages a listener to sample the next installment of a stripped program (on at the same time the next day or week) or the next segment of a mini-documentary that has been spread across multiple newsdays. Copy that reads "Tune in again tomorrow for Part 3 of . . ." is an example of horizontal promotion.

The copy for forward, cross, and horizontal promotion strategies often is similar, but their placement differs. Consider this fictitious copy for NPR's *Weekend Edition*:

> Saturday on *Weekend Edition,* the Secretary of State tells his version of why the peace negotiations broke down. This and much more when NPR correspondent John Smith holds a Washington newsmaker's feet to the fire on *Weekend Edition,* this Saturday morning, beginning at 8 o'clock here on WXXX, FM 90.

If the copy is read within Friday's *Morning Edition,* the promotion is horizontal; its purpose is to remind listeners that they can get the news at the same time on the next day. If this same promo runs on Friday afternoon during *All Things Considered,* this cross-promotion is now intended to get listeners to sample a different program with similar appeal at a quite different time of day. Finally, when the announcer reads the same promo for *Weekend Edition* very early Saturday morning before the program goes on the air, it becomes forward promotion, intended to keep listeners from tuning out.

Increasingly, local stations have been guided in their scheduling of on-air promos by adhering to concepts gleaned from research data. One of the most popular approaches to promotion spot placement is called *optimum effective scheduling* (OES). Using the station's own audience numbers, the number of times in a week a message needs to air to reach the station's entire audience can be determined. The first step is to calculate the turnover ratio by dividing the station's cumulative (cume) audience by the average quarter-hour audience (AQH). Then multiply that number (turnover ratio) by the OES spot factor of 3.29. The resulting figure is the number of times a promo needs to run each week to achieve total audience saturation.

National Promotion Support

In recent years, National Public Radio and Public Radio International, the two leading sources of nationally distributed public radio programs, have taken some cues from the more aggressive promotional leadership of PBS to help local stations signal value, promote brand loyalty, and both hold and increase audiences. Both NPR and PRI maintain web sites designed to assist member stations access promotional materials and request guidance for their individual station initiatives. Promotion workshops to train station personnel are scheduled in conjunction with the annual Public Radio Conference. NPR's Program Communications and Marketing department publishes a monthly newsletter, *SCOOP*, that provides program updates, promotion suggestions and marketing news.

In 1998, NPR made two important changes beyond the strengthening of its web site services. First, after target audience testing of the network's "radio waves" logo, NPR executives conceded what stations had been saying about NPR's corporate logo for many months—it was confusing, difficult to read, and did not lend itself to cobranding in print ads. The result was a new "clean" logo—designed by CKS Partners, a New York brand and identity consulting firm—that shows the NPR letters on three individual blocks. The logo permits a reverse image of the letters for black-and-white print ads.

Second, the network mounted a high-visibility national campaign—"NPR takes you there"—that built on the success of the award-winning business-to-business campaign developed to promote the benefits of underwriting on NPR and member stations. The "NPR takes you there" initiative was launched nationally in 1998 with ad placements in *Newsweek, National Journal,* and *Atlantic Monthly*. The campaign earned immediate response with a burst of people calling the toll-free telephone number listed in the ads to request information about NPR member stations in their area, and the find.NPR.org web site logged more than 17,000 visits.

NPR immediately encouraged local stations to customize the national ads with their own station logo and dial position and to run the ads in their own markets to help attract new listeners, build awareness for the station and the high-quality programming it carries, and generate interest in NPR programs and direct potential listeners to the local station.

With this campaign, public radio was very much following the path previously cleared by public television with establishing a national image and then encouraging cobranding so local stations could benefit.

SUMMARY

Given the ever-growing multichannel environment created by new technologies and the advent of expanding telecommunication services, public television and radio stations have been forced to become more sophisticated in their approach to promotion as a means of survival. At both the national and local levels, the public broadcasting enterprise has become increasingly dependent on corporate and viewer donations. That dependence underscores the importance of effective promotional strategies to build audience awareness, viewer and listener satisfaction, and program ratings. Public stations have become far more attentive to the conditions of the marketplace to bolster the number of viewers and listeners who contribute as much as one third of most stations' operating budgets.

In recent years, PBS, NPR, and their member stations have adopted the aggressive competitive strategies of commercial broadcasting, adapting them to the unique mission of noncommercial educational radio and television and the special needs of the audiences served. Public broadcasting has succeeded in carving out its own unique niche as the nation's source of the highest-quality educational and cultural programming. According to findings from research studies reported to gatherings of public television and radio promotion personnel, the brand recognition of the public networks and stations has continued to grow, and the competitive zeal of the public broadcasting establishment promises a bright forecast for the preservation and enhancement of public television and radio in America.

NOTES

1. One of the most reliable and unbiased sources of public broadcasting's internal conflicts is the *Current* newspaper, headquartered in Washington, DC. The publication maintains a web site called Current Online at http://www.current.org/.
2. On July 9, 1998, CMP, a leading publisher of computer- and Internet-related magazines, featured an article praising PBS Online on its web site.
3. The authors are indebted to David L. Crippens, John E. Sutton, and Susan Tyler Eastman for their chapter, "Public Station Promotion," from which this section draws liberally.

CHAPTER 8

Management, Research, and Budgeting in Promotion

Michael O. Wirth and Ronald J. Rizzuto

The organizational structures in broadcasting and cable are not consistent from company to company. Responsibilities in stations, networks, and systems depend on such factors as corporate policy, tradition, size, income, mission, and management style. Promotion managers often are designated creative services, advertising, or marketing directors to indicate their status and degree of involvement in management decisions.

Over time, there has been an increasing shift toward a marketing perspective for four main reasons: (1) greatly increased competition for audience attention, as the number of channels proliferate and audiences fragment; (2) higher promotion costs; (3) the Internet's increasing importance in marketing and promotion strategies; and (4) increased concern by government regulators (i.e., the FCC) with lotteries, payola, hypoing, and community relations. The continuing increase in multichannel competition (among cable, DBS, wireless cable, etc.) also has led to a much greater emphasis on marketing as competitors battle it out to acquire and retain subscribers.

ORGANIZATIONAL HIERARCHIES

Marketing and promotion have achieved a place of prominence in the organizational structures of broadcast and cable networks, stations, and broadcast and cable groups.

Network Configurations

Generally, a network vice president is responsible for corporate public relations but is not involved with program promotion or advertising. The activities at each network typically are grouped into four broad categories: on-air promotion, print advertising and promotion, affiliate advertising and promotion, and most recently, Internet advertising and promotion.

Different individuals deal with promotion for such program content as daytime, comedy, variety, specials, children's, news, and sports. Usually, within each network hierarchy is a press information unit concerned with program kits, press releases, interviews, and star tours. Altogether, several hundred people, situated on the East and West Coasts, are assigned these tasks.

Cable networks employ fewer people to cover the same tasks. The widely distributed services, such as HBO, TNT, and USA Network, have staffs of a dozen or more people to handle the various subdivisions within promotion and marketing, and they purchase large amounts of consumer and trade advertising. The small cable networks try to get by with two or three promotion and marketing employees. As a consequence, they can supply only minimal advertising support for their system affiliates in the form of on-air promos and camera-ready art or paid national advertising in program guides and other consumer publications. Most concentrate their efforts on purchasing trade advertising aimed at gaining more system affiliates. Many cable networks employ outside agencies to handle the production of their trade advertising messages and their media buys. While on-air promotion is handled by the promotion department, the materials usually are supplied to systems by a separate affiliate marketing department.

Station Staff Sizes

At broadcast stations, promotion tasks fall to just a handful of people compared to the major networks. Staffs range in size from only one to ten or more people. In the small radio station (49 employees and under) and the smaller television station (markets beyond the top 100, usually having fewer than 99 employees), promotion generally is handled by one or two people.

Major market stations have larger staffs because having more media outlets in big cities increases the promotional challenge, because more money is spent on advertising in these markets by agencies, thus creating bigger financial rewards to be gained from higher ratings and better marketing, and because larger stations produce more discretionary income, which gives management, if it desires, a greater opportunity to emphasize promotion.

Impact of the Internet

Typically, television stations, radio stations, cable systems, and cable program networks have at least one person, fully or partially assigned, to program and sell their web site. Larger stations, systems, and television and cable networks have somewhat larger web site staffs. This reflects the increase in web site advertising revenues and the integration of web sites into the marketing, promotional, and content strategies of these larger operations.

Marketing's and Promotion's Status

An important indicator of promotion's influence is its relative position in the station's personnel hierarchy. Many television stations have broadened the promotion manager's job responsibilities to include such duties as research, art, and even programming. More and more stations refer to the department head as the director of marketing.

While the 1,000 largest radio stations have evolved hierarchies similar to those at television stations, 10,000 or so are still relatively simple organizations. Market size, economics, power, automation, and commitment by top management determine the role of promotion. Many radio promotion managers continue to play dual roles in programming, advertising and sales, or station management. However, with the rise of multistation local market clusters made possible by the change in the FCC's Duopoly Rules and with increased competition, radio stations have become more sophisticated. As a result, they have established more full-time promotion departments or positions, increased promotional budgets, and increased the staff time devoted to promotion. Similarly, as group ownership of broadcasting stations and cable systems expanded between 1970 and 1998, many groups standardized their promotional and marketing efforts in their commonly owned stations and systems. This development enhanced corporate identity, allowed for greater use of research expertise, and spread marketing costs. In recent years, the acquisition of larger numbers of stations or cable systems by a single corporate owner (made possible by liberalized ownership rules) has greatly increased the demands placed on headquarters' promotion and marketing staffs. At most major broadcast groups, a unit or person at the corporate level coordinates promotional efforts, consults on local promotion problems, and conducts joint meetings among station department heads, frequently in tandem with top management.

Cable MSOs (multiple system owners) tend to be even more centralized, supplying most promotion and marketing materials in identical form to dozens or hundreds of cable systems scattered across the country. Considerable use is made of generic materials supplied by the pay cable networks. Historically, cable MSOs have spent little on local customization of materials, preferring to save on costs by using the same bill stuffers and promotional offers in all markets (see Chapter 6). As multichannel competition increases, however, MSOs increasingly are providing their divisions the autonomy to promote and brand themselves through the use of locally unique campaigns.

SALARIES

The salaries paid to broadcast and cable promotion personnel have wide variance (see Tables 8–1 through 8–3). As the tables show, cable promotion personnel are the highest paid, followed by television promotion personnel, with radio promotion personnel receiving the lowest compensation.

As reported in Table 8–1, 63 percent of those who work in television promotions reported making less than $50,000 per year (according to a 1996 mail survey of PROMAX members). The estimated average annual compensation received was about $51,000 for TV promotion personnel. For radio, the average salary paid to radio promotion directors was almost $35,000 (according to the 1996 Radio Industry Salary Survey by *R&R*), while radio promotion assistants averaged a little more than $21,000 annually in 1996, as shown in Table 8–2. Finally, only 32 percent of cable promotion personnel reported making less than $50,000 per year to PROMAX, and 28 percent reported making more than $59,000 annually in 1996, as shown in Table 8–3. The average salary paid to cable promotion employees was approximately $68,000 according to 1996 PROMAX Salary Survey respondents.

Table 8–1 *Television Promotion Personnel Annual Compensation*

Salary Range ($)	Percent of Respondents
20,000–29,000	15%
30,000–39,000	27
40,000–49,000	21
50,000–59,000	14
60,000–75,000	11
76,000–89,000	5
90,000–110,000	4
111,000+	4

Note: Estimated average salary = $51,320. Average salary estimated by taking the weighted average of the midpoints of the salary ranges reported in the 1996 PROMAX Member Salary Survey.

Percentages fail to add to 100 percent due to rounding error.

Source: 1996 PROMAX Member Salary Survey. As found at http://www.promax.org/tv-survey.html.

BUDGETS

Overall, there was significant growth in promotion budgets for television stations, radio stations, and cable systems from 1988 to 1996, as Table 8–4 reveals. In 1996, 43 percent of television station promotion budgets were $500,000 or more compared to 35 percent in 1988. Of radio station promotion budgets, 72 percent were reported to be $500,000 or more among 1996 PROMAX Salary Survey respondents, compared to 45 percent in 1988. Finally, 60 percent of cable system pro-

Table 8–2   *Radio Promotion Personnel Average Annual Compensation*

Market Size	Promotion Directors	Promotion Assistants
1–15	$48,090	$25,843
16–30	35,506	19,759
31–50	31,897	18,319
51–75	22,920	15,434
76–100	24,800	—
101–175	26,036	19,326
Average Salary	$34,739	$21,337

Source: "'96 Radio Industry Salary Survey," *R&R* (October 11, 1996), p. 32.

Table 8–3   *Cable Promotion Personnel Annual Compensation*

Salary Range	Percent of Respondents
$20–29,000	5%
30–39,000	15
40–49,000	12
50–59,000	24
60–75,000	15
76–89,000	5
90–110,000	7
111–125,000	7
126–149,000	5
150,000+	4

Note: Estimated average salary = $68,215. Average salary estimated by taking the weighted average of the midpoints of the salary ranges reported in the 1996 PROMAX Member Salary Survey.
Percentages fail to add to 100 percent due to rounding error.
Source: 1996 PROMAX Member Salary Survey. As found at http://www.promax.org/cable-survey.html.

Table 8–4   *Annual Promotion Budgets in 1996 for Broadcast Television and Radio Stations and Cable Systems*

Budget Level	Radio	Television	Cable
< $100,000	6%	3%	8%
100–299,000	17	36	12
300–499,000	4	22	—
500–999,000	43	26	16
1–2,999,000	29	13	40
3,000,000+	—	4	20

Note: Percentages fail to add to 100 percent due to rounding error.

Source: 1996 PROMAX Member Salary Survey. As found at http://www.promax.org/tv-survey.html, at http://www.promax.org/radio-survey.html, and at http://www.promax.org/cable-survey.html.

motion budgets were reported to be $1 million or more in 1996 (no comparable cable data are available for 1988). In general, cable respondents had larger promotion budgets than those available to television and radio respondents to PROMAX's survey.

RESPONSIBILITIES

Whether a person is situated at a network, group, system, or station, the diverse responsibilities associated with promotion require broad knowledge. In small operations, most of this expertise will be used daily, whereas specialization will be needed in larger organizations. In any case, promotion personnel generally are charged with four distinct functions to enhance the station's, system's, or network's economic position, programs, and image: *audience promotion* (including acquisition and retention), *sales promotion, community relations,* and *research.* In addition to these four functions, the duties of promotional personnel may involve station or system image, press relations, news, and general administrative responsibilities, as described in Chapters 7 and 9 about specific situations.

Audience promotion by broadcast stations is acquisitive and retentive. For broadcasters, on-air remains far more important than external advertising. About half of television stations place their on-air promos in unsold available spots while the other half work with assigned schedules. Most radio stations, on the other hand, use fixed-spot schedules for promos. Not surprisingly, television stations report that topical news and sports promotion have the highest priority among acquisitive efforts, whereas point-of-purchase promotions (games and contests in retail stores paid for by advertisers) rank highest for radio promotion managers.

In the case of cable in the 1990s, as the traditional business matured, the emphasis shifted from acquisition to retention. However, as cable systems have begun to offer bundled packages of telecommunication services (e.g., digital tiers including near video on demand and video on demand, high-speed Internet access, IP telephony, and other interactive service offerings), acquisition marketing strategies and techniques are back at the forefront. Tune-in promotion, so basic to TV and radio, has taken on increasing importance in cable—not only for building program ratings but also as a continuous reminder to subscribers of the value received. In the multichannel world of cable, branding of both cable systems and cable program networks is an essential part of any promotional strategy.

Television stations continue to use station image and news campaigns, but on-air contests have become another crucial element in television station efforts to build bigger audiences. Contests remain essential to audience maintenance in radio; station image campaigns have become more important to gaining new radio audiences. Community involvement now is an element in three quarters of acquisitive and retentive promotions for radio stations and over half of all television promotions.

PROMOTION AND MARKETING RESEARCH

Promotion and marketing require research because the risk of failure has become too great for uninformed efforts. The image of a network, system, or station to its audience and advertisers is crucial to its success, and profitability usually rides on program ratings and satisfied subscribers. In addition to research focused on programming and personalities, networks, systems, and stations use research to ensure the success of their promotion and marketing campaigns.

Research affecting promotion and marketing can occur at four points in relation to any specific project. Research can provide a benchmark to measure the marketplace at a project's outset, it can be used to isolate an achievable goal for promotional or marketing efforts, it can pretest the effectiveness of a campaign concept, and it can measure campaign performance after the campaign has occurred. Stations, systems, and networks use two kinds of research affecting promotion and marketing: *primary* research to aid in developing and evaluating advertising and promotional campaigns and *syndicated* (or secondary) research to determine audience composition and viewing patterns. Primary research (so named because it is not recycled from some other use) usually is conducted by the station, system, or network producing the campaign or sometimes by a research firm it hires to collect information on a particular campaign or a local market. The research focuses on concept testing, image, product, and segmentation or audience identification. Concept testing tests an idea on a small sample of people before it is launched to the public at large. Image research measures how effectively an image campaign is working, after the idea passes the concept stage. Product research examines public attitudes and behavior regarding purchases. Segmentation or audience identification research refines the general public into target audiences more desirable to advertisers.

Syndicated research, on the other hand, is conducted by national ratings and research companies, such as Arbitron or Nielsen. Stations, systems, and networks purchase relevant portions of their national or marketwide databases. Beyond the ratings, which measure the size of the audience, research companies supply special reports on request, but the information still is secondary because it is based on data collected for some other purpose.

Image versus Product Research

Image research examines how the audience thinks about a network, station, cable company, newscast, or program. It can focus on an institution's image or on a specific product's image. Image research is concerned with the audience's perceptions and how to tap into audience attitudes. Research into images investigates an audience's interests and needs and then addresses questions about the degree to which a network, station, or cable system appeals to those interests and meets those needs.

Benchmark image research tells what the audience already thinks; the next step is to understand how to change attitudes and, hence, behavior. This requires research into the product. For networks, stations, and systems, the product usually is a particular entertainment program or mix of programs, a newscast, or service activity. A marketing campaign that carries a message that the product does not deliver cannot succeed. The promotion manager's job is to base the decision on whether to proceed with a campaign primarily on the basis of the research, although experience and instinct also can play a role.

The flip side is that a particular product's *identity* (i.e., the true nature of a product) may have more to offer than its *image* (i.e., the manufactured and marketed perception of a product) among its audience or subscribers suggests. Basing marketing strategy solely on a current perceived image could miss an opportunity to build on unknown (to the audience or subscribers), but highly desirable, elements of a product's identity. Congruence between identity and image is the ultimate goal.

Concept Testing

Concept testing explores the appropriateness of specific campaign ideas for current viewers, listeners, or subscribers. Acquisitive promotional concepts should be tested with members of the target demographic group who do not now view, listen, or subscribe to the client network, station, or system. Retentive concepts, on the other hand, can be tested with the potential audience as well as with current viewers, listeners, or subscribers. Concept research includes the testing of formats, slogans, campaign concepts, music, and graphic styles. It may include matching an existing image to new promotional messages and finding out how audiences respond to new image elements.

Concept testing is controversial among both creative staff members and management because the results so often are misjudged or misused. For example, a common misuse of concept testing is to assume that qualitative test results will predict how well a subsequent promotional campaign will perform in a quantitative sense. Concept testing does not necessarily produce a "winner." It is most helpful in doing two things: locating strengths and running up red flags in any given creative approach, and establishing a first-read from the audience on what the content of different campaigns means to them. Qualitative concept testing of audience acceptance of particular images as they are associated with a given product or promotion can be important in shaping a campaign. However, the degree of acceptance should not be used as the final, deciding factor in accepting or rejecting further development of a campaign. Tiny changes can mean subtle changes in audience response.

Segmentation: Targeting and Reaching Key Audience Portions

Research comparing the effectiveness of various external media in targeting particular audience segments is conducted more often by advertising agencies and national ratings companies than by individual broadcasters. However, ad agencies and ratings firms focus on the effectiveness of newspapers, magazines, direct mail, or outdoor in selling their clients' products. TV networks and affiliates, on the other hand, rely heavily on their own air because of their great reach and message frequency. Most radio stations and cable networks and systems emphasize external media when they want to attract new audience groups because they reach only their existing audience with their on-air messages. It takes external media to reach new people. However, cross-channel promotion by large cable programmers such as Liberty Media, Time Warner, and Viacom allow these entities to more effectively utilize on-air promotion strategies than smaller cable programmers. Stations and cable systems have somewhat different concerns because "selling news" or "selling subscriberships" are not the same as selling clothing or cars. Media that work well for consumer products and services may not be cost effective for marketing station images or gaining program tune-ins or subscriptions. Local market ratings books carry some information about the audience segments reached by various media in the market, but the detail usually is insufficient to serve individual station or system needs. Occasionally, therefore, research on the audience reached by various media is commissioned by a network, station, or cable system.

For example, studies undertaken for individual television stations will show which media their particular viewers use to learn about TV programs. Public radio and television have special media research needs because they want to learn which media most effectively generate memberships. Cable systems require media evaluation to determine which media perform best in reaching nonsubscribers and potential upgrades (current subscribers who can be persuaded to add pay services).

Primary Research Methods

Research designs and data collection and analysis methods need to fit the research objectives. Qualitative research uses open-ended questions and is analyzed informally. This method is employed with small groups of people because it is time consuming. Quantitative research uses fixed responses on a written or oral questionnaire. It lends itself to statistical analysis if the random sample of survey respondents is large enough. Networks, stations, and systems use both quantitative and qualitative research, although certain topics and types of questions lend themselves to different research designs and methods. Questions about image and concepts tend to be answered most effectively by qualitative research while questions about media usage tend to be best answered by using quantitative analysis. For example, if a television or radio station wants information about its image or about the image of its on-air personalities, a series of focus groups may be held with viewers or listeners to obtain in-depth qualitative information on viewer perceptions. On the other hand, if a television or radio station wants to know how many people are watching or listening to a particular program or during a particular daypart, some type of fixed-choice questionnaire will be used to gather the desired quantitative information. Questions about news and program product often use a combination of research methods.

Broadcast and cable networks and television stations usually focus their quantitative research efforts on surveys that reach very large random samples of television viewers. Radio stations focus their quantitative research efforts on surveys that reach only listeners to a particular format or a particular age group. For example, a radio station whose target audience is women 25–34 may conduct ongoing telephone surveys of women 25–34 within the station's market area to help identify which songs in its format are most preferred by the target audience.

All types of networks, stations, and systems also use small focus groups to obtain qualitative information about various research questions, such as which news anchor seems most trustworthy, most professional, or most friendly. Cable systems use quantitative mail or telephone surveys when seeking to increase subscriptions or to measure customer satisfaction.

The remainder of this section reviews research designs and methods only as they apply to promotion and marketing questions. Promotion managers are wise to choose a variety of methods, depending on the questions to be answered.

Telephone Surveys

Telephone surveys are probably the most common method of primary research by broadcast and cable television. Since most U.S. homes have telephones, researchers have access to nearly any universe or audience. Telephone surveys are the most cost-effective, time-efficient way of reaching a large, representative sample of television viewers, radio listeners, or cable subscribers. Unfortunately, a lot of people are besieged by intrusive sales solicitations and simply hang up on innocent researchers.

Mail Surveys

Mail surveys take longer to conduct and achieve much lower return rates than telephone surveys. Mail is used relatively infrequently in local station research because of its high cost, but it is especially convenient and cost effective for cable companies who can conduct mail surveys of their subscribers inside the monthly bills. Mail surveys may be the only way to elicit responses on complex issues or answers to lengthy lifestyle questionnaires. Asking viewers to document their viewing patterns across a week (as in a diary) also necessitates a written and mailed questionnaire. Generally, telephone surveys are somewhat cheaper and yield more generalizable results for broadcasters and cable systems or networks than mail surveys if the questions are appropriate for telephone and the desired population can be reached. For example, a cable television system that wants to measure subscriber satisfaction could include a questionnaire in its monthly billing statement or make telephone calls to a sample of subscribers and ask the questions. The mail questionnaire approach likely will achieve a very low response rate (about 20–30 percent) and the results could be very misleading because the type of person who completes the survey may not represent that vast majority of people who did not. A properly conducted telephone survey will achieve a much higher response rate (up to 75 percent), and the results can be more representative of the entire population of subscribers. Sometimes, the problem of people simply hanging up when they are called is remedied by informing them in advance (by mail) that a survey telephone call will soon be placed.

In-Home Surveys

In-home surveys are similar to telephone surveys in that they usually involve large samples of people and utilize random selection of respondents. For this method, researchers go to private homes and conduct one-on-one interviews with selected participants. The types of questions asked in telephone and in-home surveys are similar, but in-home surveys have the advantage of permitting the use of pictures (aided recall) and actual copies of printed ads. The high cost of in-home studies has limited their use. However, some research firms favor this approach because of the advantages of showing pictures and gathering in-depth interview information. People can make comments about matters the questionnaire might not address but could be useful.

Focus Groups

Focus groups are an often-used tool in broadcast and cable promotional research. The research is qualitative research and typically uses samples of fewer than 100 people, usually in small groups of 8–12 at a time. Participants often are located in malls or office buildings and asked to come to a public place at a later time. They then are interviewed and tested in a controlled discussion format that may include showing videotapes or administering written questionnaires. Subjects typically are paid a fee of at least $20 for their participation. Thus, focus groups tend to attract people with a lot of time on their hands.

In promotion research, focus groups can be used before, after, or instead of surveys. Prior to large-scale telephone or mail surveys, focus groups can help identify issues and pretest the wording of questions. They also can be used as follow-ups to surveys to gather open-ended responses on key items, providing a further qualitative explanation of the responses. Focus groups permit testing of visual and auditory materials (such as pictures, videotapes, print layouts, and music selections), and they commonly elicit insightful qualitative responses that are difficult to obtain in quantitative surveys. However, focus groups often are used without support from more systematic quantitative studies. This can lead to problems of bias and lack of generalizability. Focus group samples rarely are selected randomly and thus have a built-in bias.

Auditorium and Theater Testing

Theater testing usually involves test groups of 50–100 people or more. A written questionnaire may be administered before and after a videotape screening or between playback of song fragments. As with other research, these groups must be selected at random to represent the desired population. The theater approach has the advantage of permitting both image and product testing; its disadvantage is that the large size of these groups often prevents extended interviewing to obtain related qualitative data. The theater testing method is widely utilized to test the pilots for television shows as well as the popularity of rock and country song selections. The method is used infrequently in promotion and marketing research.

Cable Testing

Cable testing has become popular for program testing and can be applied to evaluating promotional concepts and campaigns. Typically, researchers contact participants in advance of a program's air date and request them to view a specific program on a designated cable channel. The program readily can incorporate promotional (and advertising) spots. After the program, participants are called on the telephone for an interview. Unfortunately, few cable companies authorize such use of their channels.

Syndicated Research

All broadcast stations, broadcast and cable networks, and most cable system operators have access to syndicated ratings. The major ratings companies also provide standardized market research of many types each year and conduct customized research studies on request. Their fees, however, tend to be much higher than those of small firms specializing in customized studies.

Three companies provide most of the competitive ratings information in America. Nielsen rates the national broadcast TV and cable networks; SRI's RADAR rates the national radio networks; Nielsen supplies local market television ratings; and Arbitron supplies local market radio ratings. Their methodologies have a big influence on promotional practices, especially at the local level. So, understanding their terminology has become essential to those who create promotional and marketing materials that apply ratings information.

Television Ratings

National broadcast and cable television network ratings derive from Nielsen's metered households. These homes and apartments usually keep their peoplemeters for up to 5 years, and viewing is measured constantly.

Because ratings come daily (called *overnights*) in large markets, many TV stations hold daily tactical meetings to maximize both programming and promotional opportunities and priorities. Midsized and smaller markets, however, are rated only during portions of each year (varying from four to eight or more 4-week periods), utilizing in-home diaries. Stations plan increased promotion preceding and during ratings sweeps. Since local television ratings in most markets still come from diaries filled out by viewers, stations heavily promote their channel numbers as well as individual programs. The numbers are important to stations because one rating point can bring in many thousands of dollars in additional sales revenue.

Radio Ratings

Arbitron provides local radio ratings. Arbitron uses a pocket-sized 7-day diary in which listeners are expected to record their daily radio listening both in and out of the home. The listener then mails the completed diary back to Arbitron for analysis. Arbitron obtains random samples of listeners in each market, and sample sizes are as large as the stations (and advertising agencies and other purchasers) are willing to pay for.

Arbitron's data collection methods influence some stations' promotional activities. For example, stations often utilize promotional slogans such as "WXXX— write it down!" or engage in heavier promotion on Thursdays (when diaries begin) and on Wednesdays (when many laggard diary-keepers are attempting to remember their radio listening for the previous week). Many stations distribute promotional items such as refrigerator magnets, emergency phone number stickers, and coffee or beer mugs in the expectation that most diaries are filled out in kitchens. Figure 8–1 illustrates one of the common ways radio stations use Arbitron ratings information in ads addressing potential advertisers.

Diary Examination

Both Nielsen and Arbitron let station representatives have access to the actual station diaries for a market, and stations can hire specialized consultants to review their diaries to look for mistaken attributions and other clues to the causes of low ratings. Promotional success can be judged from the number of diary-keepers who correctly record the station's identifier or slogan.

PROMOTION BUDGET STRATEGY AND PROCESS

The myths that surround the budgeting process can be dispelled by analyzing exactly what a budget is. In simple terms, a budget is a management tool, a plan for what a station or system wants to do expressed in numbers. Marketing and promotion managers must formulate and execute campaigns that will increase audiences, solidify local identity, and promote the station or system image in the local market. To meet this challenge, a plan of action is needed. Promotion budgets are the monetary guidelines within which promotion departments accomplish their goals.

Figure 8–1 *Trade Ad for Radio. WOWO. Used with permission.*

Budgeting Objectives

Marketing and promotion departments usually are regarded as "support" arms for stations and systems. Therefore, promotion and marketing managers need to know the goals of all other departments before devising their plan of action. Answers to the following questions provide essential information:

- How many sales promotion or client parties are forecast for the coming year?
- Will there be a major revision in the programming or channel lineup—and if so, when?

- How will the new fall season be advertised?
- Is the news department planning a change in format or style?
- Is the station or system intending to add new features, services, or on-air personnel?
- What kind of community activities are planned for the coming year?
- What major changes are expected in the competition's programming?

The promotion or marketing manager should spend time with each department head searching for information about projects that may need promotional support. Of course, records from previous years provide many clues. After gathering facts and figures, the manager combines the overall goals with the promotion department's plan for routine advertising and promotion expenses.

Promotion managers must understand their position in the market, know the potential weaknesses in programming that will need substantial promotional support, and anticipate promotional and programming moves by the competition. Detailed discussion with other department managers should provide the critical information for effective promotion budgeting.

A formal system for promotional planning requires information about four areas: the *plant* (i.e., the promotion department's work area), the on-air and print promotional *product* (i.e., in-house and out-of-house promotional production needs and sales support needs), the department's *personnel* (i.e., hiring, training and personnel evaluation needs), and its measures of *productivity* (i.e., research and other information needed to assess achievement of its productivity goals). These four areas should guide strategic planning sessions and systematize budgetary considerations in the marketing or promotion department.

Promotional goals must be measurable. Promotion managers should assign a date for completion of the tasks necessary to achieve the goals and indicate who is responsible for each task. In large departments, a detailed written plan is an effective motivational tool for staff members and should be presented to the station or system manager for approval. When the plan is approved, the promotion or marketing manager can move on to the next step. For example, a television station may want to increase favorable publicity about its major evening news anchors. To accomplish this promotional goal, specific tactics must be developed with respect to advertising (e.g., radio, print, outdoor), on-air promotion, and public relations. Measurable goals could include the following: (1) increased audience recognition of the station's news anchors, (2) increased ratings for the station's evening news, (3) increased number of favorable newspaper stories about the station's evening news anchors, and (4) increased qualitative ratings (measuring likability) of the news anchors.

Applying Dollar Figures to Goals

Once the marketing or promotion manager has a firm grip on overall goals, other departments' plans for operation, and promotion's own plan of action, in written form and approved, the basic framework for budgeting exists. The next step is to apply dollar figures to each goal.

The first step in the mechanics of budgeting is direct contact with the business office. It will supply the proper forms, a chart of account numbers, and the administrative information needed to complete sections of the promotion or marketing department's budget. The forms for budgeting generally are broken down into about nine categories: Personnel Administration, Office Administration, Travel and Entertainment, Technical Supplies, Advertising Expenses, Printing, Sales Promotion, Research and Other Advertising and Promotion.

Accounting for Tradeouts

In addition to cash expenses, there are many ways to pursue advertising, promotion, and publicity by using trade (barter) agreements. Each station or system has its own philosophy regarding tradeout agreements. Some do it, and some do not.

Trade maneuvering is limited only by imagination and attitude. It is crucial to understand that the on-air inventory is being traded away, typically for (1) air time on a radio or TV station or on a cable system, (2) newspaper space, (3) outdoor billboard space, or (4) concert or sporting event tickets.

The station or system manager and sales manager should be consulted before entering into any trade agreement. Contracts must be drawn up, signed, and kept on file; oral agreements are absolutely inadequate. Although no cash changes hands, the sales and accounting departments must specify the dollar value of traded air time and whatever was received in return (because of IRS reporting requirements). If a station or system trades for 500 circus tickets to distribute in an over-the-air contest, the sales department must know the total worth of the tickets so that equivalent value in spots for the circus show can be scheduled.

Preparing the Presentation

After reviewing the various line-item expenses, the marketing or promotion manager should write a detailed explanation of proposed expenditures. Making notes during the formulation of costs aids in writing the explanation. Under the heading of Travel and Entertainment, for example, only total figures such as $23,750 appear, but the promotion manager must attach a description of how that $23,750 will be spent over the course of the year. A narrative description is nec-

Figure 8–2 *Example of Line-Item Budget*

2000 Proposed Budget

Account Number

0010	Base Salaries Salaries for Promotion Manager, Assistant Promotion Manager, & Part-time Secretary		$85,616
0020	Overtime Client Reception Premiere Party Community Project	600 600 600	1,800
0130	FICA .0765 on wages up to $65,400 per employee		6,687
0140	Unemployment Taxes 2.35% of first $6,000 in earnings per employee		423
0200	Travel and Entertainment Client Reception (January) Network regional meeting PROMAX Seminar (New York) Premiere Party Local Travel Community Project	 1,500 1,000 2,000 11,000 750 7,500	23,750

essary for each line item and will be particularly helpful when the promotion or marketing manager has to make the formal budget presentation. Figure 8–2 shows a typical line-item budget.

Monthly Spreads

After the marketing or promotion manager has applied dollar figures to goals, arrived at totals for each line item, and written a short descriptive narrative for each expenditure, the budget must be spread across the total year to produce the monthly spreads.

It is crucial to know not only how much the department wants to spend for the whole year but also when it wants to spend it. Estimating expenses month by month will indicate key periods of heavy expenditure and give an accurate picture of activities to be accomplished on a monthly basis. While every company's budget form varies, basic accounting principles require (1) information for the current budget, (2) estimates of how close to budget a department anticipates being at the end of the current budget year, and (3) the figures the promotion or marketing manager is preparing for the next budget year.

When line items have been tallied and cross-checked and the narrative description of each line-item expense has been drawn up, the first draft of the budget is complete. Research, computation, and creativity should come together in a neat package that describes the promotion or marketing manager's plans for the next 12 months.

Formal Presentation

Department heads should approach the budget presentation session in a positive and flexible frame of mind. The presentation allows three things: (1) a chance for the marketing or promotion manager to identify opportunities, define problems, help coordinate efforts, formulate new programs, and propose new actions; (2) an illustration to top management of how creative and practical the department's plans are; and (3) an opportunity to push for acceptance of promotion's proposed budget and to defend its programs.

After the presentation, the marketing or promotion manager may have to make structural or dollar changes before receiving final approval. Once this occurs, the business office usually issues the final copy of the budget to each department.

Budget Execution

Forecasting

Forecasting is of considerable value in administering budgets effectively. The promotion or marketing manager should set aside one day a month (say, the 15th or 20th) to analyze the activities and expenditures planned for the upcoming month. This practice invites advance planning to make sure that projects are completed on time and to ensure that expenses are accounted for in the correct month.

Accountability

A successfully executed budget requires a built-in system of accountability. This system should provide information that permits monitoring and directing the activities of a large department. Usually, such a system is called a monthly *variance report*. Variance reports tend to be per job and typically are a bunch of slips in a drawer that are saved for the monthly report and next year's budget planning. Some companies do it quarterly, some weekly. A variance report allows the department head and top management to keep tabs on expenses.

To fill out a variance report, the department head needs to know the budgeted amounts (projected) for the month versus what was actually expended during the month. The station's business office provides this information after it has closed the books for the month. It is the manager's responsibility to explain any variances between budget forecasts and actual expense, that is, whether the amount is higher or lower than projected. This information lets department heads know exactly where they stand at any given time during the year. Frequently, companies ask for a quarterly report on departmental budgets as well as a report at midyear. Reports of this type should be regarded as "promise versus performance" reports. Those who are behind will be the first to know and can revise their plans accordingly.

CONCLUSIONS

As competition within the telecommunications marketplace continues to grow and as the role and importance of the Internet continues to spread, promotion and marketing staff at television stations, radio stations, and cable systems will need to become increasingly sophisticated in how they manage and implement their marketing and promotion plans. Likewise, as the competitive landscape (encompassing both large and small market stations and systems) becomes more complex, promotion and marketing managers will need access to a wide array of primary and secondary research to be successful in the marketplace. Finally, increased competition and complexity also will require promotion and marketing managers to become better financial managers to maximize the efficiency with which their departments operate.

CHAPTER 9

Marketing to Affiliates, Buyers, and Advertisers

William Jenson Adams

Although the most visible forms of promotion are those targeted toward the public, as far as most broadcasters are concerned, that public is just there to watch commercials. Despite the second stream of income from subscriber fees for cable and satellite television distributors, most of the media, including the cable and satellite networks, still make the bulk of their money from advertisers. As a result, most of any medium's promotional budget must be used to convince potential sponsors to buy time.

Also true is that the days when networks sent shows and affiliates automatically ran them are fast coming to an end. Nowadays, a wide range of sources for programming are available to stations. At the same time, the competitive situation has tightened up. Well-run independent stations can outperform some network affiliates in some markets. As a result, local stations are taking more and more control over their own schedules.

Hundreds of television and radio program syndicators distribute syndicated programs and movies to stations and cable. Before such distributors can begin to sell their programs to the public, they first have to sell them to the stations. Most of the syndicators' promotional efforts are targeted at buyers, because stations and cable provide access to audiences.

When it comes to selling time or shows, promotion plays an enormous part. In both situations, the same three goals apply: maximize strengths, minimize weaknesses, and establish (and maintain) a desirable image. How promotion professionals go about meeting those three goals varies, based on what is being promoted, to whom, and who or what is delivering the message.

MARKETING NETWORK PROGRAMMING TO AFFILIATES

Established broadcast networks use marketing to maintain and expand the coverage of their programming lineup by their existing affiliates, but cable and satellite networks and the newer broadcast networks are central to looking at how networks market to affiliates. This section explains both maintenance and entrepreneurial approaches to network-affiliate marketing.

Broadcast Affiliates

The big four broadcast networks (ABC, CBS, Fox, and NBC) provide information to their affiliates about new and returning programs. As discussed in Chapters 4 and 5, video and printed materials are supplied prior to the launch of new programming seasons, particularly in the fall but also in mid-January each year. Networks also maintain private web sites to disseminate information about upcoming programming.

The newer broadcast networks (UPN, the WB, Univision, Pax TV) present a different challenge to marketing network programming to broadcast and cable affiliates. The quantity of affiliates and the quality of stations (in terms of over-the-air reception) both are key to the success of a network, because the entire program delivery system is only as strong as the individual stations that make up the network. Thus, the "netlets" battle one another for the right to claim a particular independent station that wants to carry a few hours of network programming.

Fox began in 1987 with a limited number of stations that slowly grew as the network expanded to seven nights and purchased the rights to many top-notch sporting events (e.g., NFL football, NHL hockey). The Fox network supplemented its lineup of broadcast stations with cable channels in markets where no additional affiliates were available. Marketing and promotion were the keys to developing its now-impressive lineup of stations. For example, Fox would send promotional materials to prospective stations and then take steps to solidify a budding relationship. Touting the youthful demographic appeal of Fox viewers, through print and video promotion, was important in convincing prospective affiliates that carrying the Fox program lineup would generate high revenues for the station. Fox's pattern is now being imitated by the WB and UPN.

Cable and Satellite Affiliates

The cable networks present a different situation, because they all clamor to gain exposure on the channel lineups of nearly 12,000 cable systems in the United States. The established networks are somewhat less concerned than new competitors with marketing, beyond maintaining good relations with the cable operators. Even so, cable networks must worry about the amount of *shelf space*—the number of available channels on potential cable systems. Many cable operators lack the ability to add additional channels because, metaphorically, their shelves are full. In some instances, cable systems try to determine which services to drop in order to add more popular (or more profitable) channels. For example, TCI operators attempted to discontinue the VH-1 music channel in some markets to make room for Animal Planet or The Cartoon Network (both of which offered TCI high per-subscriber fees for carriage). VH-1 fought back by running newspaper ads targeted to viewers disgruntled by the loss of a music channel.

Satellite delivery of multichannel television has less of a problem with shelf space, because most DBS systems were designed to permit over 100 choices (compared with sometimes only 50 channels on terrestrial cable systems). New cable networks often can convince a satellite carrier to add their services, because increased choice helps differentiate home satellite delivery from cable delivery. But cable networks need "real" cable delivery because most multichannel homes are on traditional cable (60 million terrestrial versus 11 million satellite homes in 1998).

If carriage on both kinds of delivery systems is necessary to "wannabe" networks, then marketing to affiliated multichannel providers is crucial. Most promotion takes the form of print advertising in trade magazines. For example, a new network like ZDTV (a computer channel) presents itself as a network that viewers will want to watch: "If there's a home and garden channel, why not one for computer enthusiasts?"

Another tactic used by brand-new networks is to use the potential viewers themselves as agents to "call your local cable operator" to add the new channel. For example, HGTV (Home & Garden TV) bought a sponsorship in *Paul Harvey News & Commentary*, a widely syndicated and popular radio program on the ABC Radio Network, to enlist Mr. Harvey's personal plea to millions of listeners to request their local cable operators to carry HGTV. The indirect use of cable and satellite subscribers is a powerful marketing tool for reaching potential affiliates.

Of course, the most common tactic for prospective networks is to "buy their way" onto cable systems, as was the case with Animal Planet and Fox Network News. Nevertheless, promotion and marketing can be equally effective in creating such overwhelming demand for a service that per-subscriber fees are not weighed as heavily by the cable operator.

MARKETING SYNDICATED PROGRAMS TO BUYERS

Although most of an affiliated station's programming comes from a network, all stations must fill a certain amount of their own time with either original local programming or syndicated shows and movies. Today, most local television stations produce little more than their newscasts and perhaps a couple of occasional public service programs. The remaining nonnetwork hours are filled with syndicated materials. At present, dozens of potential programs vie for each available slot. Which programs the stations choose to buy and how much they are willing to pay has a lot to do with how the program alternatives are promoted.

Older Network Series

Syndicated materials fall into three general types, each of which is promoted slightly differently. The three types are straight cash, cash plus barter, and straight barter. *Straight cash syndication* involves older off-network series, such as *M*A*S*H* or *I Love Lucy*, which ran on a network for five or more years. Such a series is offered to local stations for money. There is no set cost for an off-network show, and each station negotiates independently for how much it is willing to pay per episode, how many runs it wants, and how many years it wishes to have exclusive rights to the series in its market. The syndicator's job is to get each station to pay more per episode, accomplished by emphasizing three things: how well the show did during its network run, how loyal the show's audience is, and how well the show has performed with key demographic groups in other (similar) markets. Such information often will be reflected in the trade magazines in full-page advertisements that focus on the numbers. The text of these print ads typically states how a series is doing in comparison to other similar programs, how much it has improved its ratings compared to last year, and how strong the program was on the network (although with older shows this last point often is considered irrelevant).

New Network Series

Cash plus barter shows are newer off-network series or long-running original syndicated programs that are in big demand by stations. Such major hit programs as *Seinfeld* or *Home Improvement* draw bids from several stations in each market, as do *Jeopardy, Wheel of Fortune,* and *Entertainment Tonight.* The syndicator wants cash for each episode, just as with the cash-only deal. But, on top of the cash, the syndicator also wants advertising time in each episode to sell on the national market and seeks the best time slots to help ensure high ratings. The trick is to get the stations bidding against each other.

Promotion for such hot syndicated shows is designed to get local management excited and in the mood to spend. In the case of *Home Improvement,* the syndicator's reps arrived in costume, presented station personnel with tool belts filled with chocolate tools, and did an entire entertainment routine before showing a videotape highlighting funniest moments from the series. The video presentation also contained a personal appeal from the stars. Because several stations already were bidding on the program, such promotion might seem like a waste of resources, but these promotional efforts were not designed to "sell" the show. Rather, they were meant to create excitement, heat up the bidding war, and increase what each station was willing to offer.

Trade publication advertisements for such hit programs often skip numbers. Everyone already knows they are great. Instead the print advertisements in trade magazines like *Broadcasting & Cable* emphasize the stars, list the markets in which stations already have gotten on board, or point out that the series finally has become available. At times, syndicators will try to create excitement by using teaser advertisements spread over several pages or even through several magazine issues. Such ads slowly build, revealing the show's title only on the final advertisement page.

Nonnetwork First-Run Series

The third type of syndication, *straight barter*, is used with original syndicated series like *Team Knight Rider* or *Earth: Final Conflict*, which are in their first or second season of original syndication. Such programs, while offering the strongest direct competition to network offerings, present a major promotional problem as they often have no track record. Promotional campaigns for series like *Babylon 5* often emphasize the unique nature of the program, something the audience cannot get from the networks. At other times, the promotional message points out how much the program is like something already successful. In recent years, the distributors for both *Conan* and *Sinbad* used the success of *Hercules* and *Xena* as major selling points for their series. Distributors also may offer package deals, combining a new program with an already successful series.

Print advertising for barter series tends to emphasize market penetration and word of mouth in the form of testimonials or media hype. The advertisements themselves often are designed to look like movie posters rather than television promotions to generate enough interest for stations to take the chance and commit time. Syndicators strive to get in on the ground floor with deals that lock in stations for several years. The selling point of such a deal is a gamble. If the syndicated series is a success, stations not locked in must pay cash-plus-barter to get or keep the program. With the enormous success of original syndicated series such as *Wheel of Fortune*, *Hercules*, and *The Highlander*, not committing early has become a potent risk for stations. On the other hand, only one in 10 or 12 such shows succeed.

Movies and Specials

Syndicators also put together temporary (*ad hoc*) networks for nontheatrical movies and other special programming. Typically, the marketing effort is focused on mail-outs to stations and print advertising in trade magazines to entice affiliates (and independents) into carrying the special or movie. One time of year when this marketing effort is prevalent is early fall, in advance of the holiday season, when broadcast stations are looking for shows (called *spot-carriers*) in which they can carry more seasonal advertising than would normally run in the preempted network programming.

An interesting benefit to marketing special programming to buyers at stations is that the print ads in trade magazines are seen by buyers at advertising agencies, who also read "the trades." The next section of this chapter looks further at marketing to advertisers.

MARKETING TO ADVERTISERS

As investigative reporters like to say, follow the money. When dealing with the media, it always is smart to start with revenues, which usually means convincing potential advertisers to buy time. On the network level, separate departments have been established for sales promotion and audience promotion. But, the two still work closely together to create a common theme, graphics style, and approach to getting the message across. After all, advertisers and agency buyers also watch some commercial television. No network wants potential buyers getting conflicting messages just because two separate departments are at work. The actual materials used may vary a great deal from simple flyers to elaborate four-color brochures, to merchandise, to full multimedia campaigns. How much of that material is produced "in house" or "farmed out" to specialists changes from network to network. As a rule, video promotion is done in-house.

PROMOTION TO NETWORK ADVERTISERS

Through a process called *up-front buying*, the vast majority of broadcast network advertising time actually is sold several months before programs air. Although the amount paid for a show is based on ratings, shares, target demographics, and so on, those numbers do not exist when the buy is made. The numbers have to be estimated based on the previous year, previous similar shows, and the characteristics of the time slot each show will have. Both the networks and the major advertising agencies produce these estimates using their own secret formulas. Of course, advertising agencies tend to push a conservative or low view of what those numbers will be, while networks like to push higher estimates. In the case of new programs, where there is no track record to build on, these estimates are hard to justify and vary markedly from agency to agency. The trick is to get both sides in a negotiation to agree. Once agreement is reached on the numbers, salespeople can concentrate on getting potential clients to buy their network's show instead of the competition's programs. Promotion plays a very large role in both processes.

Traditionally, the game begins in early spring, when each network presents its schedule to advertising agencies, large retailers, and other large buyers. Although this could be done with a simple mailing, that is not how the game is played. Potential buyers are brought to a fine hotel and plied with expensive food, free liquor, and entertainment. Finally, the actual presentation of the schedule will combine the announced lineup with production numbers, speeches from top executives, panels of producers, critics and programmers, and so on.

Many production companies maintain separate suites at the event to meet more privately with potential sponsors for programs. In one, not particularly unusual case, the producers took potential sponsors by bus to one of the finest eating establishments in town. Live entertainment was provided on the bus both coming and going. At the restaurant, potential buyers were wined and dined again with more live entertainment and a chance to personally meet the stars of the series being promoted. Photographers were on hand to snap free souvenir pictures. Hard sell? Actually, no mention of buying time was even made at this event. So why do it?

This sort of promotional activity is sometimes called "smoozing," or a "dog and pony show." It is very hard to actually measure the effectiveness of such activities on sales. However, it is generally believed that this sort of personal touch builds good will, gets potential buyers excited, and gives them that little extra push when it comes to buying one show over another or increasing the amount of money spent. In spite of a lack of any real proof that such promotional activities really make a difference, at this point no network dares stop. Tradition and expectation play a large role in much of what is done in media promotion.

Follow-up to the Schedule Presentation

Once the presentation of the schedule is done, the actual buying takes place. During this time, potential sponsors will be flooded with more traditional promotional materials. At the network level, the agencies and large buyers are very sophisticated when it comes to the media. Advertisers subscribe to the ratings on their own and have large marketing research departments. This means the materials provided by network sales promotion departments also have to be of a very sophisticated nature. Along with full-color brochures extolling the virtues of pro-

grams, the networks will provide refined computer projections of the expected audience demographics and rating or share numbers, program testing information,
network lineup strategies, and so on. Sales people will put together proposed
groups of programs and buying schedules to meet the sponsors' goals, giving
them several options they may want to consider. Minimum rating or share guarantees also may be made, although this can be risky. According to the trade press,
CBS, for example, was not able to meet the guarantees made for the 1998 Winter
Olympics and had to run a large number of make-good advertisements until the
promised numbers were reached.

To aid in sales commitments, promotional materials provide information on
how much money and effort will be committed to promoting the network schedule and specific programs to the public, the reputation of producers, the reason-
ing behind network scheduling, ratings goals, possible tie-ins with successful
series, and other information that may affect ratings or the chance for critical success. During the last few years, networks have even made deals with major sponsors to cross-promote events built around the September premieres, such as ABC
and McDonalds and CBS and K-Mart. In any case, before the start of summer, almost 90 percent of all network time will have been sold.

Promotion to Spot Buyers

Once up-front buying is completed, promotional efforts shift to emphasizing the
spot market, national cable networks, and the barter syndication market. Here,
the remaining network time is sold, often after the season actually begins and the
rating numbers start coming in. Projections are less important to spot buyers, as
promotion people instead emphasize actual performance, special events, important tie-ins with other series or holidays, and package deals. Cable networks, for
example, often are sold in groups to meet a sponsor's goals. Barter syndicated series like *Hercules* and *Xena* also often are sold to stations together. With this type
of sale, advertising efficiency measured in cost per thousand, and the special nature of the audience often is promoted as the main selling point. For example, an
ad in a trade magazine might demonstrate that the pairing of two shows helps
build and maintain an audience for an extended block of air time.

Many times promotion and marketing specialists can generate excitement to
go along with the cold financial figures put together by the advertising department. Buyers are people, too, and they respond accordingly to splashy, four-color
advertisements. Also, many promotion staffs mail out videocassettes for buyers to
watch in the office or take home to view. The impact of sight, sound, and motion
can enhance the selling effort of even the most logical campaign approach.

At the same time, on the network level, the fall programming schedule will
begin to break down with the inevitable cancellations, underperformances, and

schedule movements. The network's sales promotion staff uses trade magazine ads to calm fears and objections from agency buyers or the clients themselves, who see their advertising plans breaking down. In other cases, sales promotion staff can anticipate controversy and should prepare advertisers to deal with it. When *Ellen* decided to come out of the closet, ABC's sales promotion executives provided sponsors with research showing potential range of audience reactions and took the lead in a campaign to prepare the public and paint sponsors as heroes for standing up to unreasonable assaults on tolerance and freedom of speech.

Local Promotion to Advertisers

On the local front, promotion to potential buyers is just as important as for the networks, but there are some major differences in the way advertising is handled. The sales promotion staff, whose task is to facilitate communication between advertising staff and advertising clients, must be aware of many of these differences.

The large advertising agencies (usually in New York City) generally are not interested in buying time on individual stations or any but the very largest groups of stations. As a result, most local stations concentrate their efforts into three areas: the regional spot market, the smaller local agencies, and direct contacts (the owner of the retail or service business).

Regional Spot Market

Many large advertisers set aside a portion of their budgets for local stations. However, these companies lack the time to go from town to town placing advertisements. Instead, they have divided the country into geographic regions with similar characteristics. For example, the Midwest would be a good region for companies selling farm supplies. On the other hand, a car tire company might want to emphasize different products for a southern region with a lot of rain versus a northern one with a lot of snow. The regional spot market allows these companies to take different audiences or environmental characteristics into account when placing local advertisements.

Naturally, local television and radio stations want part of that money. But, getting it poses some unusual problems. Stations outside of the top 50 markets not only have to sell their stations' images; they also have to sell their communities. What can they offer that will set them apart from all of the other communities in the region who also want the money? Perhaps, more importantly, what can they offer a company like Pepsi that it cannot get with its national campaign? At the same time, many regional buyers place a heavy emphasis on "gross impressions" (how many spots will they have to buy to reach say 80 percent of the audience at least three times). As a result, they often overlook or do not even consider lower-rated stations, even if they have unique audiences. It took Spanish-language stations years to convince the spot market they were even worth considering. Of course, now, with sales figures to prove the Hispanic audience is worth the effort, stations targeting Latinos are major beneficiaries of regional spot sales.

In many cases, although local advertisers know about ratings, demographics, and so on, they have no idea of how to read a rating book. The truth is, these business people may not know a great deal about the audience or coverage area. They seldom are concerned about broadcast theory or overall station strategies. This means the promotional effort has to be much more personal and less technical than at the network level.

At the local level, there may be no clear division between sales, promotion, and management, as all work together and each shares part of the promotional load. For example, it is important for salespeople to remember birthdays, graduations, anniversaries, and other events in the lives of clients. Station managers also often keep close social ties to their regular advertisers. Promotion people usually are involved both in promoting programs and preparing the materials the other two areas need for their personal contacts. It is assumed that local sponsors want to know and like the people with whom they do business. They want to think of the station as a friend, and they often develop loyalties that have very little to do with audience size or even past successes. In many communities, the management, sales, and promotion people go to the same church, belong to the same clubs, and have kids on the same teams as the potential sponsors.

This unique relationship produces a unique problem. Many of these local sponsors see the people at the station as the experts they can turn to with their advertising problems. They want their advice and suggestions for what types of campaigns to run or at whom they should be aiming their messages. Most local stations work closely with the clients when it comes to actually producing the advertisements. Radio stations regularly help produce the advertising spots they air, and stations sales personnel may be asked to help a client choose print, billboard, or other nonbroadcast advertising campaigns that they want to use in combination with the messages being run on the station.

BASIC AND SPECIALIZED MATERIALS

Types of materials produced by the local sales promotion people fall into two areas: basic and specialized. *Basic* (or tangible) *materials* are provided to nearly all clients and agencies and can be revised as needed. These materials include rate cards, information sheets on special opportunities (e.g., package deals offering quantity discounts), coverage maps showing the station's signal coverage area,

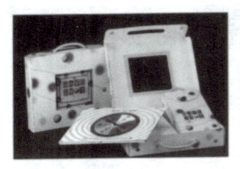

AWARD TYPE:
Silver
TITLE:
Game Show Network Affiliate Kit
CREATIVE DIRECTORS:
Cheri Dorr
David Seeley
DESIGNER:
Colleen Bothwell
PRODUCER:
Lynn Sadofsky
OTHER:
Elena Olivares - Project Manager
COMPANY:
Lee Hunt Associates

AWARD TYPE:
Silver
TITLE:
MTV Media Kit
CREATIVE DIRECTOR:
Jeffery Keyton
ART DIRECTOR:
Johan Vipper
DESIGNER:
Josh Nichols
COMPANY:
MTV Off-Air Creative

Figure 9–1 *Game Show Affiliate Kit and MTV Media Kit.*

program schedules, often separating network series from the locally produced or purchased ones, and audience data. Of course, the audience data includes ratings, shares, and demographics. However, this material often is reduced to graphs or charts that are easy to understand. Such materials also often include comparisons with the competition. For a radio station, basic materials would also include format information and examples of the play list.

Specialized (or intangible) *materials* are selected by the sales staff to meet the needs or desires of specific clients (Figure 9–1). Such materials include information on specific shows, biographical data on personalities or stars, success stories and testimonials, and clippings from newspapers and trade publications. Sometimes client lists are included to show who else is buying time. Other times specialized demographic or sales data may be included.

The Simpsons

Production Company:
Gracie Films/20th Century Fox Television

Executive Producers:
James L. Brooks, Matt Groening, Michael Scully

Cast:
Julie Kavner as Marge Simpson
Dan Castellaneta as Homer Simpson
Nancy Cartwright as Bart Simpson
Yeardley Smith as Lisa Simpson

"This is one of the sharpest, most purely pleasurable television series ever."

- Entertainment Weekly, 4/4/97

For eight seasons, THE SIMPSONS has grown to become an award-winning, critically acclaimed series that offers biting social and political satire while delivering multi-leveled humor and insight for audiences of all ages. This year the series was honored with the coveted George Foster Peabody Award, given in recognition of excellence in broadcasting.

Entering its ninth season, the irreverence in Springfield kicks off as the Simpsons travel to New York City where HOMER must retrieve his car from an impound lot, while the family takes in the sights. MARGE works as a real estate agent and sells a questionable home to the happy-go-lucky FLANDERS family. BART gets bumped up to quarterback on his pee-wee football team when Homer takes over coaching duties from NED FLANDERS. LISA uncovers the fossils of what appears to be an angel while trying to save some land from development. Even APU gets in on the action when Homer lends him the family to save him from an arranged marriage.

Join us for another hilarious season of FOX's first family... THE SIMPSONS.

Sundays 7:00PM

Figure 9–2   *Fox 6 Shell Example.*

To keep a consistent image, even with this specialized material, stations usually produce *shells*, preprinted sheets that can be filled in with whatever information is needed (Figure 9–2). These sheets usually have the station's logo and identifier, perhaps a slogan or brief selling point, and a contact person. The materials are placed in an elaborate preproduced four-color cover or in a professionally designed folder as a *leave-behind* for the client.

The actual information provided in the promotion materials often comes from the affiliate's network or from the syndicator of the program, as part of its promotional effort to keep the station happy. Fox, for example, provides a members-only web site where affiliates can download pictures, numbers, brochures, and so on for any program on the Fox network. The information then can be tailored to specific clients. The Fox web site features a section where local affiliates can file examples of successful sales or other promotional campaigns they developed. Other affiliated stations can use or adapt these ideas. The web site also provides nonpublic access to the network's top promotional people, who will help with local campaigns. Along with such private web sites, networks provide a wide array of computer-based CD-ROM and video materials that affiliates can run on a laptop computer to impress a potential sponsor. These materials usually are produced by the network's sales promotion department and are free, with very few restrictions on how they can be used.

Television stations still have to do a great deal of their own research because they are rated only four or six times a year, and only radio stations in the large markets have 48-week ratings. Nationally produced numbers also may represent only a handful of people in any radio station's real market. As a result, stations must do additional audience research to develop their own comparisons to other local stations and to find out who the viewers or listeners are and what their shopping habits are like. Such promotional information often is reduced to attractive graphs and short statements that salespeople can then leave behind when they visit potential advertisers or their agencies.

Remotes, Contests, and Gimmicks

Often, local advertisers lack the resources to understand how well an advertising campaign is working. As a result, many stations design unique kinds of sponsor-public promotional events to visibly prove the effectiveness of advertising on the station. The method originally was developed for radio but, thanks to a tightening competitive situation, has been adopted by television stations as well. The idea is to create a visible increase in foot traffic coming into the advertiser's stores. Traditionally, foot traffic was created through the use of *remotes*. Stations would broadcast live from the location of businesses, giving away things like T-shirts,

CDs, and gift certificates to people who came in, thus increasing the number of people in the store. Variations on the traditional remote have now taken on an extraordinary level of creativity. Almost anything the sales promotion staff dreams up can be done. For example, one type of popular promotional event bears a strong resemblance to 1930's marathon dancing. Contestants vie to win a big prize, such as a car, through sheer endurance. The last one standing, or in the case of at least one Kansas and one California station sitting in a tub of ice, wins. The ice contests were tied to the heat wave of 1998 but are only examples of the variations possible on this common promotion. This type of event may go on for days, pulling people in to see how it's going and even generating news coverage.

More commonly, traffic-creating events feature such things as contests where participants must visit participating stores to get clues. The KPIX elves, for example, became a major Christmas event for one market, eventually involving most of the merchants in town. In this contest variation, a couple of Santa's elves were kidnapped each year. Merchants would offer items as a reward for their return, and people had to listen to the station and visit stores to get clues to the elves' locations. In another case, a station printed its own money that listeners could buy for 75 cents on the dollar. The station dollars were sold at remotes set up at any business that purchased a certain amount of time and then could be spent like real money at participating merchants. The promotion not only increased foot traffic, but left a visible piece of paper to prove how well the campaign was working.

Television and cable have been slow to get into this radio-style sales-audience promotion, but a few are beginning to try variations of their own. *Wheel of Fortune*, for example, has encouraged stations carrying the program to make their own wheel. This wheel, minus Vanna White, can be used to reward local businesses by providing a type of remote without TV cameras. People coming through the store play a short game or answer media questions to win the right to spin the wheel for prizes.

Gimmicks, or created media events other than contests, generally have been used more to draw audience than to create sales. However, promotion people have begun to realize they can do both. For example, a Midwestern country station took an enormous risk by putting together a three-day country music festival with top talent playing ten hours a day. Tens of thousands of people bought tickets, the media gave the station statewide coverage, and the festival became an annual event. But, the festival was done only partly for the public. The station made its real money on the event from advertisers who, by the second year, fought to buy the right to set up booths at the festival or who bought station time to support the event. In short, it was a sales promotion. In less risky examples of such gimmicks, the station might supply a personality to sit on a billboard or tower at a local car dealer until the local team wins a game, or it might have an Elvis impersonator show up at the mall to tie-in with some station promotion. Gimmicks and created events are limited only by the imagination of the promotion staff thinking them up (provided the events are not lotteries, as discussed in Chapter 1).

Community Image

Image is even more important on the local level than to the networks. Advertising agencies serving large markets buy time on stations they don't watch or listen to because they are the best way to reach large audiences. But, on a local level, if the potential advertisers do not like the station, they do not buy because there are many other ways to reach their customers. As a result, much of a station's promotional budget must be spent to convince clients that the station is a good citizen, that it is a valuable part of the community. It is impossible to distinguish this type of promotion from sales or audience promotion as image efforts usually target both groups. Examples of image promotion include fund-raising for local charities, sponsoring local teams, covering high school sports, and sometimes donating equipment to schools to help with their school-run stations. Because local on-air people are celebrities, there are image advantages from getting them to speak to clubs, to host local pageants, to appear in parades, and so on. Building a positive community image also means becoming a community booster. For example, small and middle-size market news reporters who dig up dirt in their communities may soon find their advertisers falling away. Such considerations can lead to difficult editorial decisions when it comes to what is news and what will damage the station's revenues.

SOME PRACTICAL GUIDELINES

Like an iceberg, much of the promotional effort is below the public surface, unseen to the public, but vital to success. Rules, guidelines, and practices are hard to summarize because they cover so many methods of promotion. They also change according to program type, network, station, target audience, and so on. However, there are some general guidelines.

In 1994 Jim Janicek, the creator of ABC's T.G.I.F. campaign created a list of ten guidelines for successful promotional efforts and enumerated them in an article for the conference publication of the 1994 PROMAX Image Conference. That list can be paraphrased for promotion by syndicators to networks, networks to affiliates, or stations to advertisers:

1. Always make emotional contact with clients. Stations and advertisers are seldom sold by lists of benefits or numbers alone. They are motivated by a desire to be part of the experience.

2. Find an angle to set your station apart from the competition but not too far apart. Originality is not a great selling point with either stations or advertisers.
3. Get to know the clients. Personal contact is essential, and records indexing the names of children, past buying behavior, and other background are useful.
4. Create a strong, easily recognized and coordinated image to guide the entire campaign.
5. Test new ideas on small groups before going big. Ask yourself, "Would I enjoy this idea if it were presented to me?" Remember to make the product emotionally more appealing than the competition's product. If you don't buy the pitch, neither will anyone else.
6. Challenge the ways things have been done in the past. Make your promotions stand out, but be careful not to go too far. You don't sell by offending or by breaking broadcast or cable tradition.
7. When the competition gets tough, shift the battlefield in your favor. What can you offer that is unique about your station's product?
8. Build an army of supporters. If you can get the receptionist, secretaries, sales, production and promotion people behind you, it is a lot easier to sell management.
9. Deliver the same message over and over, every chance you get. Resist the urge to change focus or add something new unless you have absolute proof that the original strategy isn't working. Too many messages just confuse your audience.
10. Take the word *fear* out of your dictionary, and don't rely on "experts." Many great ideas have been lost because promotion people were afraid to try something new or because the experts already knew it wouldn't work. Promotion is a creative endeavor and promotional staff cannot be creative if all it does is copy other people's work.

SUMMARY

Marketing and promotion are much more than selling media information and entertainment to the hungry public. At the heart of everything is communication. Programming and advertising are combined on media outlets in complicated ways, and communication to various interested constituents is key. Communication must be factual, but it also must be interesting. Effective marketing and promotion, like effective advertising, must attract attention before it can be interpreted. Marketing and promotion also must build constituencies, partnerships of people working to bring mass media products to market.

CHAPTER 10

Global Promotion and Marketing of Television

Robert V. Bellamy, Jr., and James B. Chabin

Even a cursory glance at the trade press reveals the increased importance of globalization to the television industry. *Globalization*, in this context, is defined as the connection of economic interests of individual countries with one another into an interrelated worldwide system of commerce. Rarely does a week pass without news of another deal being made to extend programming from one nation to others, either through the introduction of new services or channels or coventure or licensing arrangements with existing content providers. Despite notable failures in the global expansion of television programming, there is little doubt that the trend toward globalization is accelerating as television content providers seek newly available audiences. Promotion is a key element in this process, as it is the primary if not exclusive means of differentiating programming in a multichannel environment and of making the program or service locally and personally relevant.

Understanding the global activities of U.S.-based corporations is crucial to functioning in the media world of the next decade. America clearly was the source of most of global television promotion and marketing through the late 1990s. Its influence can be seen in *Advertising Age*'s list of the top 100 global media companies. In 1996, 9 of the top 10 and 22 of the top 25 firms were U.S. based. *True* television globalization, implying a relatively free and fair exchange of programming, had arrived by the late 1990s for long-standing political and economic reasons. The highly developed, successful, and popular U.S. television industry is the dominant force in television globalization, while also a barrier to the success of programming imported into the United States.

At the same time, the descriptive name of international marketing television efforts should remain *globalization* rather than *Americanization*. The industry is in a state of operational and economic flux that makes such labeling problematic because mergers, consolidations, and coventures have brought forth a more truly global industry (although with a pivotal and perhaps dominant role played by American firms). One indicator of the emergence of a more global television industry is the continued growth and international expansion of PROMAX, the trade association for electronic media promotion and marketing executives. The organization now has members from over 50 nations and sponsors separate meetings in Asia, Europe, and the United Kingdom. In addition, the organization's Gold Awards for excellence in promotion increasingly are going to non-U.S. promotional spots or campaigns. News Corporation provides another example of media globalization. This Australian firm headed by a naturalized American (Rupert Murdoch), who needed U.S. citizenship to create the Fox Broadcasting Company, has operations in almost every part of the globe and controls such international brand names as Fox, Sky, and Star.

The basics and commonalties of promotion (content, brand, image, time, date) in global television *do not differ substantially* from domestic (i.e., U.S.) promotion. The fundamental rules of promotion are not owned by any country or culture, even if the rules were developed primarily in the United States. Successful and unsuccessful promotion and marketing practices, while taking account of cultural differences related to lifestyles and backgrounds that can affect the content of promotion, apply both to domestic *and* global promotion.

The dichotomy of global television is the coexistence of an increasing amount of global (or at least U.S.) programming combined with local promotion and marketing. Although domestic television promotion and marketing is increasing most everywhere, the role of promotion and marketing is even more important in global efforts, where it must fulfill its basic functions of generating interest and action while often being the only local connection or bridge from programming to viewer.

THE GLOBAL IMPERATIVE

The ongoing globalization of the television industry is part of a trend in most businesses, fueled by the privatization of once state-owned firms in many parts of the world, the consequent deregulation of markets, the diffusion of new technology, and the generally rising living standards of the "middle class" in many parts of the world. Globalization has been identified as one of the six "imperatives of marketing" of the present era, as important as productivity, innovation, distribution, alliances, and quality.

As in the case of many other industries, television globalization is an enhancement of long-existing business practices rather than a new practice. The U.S. television industry has distributed programming abroad, a practice that began in radio with the formation of CBS and NBC Latin American radio networks in the 1930s. In television, observers in the 1970s described and decried the standardization of global television and the U.S. domination of substantial portions of the world television market (Table 10–1). What is new is (1) the enormous importance assigned to globalization by the industry, scholars, trade press, and the popular media beginning in the mid-1990s and (2) the increased focus in worldwide recognition of brand names and images of both programming and content providers. Several interrelated factors led to these increased emphases.

Political Change

The late 1980s and early 1990s were a time of enormous global political change, by far the most far-reaching since the establishment of commercial broadcasting in the 1920s. The replacement of communist governments in the former Soviet Union and Eastern Europe led to the ascendancy of a capitalistic market system in most parts of the globe. Enormous markets that before had been all but closed to Western media companies were opened, as the former statist nations generally welcomed foreign investment to build new market economies.

Deregulation

Even before the political shift, the United States and certain other Western European and Asian nations had begun relying on market mechanisms rather than regulation as a matter of national policy in many areas of their economies. The result of this philosophy in the United States was government-fueled structural changes that altered the conduct and performance of the television industry—changes that actually were set in motion decades earlier in an age often perceived to be one of the most heavily regulated eras in U.S. telecommunications. Beginning with the first "definitive" cable rules and the partial deregulation of domestic satellites in 1972, the Federal Communications Commission (FCC) provided the impetus for entrepreneurs and investors to challenge the dominance of the Big 3 network television oligopoly. The emergence of an increasingly powerful cable television industry led to that industry's subsequent arguments for more open markets and access to viewers, an argument sometimes echoed by the Big 3, which wanted to enter new businesses. Such arguments were accepted and acted on by an FCC and (sometimes) a Congress increasingly predisposed to equating the poorly defined "public-interest doctrine" in broadcasting with whatever the market would provide. Eventually, many of the barriers between the once dis-

Table 10–1 *U.S. Television Brand Names in the Global Marketplace by Major and Key Players*

BET holdings
    BET on Jazz International (Europe, South Africa, U.K., Caribbean)

Bloomberg L.P.
    Bloomberg TV (Asia Pacific, Brasil, France, Germany, Italy, Japan, Latin America, Middle East, Spain, U.K.)

Cablevision
    Bravo Latin America

CBS
    CBS TeleNoticias
    CMT (Canada, Australia Pacific, Europe, Latin America)

Hallmark Entertainment
    Hallmark Entertainment Channel (Europe, Mexico, Australia/New Zealand, Malaysia, South Africa, Middle East, Central America, Latin America, Scandinavia)

Hearst
    History Channel U.K.

Landmark Communications
    The Travel Channel (Latin America, U.K.)
    The Weather Channel (Latin America, U.K.–Ireland, Germany–Austria, Belgium–Netherlands–Luxembourg)

NBC
    Canal de Noticias NBC, National Geographic Channel
    CNBC Asia, NBC Asia
    CNBC Europe, NBC Europe
    CNBC Brasil

News Corp.
    El Canal Fox (Latin America)
    ESPN Star Sports
    Family Channel Latin America
    Fox Kids (U.K., Latin America, Australia)
    Fox Sports (Australia, Americas, Brasil)

Playboy Enterprises, Inc.
    The Playboy Channel Japan
    Playboy TV (Latin America, Scandinavia, U.K.)

Seagram
    Sci-Fi Channel Europe
    USA Network (Latin America, Brasil)

Table 10–1   *(continued)*

TCI

    Animal Planet (Latin America, Europe)

    Discovery Channel (Europe, Africa, Latin America, Middle East, Australia–New Zealand, Asia, India, Canada, Brasil, Italy, Japan, Germany)

    Discovery Kids Latin America

    Home Shopping Network Germany

Time Warner

    Cartoon Network Japan

    Cinemax (Latin America, Brasil, Asia)

    CNN International

    E! Latin America

    HBO (Ole [Latin America], Brasil, Poland, Asia)

    HBO 2 Brasil

    TNT/Cartoon Network (Latin America, Europe, Asia)

United International Holdings

    HBO (Hungary, Czech Rep.)

US West

    Food Network Canada

Viacom

    M2 (U.K., Scandinavia)

    MTV (U.K., Europe, Asia, Mandarin, India, Brasil, Latin America, Japan, New Zealand, Australia)

    Nickelodeon (Nordic, Latin America, Australia, U.K., Turkey)

    VH1 U.K.

Walt Disney Co.

    Disney Channel (Australia, France, Malaysia, Middle East, U.K.)

    Disney Taiwan

    ESPN (Latin America, Brasil, SUR [Latin America], Orbit [Middle East–North Africa], Asia, Pacific Rim, Africa, India, Australia)

    ESPN 2 (Northern Latin America)

Notes: Major television players are in **bold italics**. Key television players are in *italics*. Other companies are in plain type.

Channels and program services are listed under their majority owner. Channels owned by even partnerships will be listed under both companies.

Source: Information from "U.S. Program Network Connections." Table compiled and copyrighted by *Multichannel News International*. Information was current as of November 1997. The reader is cautioned that the rapidly evolving nature of the global television business virtually ensures that this information will be somewhat out of date by the time it is read. However, the chart does give an overview of the extent of U.S. television provider global efforts in the late 1990s. The major, key, and other player designations are those of *Multichannel News International*.

parate industries of broadcasting, cable, satellites, and telephony were weakened or eliminated. This was a major factor in the proliferation of new services and channels.

Competition

With regulatory protection weakened in many areas, the television industry had to cope with previously unknown levels of competition. Globalization is one of the two major ways of coping because it offers the possibility of extending image, product, and revenue generation to previously unavailable markets, a process perceived as a necessity in a competitive domestic and global market. The second way of coping has been the continuing consolidation of the television industry both domestically and globally. Such combinations as Time Warner/Turner and Disney/ABC/ESPN, as well as the continuing expansion of Murdoch's Fox/Sky/Star empire, are indicators of the ongoing formation of what can be labeled the *new oligopoly*. This trend essentially is the combination of well-known media companies across once disparate media boundaries as a means of gaining competitive edge and of ensuring a role in the developing global structure of media corporations.

The near-global shift to reliance on market mechanisms had a direct effect on promotion in that promotion always is a *product of competition*, and *the amount and importance of promotion increases in direct proportion to the amount of competition for the time of the television viewer or user.*

Technological Diffusion

As mentioned, the diffusion of cable television to about two thirds of U.S. households and the development of geosynchronous communications satellites that allowed for the consistent and relatively inexpensive delivery of television content to cable systems, terrestrial broadcasters, and to a lesser extent, directly to the viewer were instrumental in setting in motion the regulatory changes that have led to many of the structural changes in the television industry. The videocassette recorder (VCR) and the remote control device (RCD) are two other technological items that have had a significant impact on the evolving global television industry.

The VCR gave the viewer of television control over the time element of programming and created a new market for theatrical motion pictures and other off-air programming that provided more competition for the attention of the viewer. Perhaps the key factor in the diffusion of the VCR that affected promotion was the level of control the device gave viewers or users to alter their viewing habits. No longer could the viewer be seen mainly as a passive conduit for the wares of a limited number of television content providers. Now, those providers would have to show reasons (*benefits*, see Chapter 2) for the viewer to pay attention to programs and accompanying advertising, which was easy to *zip* (running the VCR in fast-forward mode) on videotape.

The increased program choice and program-manipulation options of the VCR, cable, and satellites required a simple consumer-friendly navigation device for their full benefit to be realized. The remote control device, once an add-on to more expensive television receivers, became standard on virtually every VCR, cable converter box, and television receiver in the 1980s. Although not a programming conduit, the simple and ubiquitous RCD made it possible for the television viewer to become a user of the new technology. Key television programming strategies that relied on a relatively passive audience to "flow" from one program to the next and, most important, from one advertisement to the next suddenly were open to reinterpretation and questioning by a combination of technologies that allowed the viewer to instantly *zap* (change) from one channel to many others.

To stem viewer defection and combat the myriad of new viewing options, the U.S. television and advertising industries adopted modified or new methods of scheduling (e.g., NBC's "seamless" prime-time scheduling), program content (e.g., "hot" program openings), and advertising content (e.g., 15-second spots, continuing narrative spots, more advertiser-program integration) to maintain or regain the attention of the "restless" RCD-armed viewer. Not surprisingly, viewers who *grazed* (i.e., used the RCD to both zap, zip, and create a self-designed viewing menu) often found themselves watching, if even momentarily, one of the many new television services, further eroding the audience and traditional scheduling and programming strategies of the conventional content providers. More troubling for traditional industry power centers and practices, younger audiences were more likely to graze than older ones, meaning that television's most desirable demographic was increasingly the most difficult one to reach.

NEW MARKETING EMPHASES

Once captive, or perceived to be captive, viewers seemingly "up for grabs" demonstrated less and less loyalty to specific channels or services, causing the role of effective promotion to increase exponentially in several ways. First, advertisers, beginning in the early 1980s, shifted increasing portions of their budgets to promotional and other nonspot marketing activities. For example, sponsors began to lend their names to sporting events rather than buy one or two commercial messages in them. By the early 1990s, *integrated marketing*, the combination of the once relatively disparate practices of advertising, public relations, and promotion, had become a key concept in sales. Second, the emphasis on promotion of television content became a primary strategic element within the television industry. For example, broadcast and cable networks sought identifiable branding to unify their promotional messages. Although the flush domestic economy of the middle to late 1990s saw ever-increasing television advertising prices, the recession of the late 1980s and early 1990s showed that the television industry could no longer assume that big annual increases in advertising revenues were a "birthright." This economic reality, combined with the possibility that the domestic market may become saturated, makes expansion to new markets a necessity if the industry is to continue growing.

In addition, the wide availability of alternative home media (videotape, videogames, computers, and Internet) made even the traditional viewing of television (as well as listening to radio) more a competitive battleground, as advertisers experimented with and even shifted budgets to advertise on or within these new media. The many television providers both domestically and internationally began fighting to gain the attention of the viewers, with promotion being the main weapon.

Branding Strategy

Capturing the attention of an active and perhaps distracted audience took on vital importance as the many providers of television services began to understand that, to attract these viewers, they would have to have not only appealing programming but have to ensure that the target audience for that programming was made aware of its availability (date and time), was given reason to believe that the program was important to them (benefit in content, image), and perhaps most important, given reason to identify with the content provider (brand identity). Channel and service branding is vital in a crowded television environment, because research indicates that most people, even those who graze, pay attention to only a limited number of channels, which then become part of the individual or family *channel repertoire*. Branding (discussed later in this chapter) creates for a program service an image that communicates what type of content is offered to a particular target audience. A highly targeted service with a strongly recognizable brand image has a much better chance of becoming part of the channel repertoire of the intended viewer. Obviously programs and accompanying advertising on a repertoire channel have a much greater chance of being consumed by the viewer.

Because of the many choices and the easy means of television manipulation available to viewers, promotion must be able to capture the attention of, and ideally elicit a reaction from, the viewer in a very short amount of time. Industry research studies have found that people use promotion more than previewing the actual program to make decisions about whether or not to attend to the entire program. Promotional spots have been described as the road signs on a very fast moving highway of entertainment options. In fact, conventional promotional wisdom, supported by several research studies, supports "The Big Bang" theory, which says that *a promotional spot has 3 seconds to attract and hold the attention of viewers, before they zap to another channel.*

Television globalization, then, is a product of political economic changes that have privileged market mechanisms and led to an unparalleled level of competition in the once monopolistic or oligopolistic television industry. These changes have encouraged or been directly responsible for the technological convergence, economic consolidation, and market competition that have encouraged the industry to seek new markets both domestically and globally. The present structure of the global television industry is somewhat in flux, with a new oligopoly structure a likely outcome. However the structure eventually solidifies, there is no doubt that the role of promotion, as a by-product of greater competition for television viewers or users and for advertisers, has become integral to the success of television content providers.

LESSONS IN GLOBAL TELEVISION PROMOTION AND MARKETING

Promotional strategies must take into account that global television can take several forms. First, there are the "full-time" television channels and services that compete for viewers and advertisers along with a variety of other domestic and international channels. Examples include Fox Sports Americas (Latin America) and MTV Mandarin. Second, a content provider can acquire time on an existing service through a partnership arrangement to present a selection of its programs. This also was the tactic of the now-collapsed Nickelodeon Germany service. Third is the long-existing business of selling (i.e., syndicating) individual programs to a variety of channels. Fourth, the format of a successful program can be "franchised." The many international versions of *Wheel of Fortune* are a good example of this approach. Media businesses are expanding as the privatization and deregulation of television combined with the continual diffusion of enhanced technology contribute to the proliferation of available television outlets. Promotion and marketing are vital in introducing little-known brand names to large audiences that usually have their own well-established television favorites and are just beginning to adapt to a wide and confusing array of commercial television services.

Some common tactics used by marketing and promotion staffs include direct mail, trade magazines advertising, cross-promotion, and international programming conferences like NATPE (National Association of Television Program Executives) and MIP-TV. Marketing and promotion staffs work closely with programming strategists, planning a campaign to reach the key decision makers for a geographical area.

The major issues in global promotion and marketing are establishing an effective brand image, establishing effective local partnerships, and understanding cultural differences and demonstrating sensitivity to them.

Brand Identity and Image Building

Many well-known television brand names in the United States are barely known in other nations. This combined with the newness of multichannel television in many countries is why branding is so vital in global television marketing. Although branding is "no miracle cure," it is essential to cutting through the clutter of advertising messages.

Effective branding campaigns begin with settling on one key message because multiple messages confuse the viewer and dilute the value of brand equity. The various global versions of MTV, for example, all promote themselves as the voice of youth culture, a culturally transcendent message. In Canada, CityTV's key message to "reflect the contemporary urban lifestyle" is similarly transcendent of different cultures.

Although CityTV's potential appeal is broad, more market-specific approaches are important and utilized by ChumCity International, a division of the Canadian media conglomerate that includes CityTV. While ChumCity continues to derive approximately 50 percent of its international revenues from individual program sales (e.g., *FT: Fashion Television* on VH-1 in the United States), it increasingly concentrates on "extending the Mother Ship" through format licensing agreements and franchising. Examples include *Jyrki* on MTV3 in Finland ("a show within a show"), the proposed CityTV Helsinki service, Channel 21 in Sao Paulo, and the MuchaMusica music video service in Buenos Aires. In each of these, ChumCity entered into partnerships (including either equity or financial option considerations) where it offered consultation and expertise to program services operated by locals. Branding in these scenarios becomes the primary responsibility of locals, who use many of the materials, media, and on-air tools discussed in earlier chapters.

Local and Strategic Partners

ChumCity International provides a good example of the necessity of developing local partners. Programs that seek to cross national borders need a promotional strategy that fosters joint creative goals. However, partnerships are just as important, if not more important, for full-service television services seeking to expand globally than they are for the relative "loose" structures employed globally by ChumCity. Nickelodeon Latin America, for example, spends considerable time in simply convincing television exhibitors to consider themselves partners responsible for the network's success. This concept is quite elusive in countries with little history of competition and subsequent promotion. Nick LA attempts to get the system operators and exhibitors to think of themselves more as a software (programming) provider, rather than simply as a supplier of hardware for campaigns and the sales effort. Local marketing campaigns serve local audiences with custom messages targeted to local needs.

In addition, local operators are in a position to provide information on local events (i.e., off-air marketing opportunities) that are not known to the network. Nick LA found out about Peru's major consumer products trade show (which draws 1 million attendees) and Panama's Holiday Parade (200,000 attendees), major events for marketing efforts, by speaking with and listening to distributors in those two nations. Clearly, maintaining open lines of communication to distributors and exhibitors is essential to learning about the local market and in "educating" the operator as to contemporary promotional campaigns.

Strategic partnerships also are common among content providers. NBC Europe, for example, ended its full-channel service in 1998 to enter into a partnership with the National Geographic Channel (NGC) whereby blocks of NBC and CNBC programming would appear on NGC. At the same time, NBC entered into an agreement with German television company DFA for a new channel or channels to replace NBC Europe in part of the continent.

ECONOMIC INTEGRATION

Co-owned channels are an increasing reality around the world, although their appeals may be "radically" different (e.g., the co-owned MTV and Nickelodeon services) or quite similar (e.g., CNN and CNN International, NBC and NBC Europe). A "family of design" approach often is employed to brand co-owned services. This involves positioning the channels as complementary to each other and offering "added value" to the other in the minds of the viewer.

Some economic combinations that likely would have raised antitrust concerns in the United States and other nations a few years ago are now heralded as good for the public. News Corporation, for example, declares itself the "only vertically integrated media company on a global scale." A company that controls production, distribution, and exhibition obviously has more marketing clout than one that does not. Concerns about gaining and keeping local distributors and other questions of access are not relevant to vertically integrated companies. Obviously, this type of structure encourages a similarity of promotion, as lessons learned in one location with one service often are transplanted to other services within the same family.

Another form of economic integration appears in the horizontal relationships of such companies as Fox and Viacom (see Box 10–1). Fox's ownership of the distribution system in some nations enables it to negotiate an ownership interest in program services in other countries that are its own rivals within the United States. Such "offshore" combinations are a hallmark of emerging structure of the new global media oligopoly.

Promotion, of course, is part of a larger marketing effort for program services. Considerable amounts of time and attention are invested in such ventures as MTV-branded clothing in Chile and Nickelodeon-related theme park attractions in Australia and the United Kingdom. Keeping the brand name visible off air is regarded as an integral component of promotion and advertising (i.e., integrated marketing) both in the United States and around the world.

CULTURAL SENSIBILITIES

There is general consensus in the industry that local people at stations and networks must be involved in designing and implementing promotional campaigns because only they truly know and understand local conditions, issues, and general culture. Cultural ignorance is by definition insensitive and often perceived as arrogance, a very bad position for a channel attempting to carve out a niche in a crowded marketplace.

Exported programming, to a limited degree, can be "localized" through careful editing and state-of-the-art dubbing. However, *promotion generally is the key to localizing*. The first step in creative localizing is for nonnative people working on the campaign to avoid cultural errors by immersion in the culture or, optimally, empowering natives to make creative decisions.

Any discussion of cultural differences is certain to be incomplete and in some ways stereotypical because the differences often are regional, rather than national, and because they often are the opinion of a small number of people. Nonetheless, some reporting of observed differences will be instructive of the types of issues that can arise when developing promotion for international markets.

Asia has been called the most culturally complex area of the world because of the dozens of separate cultures that make up the continent. As learned by Murdoch's Star TV and other pan-Asian services, facial images usually are to be avoided on-air and in print materials because of the many different people in Asia who do not identify with each other. Instead, commonalties of culture used in

BOX 10–1   **Globalization or Americanization, Examples (as of July 1998)**

The News Corporation and Viacom are two of the largest media companies in the world. The selected list of non-U.S. holdings that follows demonstrates the scope and reach of U.S.-originated brand names, the development of services (Sky, Star) that distribute and exhibit U.S. product, and the relationships between these ostensibly rival corporations.

Brand	Where
News Corporation	
ESPN	Asia
Fox	Australia, Latin America
Fox Kids	Latin America, U.K.
Fox Sports	Australia, Latin America (Americas)
FX	Australia
History Channel**	U.K.
National Geographic Channel**	U.K.
Nickelodeon	Australia, U.K.
Paramount Channel*	U.K.
Playboy Channel**	U.K.
Sky	Australia, India, Latin America, U.K.
Star	China, Japan, North Asia, South Asia, South East Asia
Viacom	
Bloomberg Information TV**	Middle East
HBO**	Asia
MTV	Asia, Australia, Brazil, Europe (to Middle East), India, Japan, Latin America, Mandarin (China), U.K.
The Movie Channel	Middle East
Nickelodeon	Australia, Japan, Latin America, Middle East, Nordic region, Philippines, Turkey, U.K.
Paramount Channel	Middle East, U.K.
VH-1	Germany, U.K. (also Middle East)

* Viacom is the majority owner of these services.
** Minority ownership position for non-U.S. operations.
Sources: Steve Donahue, "Nickelodeon Bound for Asia," *Electronic Media* (July 20, 1998), pp. 3–42. News Corporation web site: http://www.newscorp.com/public/cor/cor_cns.htm. Viacom web site: http://www.viacom.com/global.tin.

promotional campaigns are natural imagery such as the sky, clouds, water, or trees. Pan-Asian promotion also must be aware how interpretations of such imagery varies from nation to nation. Other observed differences are the Pan-Asian disdain for the word *disaster*, the preference in Hong Kong for long promos and trailers, and the avoidance in China of promotion that demonstrates disrespect for elders such as *Dennis the Menace*.

Disrespect for elders, or more specifically monarchs, also is a problem in much of the Middle East, where *Archie* is not shown because of the crownlike hat worn by the Jughead character. Motion pictures and television programs featuring female lead characters have been a tough sell in many Middle Eastern and African nations, although this appears to be one of the differences being "leveled" by television.

Europe includes some of the most difficult markets to enter by nonnative program suppliers because of the highly developed television and film industries in many nations and national and supra-national restrictions on imported content. In addition, Martin Poole of Novacom, one of the major global television promotion companies, has observed that, in most of Europe, a neon or electric style of design is not well liked, especially among the older population. Older Europeans, whose television viewing experience has been defined by limited and often noncommercial channels, have a tendency to regard most modern design imagery as too brash, "too American." This difference is likely to dissipate over time as younger people, exposed to MTV-like visuals, show no such tendency. In addition, the recent increase in numbers of American-based channels and corresponding promotion available to Europeans serves to level such attitudes through cultural adaptation.

Disliked in most of Europe (with the exception of the United Kingdom) is the use of fire or flames in marketing material. Two national differences are the need to avoid purple, the color of death, in Italy and the dislike of the British for program recaps in promotion.

OTHER MARKETING ISSUES

Several U.S.-based television services have withdrawn from the European marketplace, including Nickelodeon Germany, The Weather Channel, and CMT—Country Music Television. Among the major reasons given for the withdrawal are government regulations that make access to audiences difficult. These typically are some combination of restrictions on imported content and alleged favoritism to domestic channels in terms of carriage. In addition, the wide availability of programmable remote control devices in Europe allows viewers to completely avoid certain channels and makes it difficult for new services to obtain sampling. So cross-promotion on other channels and advertising in external media to attract attention is essential. Regulatory and technological problems are considered less serious in Asia and Latin America, despite the late 1990s economic problems in the former. Asia and Latin America are experiencing a large increase in new television service launches and extensive promotion in all media.

Understanding how the local market conditions are affected by regulation and economics is essential to determining if expanding into a new market is viable. If it is, the level of viability will determine whether a fully branded channel, a channel within a channel, a local licensing agreement or franchise, or straight program syndication is the best approach to reaching an audience. Promotion and marketing obviously will differ depending on the system implemented, but no amount of promotion and marketing will be successful if the targeted audience cannot receive the channel. In cases where the audience does not yet receive a proposed channel or service, promotion and marketing may build demand among targeted viewers with advertising messages, not unlike the American technique of television and radio commercials asking cable subscribers to "call your local operator to add this channel."

Despite its enormous contribution to these types of cultural commonalties and its demonstrated power to affect politics, economics, and most other areas of life, there are limits to television's ability to impose cultural domination over viewers. For example, local programming almost always is preferred over imported material. The Sony Corporation, for example, regards local programming as the "passport to success offshore." This viewer preference does not necessarily cause a reduction in program importation because of the cost advantage of imports to domestic products in many nations. However, as most of the world now experiences the proliferation of television channels, the U.S. television program supplier and other out-of-country suppliers find themselves in a situation where they have to *creatively localize* their product to gain a spot in viewer repertoires. Therefore, U.S. television providers typically do not simply make deals for the transmission of the domestic feed to other markets. Rather, new services are created that are branded as local or regional even if much of the programming is not.

Nickelodeon Latin America (Nick LA), for instance, claims 75 percent original programming, although most of the programming is from the United States. Nick LA localizes by scheduling differently than in the United States in both time slot and program sequence. Although the network spends a great deal of money and time in having English-language programming dubbed into Spanish or Portuguese, the main element of localism is promotion and marketing both to target audiences and to cable system operators, the gatekeepers for the distribution of programming in many nations. Box 10–2 examines Nick LA.

Box 10–2   Nickelodeon Latin America

Viacom's Nickelodeon (Nick) is one of the most valuable brand names to emerge in the cable-multichannel age. Established in 1979, Nick is now available in 70 million U.S. households and consistently is one of the highest-rated basic cable networks. It reaches over 55 percent of all U.S. children between ages 2 and 11.[1] In addition to its core mission of reaching children (which Nickelodeon always refers to as *kids*), Nick has developed a successful night-time programming block ("Nick at Nite") consisting of old family-oriented television series that reaches young adults. The success of "Nick at Nite" has led to the establishment of a separate "TV Land" basic service.

Nickelodeon entered the global television market through dedicated channels, programming blocks, and individual program syndication. As of early 1999, Nickelodeon programming had a potential reach of approximately 100 million households in about 100 countries. Dedicated channels are in operation or in the planning stages in Australia, Japan, Hungary, Italy, Latin America, the Nordic Countries, the Philippines, Turkey, and the United Kingdom, in addition to the United States.[2]

The key operational philosophy of Nickelodeon is that it "Puts Kids First," a culturally transcendent premise that applies to operations anywhere in the world. Extensive research is conducted to identify the interests of the children in each market. This information then is used to develop program schedules and promotional or marketing campaigns.[3]

Nickelodeon Latin America (Nick LA) provides a good example of the operational philosophy in action (Figure 10–1). The Miami-based Nick LA was launched in late December 1996 and, by early 1998, could boast of being Latin America's "fastest growing multichannel program service," reaching 6.5 million homes in 20 Central and South American countries.[4] The distribution breakdown is approximately 41 percent in the "Southern Cone" (Argentina, Bolivia, Chile, Paraguay, Uruguay), 43 percent in the "Northern Cone" (Colombia, Ecuador, Mexico, Peru, Venezuela, and Central America), and 16 percent in Brazil.[5] Nick LA was conceived as a pan-regional (versus a national) service after research showed that Central and South American nations are more homogenous in language (Spanish and Portuguese [Brazil] with a substantial English-speaking minority—the three languages of Nick LA) and other cultural variables than in Europe or Asia. Latin America also was seen as a desirable market due to the long attraction of U.S. television and popular culture in most of the area, the high percentage of children in the population, and relatively nonrestrictive entry policies.[6]

Figure 10–1   *Nickelodeon Latin America Logo. Nickelodeon. Used by permission.*

Operationalizing the message of "Put[ting] Kids First" into local terms was a vital step in effective branding. Nick LA used extensive focus group interviewing of children in Argentina, Brazil, and Mexico to discover similarities among children in quite distinct nations. The main finding was that children had a "real interest in learning about kids in other places."[7] This led to the adoption of "Nickelodeon Te Conecta a Tu Mundo" ["Nickelodeon Connects You to Your World"] as the channel's major promotional slogan and the use of footage showing children in many Latin American nations in on-air promotions.

Nickelodeon Latin America relies heavily on research of various types from telephone surveys to focus groups to "photo surveys," that involve the analysis of subject-submitted photographs of areas of interest and personal importance. In addition, every letter, e-mail, and contest entry is entered into a database. The result is a service that attempts to be "in touch" with the desires and concerns of children in the region.[8]

Although 75 percent of Nickelodeon Latin America's programming is original for the Latin American market, most of it was produced in the United States. Nick LA acquired some "local" programming and has long-term plans to develop programs with local or regional television providers. An interesting global effort of Nickelodeon is the "Global Character Lab," described as an attempt to "break up the New York–Los Angeles–London creative axis" by presenting short videos, and perhaps longer form programming over time, developed in the countries where Nickelodeon operates.[9]

Despite these efforts, ways other than program acquisition have been the keys to localizing the service. Many of these efforts are related to cultural differences. For example, the program schedule of Nick LA differs considerably from the U.S. service to adapt to local school times, to parental content concerns that are often greater than in the United States, and to the fact that children in Latin America tend to stay up later at night than their U.S. counterparts. In addition such U.S. broadcast network programs as *Sabrina, the Teenage Witch* and *Clueless* are scheduled in the evening rather than Nick at Nite's tongue-in-cheek presentation of "Classic TV."[10]

As explained by Steve Grieder, vice president and creative director, "Localization is not specifically a programming acquisitions issue. We don't feel we have to buy shows from the region; we look for the best stuff to serve the audience from everywhere. Our responsibility is to make it local through very high quality dubbing and adaptation."[11] The main burden of localizing Nickelodeon Latin America falls on promotion and marketing, with most of the campaigns localized versions of campaigns that have been successful in the United States. Key examples include

1. "Nickelodeon En Vivo" ["Nickelodeon Live"], a traveling live theatrical show with interactive games based on such popular programs as *Rugrats* and *Clarissa*.
2. "Ayuda a Tu Mundo" ["Help Your World"], a "pro-social initiative" that encourages children to get involved in volunteer helping activities. "Ayuda a Tu Mundo" provides a good example of corporate "synergy" or integrated marketing as Viacom-owned corporate siblings Blockbuster Video (as information center) and Simon & Schuster (through educational material designed for Mexican teachers) were employed to support the effort.
3. "Director por un Dia" ["Director for a Day"], a regional sweepstakes.[12]

Cultural differences had to be accounted for in these and other campaigns. For example, "Ayuda a Tu Mundo," based on "The Big Help" initiative in the United States, had to be carefully positioned in Latin America because, while "helping" others is understood, volunteerism is a relatively vague concept. The "Super Toy Run" promotion that was popular in the United States was not attempted in Latin America due to the general absence of toy superstores. References to "milk and cookies" as a common snack were changed because few children in Latin America drink milk after infancy.[13]

Merchandising is an important component of Nickelodeon in the United States and increasingly in other countries. Magazines, books, videos, videogames, clothing, toys, and other licensed merchandise follows the service to new markets. Theme park attractions and retail stores are likely to be added to the Nickelodeon presence in Latin America in the near future, as they have been elsewhere.[14]

Nickelodeon Latin America provides a good example of the importance of knowledge of and sensitivity to market conditions and cultural factors in building a brand. In addition, Nick LA is an example of how continuing research and canny promotion and marketing campaigns can make a service "local," even if most of the programming is from outside the region.

Sources

1. "Nickelodeon Latin America Fact Sheet," press release. Miami: Nickelodeon Latin America, February 1998.
2. Donna Friedman, vice president of marketing and associate creative director, Nickelodeon Latin America. Telephone interview, August 24, 1998.
3. Jimena Fridman, "The U.S. Invasion of Latin American Kids' TV," *The Big Blue Box* (Fall 1997 [reprint]); Donna Friedman, vice president of marketing and associate creative director, and Valerie G. McCarty, vice president, Marketing and Communications, Nickelodeon Latin America, joint telephone interview, March 4, 1998.
4. Friedman; "Nickelodeon Latin America Fact Sheet."
5. Friedman.
6. Friedman and McCarty.
7. Friedman and McCarty.
8. "Nickelodeon Latin America Fact Sheet."
9. Steven Grieder, vice president and creative director, Nickelodeon Latin America, telephone interview, March 30, 1998; "Nickelodeon Worldwide Development Group Announces Creation Of Nickelodeon's Global Character Lab," press release. Miami: Nickelodeon Latin America, July 29, 1997.
10. "Nickelodeon Latin America Celebrates the New Year by Premiering Two New Acquisitions," press release. Miami: Nickelodeon Latin America, December 23, 1997.
11. Grieder; Ed Kirchdoerffer, "Courting Latin America," *KidScreen* (January 1998 [reprint]).
12. "Ayuda a Tu Mundo," press release, Miami: Nickelodeon Latin America, January 1998; "Nickelodeon Latin America Fact Sheet."
13. Friedman and McCarty.
14. Viacom web site: http://www.viacom.com/global.tin, July 21, 1998.

SUMMARY

While not ignoring emerging technology and its potential effect on the viewers (users) of television and the industry, the material in this chapter is primarily and necessarily bound to the way television operates at the turn of the twenty-first century. Some combination of digital and web transmission has the potential to substantially alter the viewer–content provider relationship. Perhaps the promise of interactive television as a mass medium finally might be realized by its promoters despite its to-date rather spectacular failures. On-demand and pay-per-view (or *pay-per-connection* time) usage someday might become the dominant distribution method for television content. While the state of the future global television industry is not known to us, the major parameters affecting promotion are likely to remain essentially unchanged regardless of how the industry evolves. Although the traditional *date and time* (the *when* function) will not be as important in a true on-demand television delivery system, except to announce when the service first will become available, the *content* and *brand* and *image* functions of promotion (the *what* and *who*, as well as the *where* and *call-to-action* functions) will become more important than ever in an on-demand system. The simple and basic fact remains that, as long as advertisers use television (however distributed or delivered) to reach desirable target audiences, the traditional functions of promotion will be essential to content providers in producing those audiences.

Nevertheless, global television is the great "leveler" of cultural differences. As more people from diverse cultural environments watch the same television content and find positions in the television and advertising industries and as the television industry becomes more structurally integrated across international boundaries, the more the "rules" of television programming, promotion, and marketing become standardized (see Box 10–3). While the recognition of and reaction to cultural differences is an integral component of international television promotion and marketing, the components and fundamentals of the promotion process are rapidly becoming an understood common language among industry professionals.

Globalization is both "here and now" as well as the future of the television industry. Economic consolidation and technological convergence will continue to fuel global expansion by major television providers, as will the eventual maximization of domestic growth in the world's most developed television markets.

Global consolidation is leading to a new oligopoly, whereby a limited number of giant media companies will control much of the world's access to and content of television, with U.S. firms in a privileged, if not dominant, position. However, the operational parameters of this oligopoly still are in flux and subject to both political action within individual nations or regions, and the situation wherein the viewer is newly exposed to multichannel television and increasingly difficult to capture. Consolidation will not necessarily lead to the generic sameness of product usually found in oligopoly structures. In an increasingly cluttered television universe, localism is one of the most important ways for a program or a program provider to differentiate itself from all the other programs or channels. The increasing sophistication of both quantitative and qualitative lifestyle research (*psychographics*) will enable programming and promotion professionals to better target viewers culturally, ethnically, and personally.

Although the enormous market clout of the members of the emerging global television oligopoly can dominate the market, local program providers still can prosper because of their connection with the local population. As demonstrated by the recent failures of several U.S.-originated or owned services in Europe, the future is not so much about overwhelming the locals, as it is in recognizing them through copartnerships. Whether a local copartner can maintain a degree of autonomy and exist in an "equal" partnership with its large transnational partner will be a key issue within the industry in the next few years.

In any event, multichannel television is only going to expand in the near future. The viewers will have many more choices and more control over their viewing than ever before. Promotion and marketing that can persuade the viewers that a specific program or channel is worth their investment of time and attention are fundamental to the success of global and domestic television providers.

BOX 10–3   Keys to Effective Global Television Promotion and Marketing

The key considerations in effective global television promotion and marketing are as follows:

1. Promotion and marketing basics need not be reinvented for nondomestic markets. The basics of time, date, content, image, and brand are essentially the same everywhere in the world.
2. Brand extensions should be designed specifically for the host nation(s) *within* the host nation.
3. Residents of the host country should be key members of the promotion and marketing team. These individuals can help avoid embarrassing or more serious mistakes resulting from cultural insensitivity or ignorance. Local residents also are likely to be knowledgeable of and sensitive to domestic cultural indicators.
4. Optimally, nonnatives working on campaigns should have lived in the nation(s) in which the program or service is being marketed and speak the local language(s).
5. Campaigns should be congruent with the entire program chain and not just the program service or channel (the typical primary client). Particularly important is the local exhibitor. A local exhibitor's role as gatekeeper

can be essential to the success of the program or promotion and so deserves attention from any canny marketer. A local manager also often is knowledgeable of local events that present off-air marketing opportunities.

6. Local political and economic conditions should be well understood. Limitations on nondomestic content or lack of exhibitor capacity can determine the form and level of television globalization (full channel, shared channel, program blocs, or individual programs) both in terms of programming and promotion.

7. Promotional campaigns should reflect an understanding of what global television programming actually is and is not. It is rarely about globally popular programs, because individual differences among viewers and the proliferation of channels reduces the chance of any one program becoming popular all over the world. With the exception of certain news and sports events, global television programming operates on the macro-level of economic globalization, a level usually not relevant to the viewer. Standardization of promotional materials, as part of the globalization of marketing television programming, works only with the generic functions of promotion and when both product usage and culture is similar—a rare circumstance.

8. While culturally transcendent meanings should be part of any effective promotional campaign, the most important fact of global television is that the viewer or user *consumes television locally*, regardless of the source of the programming. Promotion and marketing campaigns, which often carry the burden of making nonlocal programming creatively local, must themselves reflect local conditions over often superficial global similarities. As articulated by CityTV founder Moses Znaimer and increasingly obvious, "as worldwide television expands, the demand for local television increases."

Selected Bibliography

Abelman, R., and Atkin, D. (Apr. 1998). Evaluating the impact of affiliation change on children's viewership and perceptions of network branding. Paper presented to the Broadcast Education Association, Las Vegas, NV.

Austin, B. T. (1994). The construction and transformation of the American disc jockey occupation. Unpublished doctoral dissertation, University of Massachusetts, Amherst.

Bates, B. J., and King, R. E. (Apr. 1996). Television and the web: How local television broadcasters are using the World Wide Web. Paper presented to the Broadcast Education Association, Las Vegas, NV.

Bates, B. J., Chambers, L. T., Embery, M., Jones, M., McClung, S., and Park, J. (August 1997). Television on the web, 1996: Local television stations' use of the World Wide Web. Paper presented to the Association for Education in Journalism and Mass Communication, Chicago.

Bellamy, R., Jr. (1992). Emerging images of product differentiation: Network television promotion in a time of industry change. *Feedback. 33*(3): 22–26.

Berthon, P., Leyland, F. P., and Watson, R. T. (1996). The World Wide Web as an advertising medium. *Journal of Advertising Research. 36*(1): 43–54.

Billings, A. C., Eastman, S. T, and Newton, G. D. (1998). Atlanta revisited: Prime-time promotion in the 1996 Summer Olympics. *Journal of Sports and Social Issues, 22*(1): 65–78.

Bolls, P. D., and Potter, R. F. (1998). I saw it on the radio: The effects of imagery-evoking radio commercials on listeners' allocation of attention and attitude toward the ad. In D. D. Meuhung (ed.), *Proceedings of the 1998 Conference of the American Academy of Advertising.* Pullman, WA: Washington State University.

Bolls, P. D., Potter, R. F., and Lang, A. (1998). I saw it on the radio: Listeners' physiological and cognitive responses to imagery-eliciting radio commercials. Paper presented at the Society of Psychophysiological Research.

Borzillo, C. (May 18, 1996). Beyond hot dogs: Promotions a la Harris. *Billboard*, p. 95.

Borzillo, C. (Aug. 3, 1996). Promax execs share some strategies. *Billboard*, p. 95.

Broniarczyk, S. M., and Alba, J. W. (May 1994). The importance of the brand in brand extension. *Journal of Marketing Research 31*: 214–228.

Brown, T. J., and Dacin, P. A. (Jan. 1997). The company and the product: Corporate associations and consumer product responses. *Journal of Marketing 61*: 68–84.

Bryant, J., and Rockwell, S. C. (1993). Remote control devices in television program selection: Experimental evidence. In J. R. Walker and R. V. Bellamy, Jr. (eds.), *The Remote Control in the New Age of Television* (pp. 73–85). Westport, CT: Westport.

233

Bucy, E. P., Lang, A., Potter, R. F., and Grabe, M. E. (Aug. 1998). Structural features of cyberspace: A content analysis of the World Wide Web. Paper presented to the Association for Education in Journalism and Mass Communication, Baltimore, MD.

Cameron, G. T., Schleuder, J., and Thorson, E. (1991). The role of news teasers in processing TV news and commercials. *Communication Research 18*: 667–684.

Carpenter, G. S., Glazer, R., and Nakamoto, K. (Aug. 1994). Meaningful brands from meaningless differentiation: The dependence on irrelevant attributes. *Journal of Marketing Research 31*: 339–350.

Carroll, R. L., Tuggle, C. A., McCullum, J. F., Mitrook, M. A., Arlington, K. J., and Hoerner, Jr., J. M. (1997). Consonance in local television news program content: An examination of intermarket diversity. *Journal of Broadcasting and Electronic Media 41*: 132–144.

Cooper, R. and Clark, G. (1994). Channel loyalty: An examination of audience behavior from the perspectives of broadcasters and local television viewers. Report to the National Association of Broadcasters, Washington, D.C.

Davis, D. M., and Walker, J. R. (1991). Sex, violence, and network program promotion: A content analysis. Paper presented at the national meeting of the Speech Communication Association, Atlanta, GA.

Derbaix, C. M. (Nov. 1995). The impact of affective reactions on attitudes toward the advertisement and the brand: A step toward ecological validity. *Journal of Marketing Research 32*: 470–479.

DiNucci, D., with Giudice, M., and Stiles, L. (1997). *Elements of Web Design.* Berkeley, CA: Peachpit Press.

Eastman, S. T. (1994). Evaluating premium performance. *Journal of Broadcasting and Electronic Media 28*: 201–213.

Eastman, S. T. (1998). Programming theory under stress: The active industry and the active audience. In *Communication Yearbook*, vol. 21 (pp. 323–377). Thousand Oaks, CA: Sage.

Eastman, S. T., and Neal-Lunsford, J. (1993). The RCD's impact on television programming and promotion. In J. Walker and R. Bellamy, Jr. (eds.), *The Remote Control in the New Age of Television* (pp. 189–209). Westport, CT: Praeger.

Eastman, S. T., and Newton, G. D. (1995). Delineating grazing: Observations of remote control use. *Journal of Communication 45* (1): 77–95.

Eastman, S. T., and Newton, G. D. (1998). Estimating the contributions of inheritance and promotion. In S. T. Eastman, *Report on Compilation Valuation for Distant Television Signals* (pp. 15–31), filed as part of the Statement of Case and Exhibits regarding retransmission 1998–2000, on behalf of BBC, CBRA, and CRRA, with the Copyright Board of Canada, pp. 3.15–3.27.

Eastman, S. T., and Newton, G. D. (1998). The impact of structural salience within on-air promotion. *Journal of Broadcasting and Electronic Media 42*: 50–79.

Eastman, S. T., and Newton, G. D. (1999). Hitting promotion hard: A network response to channel surfing and new competition. *Journal of Applied Communication Research 27* (1): 73–85.

Eastman, S. T., Newton, G. D., and Pack, L. (1996). Promoting prime-time programs in megasporting events. *Journal of Broadcasting and Electronic Media 40*: 366–388.

Eastman, S. T., Newton, G. D., Riggs, K. A., and Neal-Lunsford, J. (1997). Accelerating the flow: A transition effect in programming theory? *Journal of Broadcasting and Electronic Media 41*: 305–323.

Eastman, S. T., and Otteson, J. L. (1994). Promotion increases ratings, doesn't it? The impact of program promotion in the 1992 Olympics. *Journal of Broadcasting and Electronic Media 38*: 307–322.

Entman, R. 1993). Framing: Toward clarification of a fractured paradigm. *Journal of Communication 43* (4): 51–58.

Ferguson, D. A, and Perse, E. M. (1993). Media and audience influences on channel repertoire. *Journal of Broadcasting and Electronic Media 37*: 31–47.

Ferguson, D. A. (1992). Channel repertoire in the presence of remote control devices, VCRs, and cable television. *Journal of Broadcasting and Electronic Media 36*: 83–91.

Grabe, M., Zhou, S., Lang, A., and Bolls, P. (Aug. 1998) The effects of tabloid and standard television news on viewer evaluations, memory, and arousal. Paper presented to the Association for Education in Journalism and Mass Communication, Baltimore, MD.

Gunter, G. (1987). *Poor Reception: Misunderstanding and Forgetting Broadcast News.* Hillsdale, NJ: Erlbaum.

Keller, K. L. (Jan. 1993). Conceptualizing, measuring, and managing customer-based brand equity. *Journal of Marketing 57*: 1–22.

Kubey, R., and Csikszentmihalyi, M. (1990). *Television and the Quality of Life: How Viewing Shades Everyday Experiences.* Hillsdale, NJ: Erlbaum.

Lang, A., Bolls, P. D., Potter, R. F., and Kawahara, K. (in press). The effects of production pacing and arousing content on the information processing of television messages. *Journal of Broadcasting and Electronic Media.*

Lang, A., Dhillon, P., and Dong Q. (1995). Defining audio/video redundancy from a limited capacity information processing perspective. *Journal of Broadcasting and Electronic Media 38*: 1–15.

Lang, A., Geiger, S., Strickwerda, M., and Sumner, J. (1993). The effects of related and unrelated cuts on viewers' memory for television: A limited capacity theory of television viewing. *Communication Research 20* (l): 4–29.

Lang, A., Sias, P., Chantrill, P., and Burek, J. A. (1995). Tell me a story: Narrative structure and memory for television messages. *Communication Reports 8* (2): 1–9.

Lang, P. J., Simons, R. F., and Balaban, M. (Eds.). (1997). *Attention and Orienting: Sensory and Motivational Processes.* Mahwah, NJ: Erlbaum.

LeClerc, F., Schmitt, B. H., and Dube, L. (May 1994). Foreign branding and its effects on product perceptions and attitudes. *Journal of Marketing Research 31*: 263–270.

Leshner, G., Reeves, B., and Nass, C. (1998). Switching channels: The effects of television channels on the mental representations of television news. *Journal of Broadcasting and Electronic Media 42*: 21–33.

Loken, B., and John, D. R. (July 1993). Diluting brand beliefs: When do brand extensions have a negative impact? *Journal of Marketing 57*: 71–84.

Machleit, K. A., Allen, C. T., and Madden, T. J. (Oct. 1993). The mature brand and brand interest: An alternative consequence of ad-evoked effects. *Journal of Marketing 57*: 72–82.

McClung, S. R. (Oct. 1997). Information representation and local TV stations on the web: Building a better web site. Paper presented to the Ohio University Communications Research Conference, Athens.

McDaniel, L. (May 1997). Promoting for success. *Communicator 51* (5): 12–14.

Meeske, M., and Maunez-Caudra, J. (1992). Protecting radio call letters and slogans as trademarks. *Journal of Broadcasting and Electronic Media 36*: 267–277.

Mela, C. F., Gupta, S., and Lehmann, D. R. (May 1997). The long-term impact of promotion and advertising on consumer brand choice. *Journal of Marketing Research 34*: 248–261.

Miller, D. W. (1994). Imagery-evoking advertising strategies and the interrelationship among cognitive and affective responses to radio commercials. Unpublished doctoral dissertation, Kent State University, Kent, OH.

Murphy, R. (1998, April). The value of radio station web sites. Paper presented to the Broadcast Education Association, Las Vegas, NV.

Newhagen, J. E. (1998). TV news images that induce anger, fear, and disgust: Effects on approach-avoidance and memory. *Journal of Broadcasting and Electronic Media 42*: 265–276.

Niekamp, R. (Aug. 1996). Television station sites on the World Wide Web. Paper present to the Association for Education in Journalism and Mass Communication, Chicago.

Owens, J. W., and Bryant, J. (Apr. 1998). The on-air promotion of college and professional football: A content analysis. Paper presented to the Broadcast Education Association, Las Vegas, NV.

Papatla, P., and Krishnamurthi, L. (Feb. 1996). Measuring the dynamic effects of promotions on brand choice. *Journal of Marketing Research 33*: 20–35.

Park, C. W., Jun, Y., and Shocker, A. D. (Nov. 1996). Composite branding alliances: An investigation of extension and feedback effects. *Journal of Marketing Research 32*: 453–466.

Perry, S. D. (Apr. 1998). Commercial humor influence on sitcom liking: A reevaluation. Paper presented to the Broadcast Education Association, Las Vegas, NV.

Perry, S. D., Jenzowski, S. A., King, C. M., Heater, J. B., and Yi, H. (1997). The influence of commercial humor on program enjoyment and evaluation. *Journalism and Mass Communication Quarterly 74* (2): 388–399.

Piper-Aiken, K. (1997). Listener-member perceptions of marketing strategies employed by public radio stations. *Journal of Radio Studies 4*: 15–29.

Pokrywczynski, J., and Crowley, J. H. (1994). The influence of irritating commercials on radio listening habits. *Journal of Radio Studies 2*: 51–68.

Potter, R. F. (1998). The effects of voice change and production effects on attention to and memory for radio messages. Unpublished doctoral dissertation, Indiana University, Bloomington.

Potter, R. F., Lang, A., and Bolls, P. D. (1998). Orienting to structural features in auditory media messages. *Psychophysiology 35*, supplement 2: S66.

Potter, R., Lang, A., and Bolls, P. (1998). Identifying structural features of radio: Orienting and memory for radio messages, Paper presented at the Association for Education in Journalism and Mass Communication, Baltimore, MD.

Rank, H. (1991). *The Pitch: A Simple Way to Understand the Basic Pattern of Persuasion in Advertising.* Park Forest, IL: Counter-Propaganda Press.

Reese, D. (June 21, 1997). Radio execs upbeat at Promax confab. *Billboard*, p. 75.

Ridgway, J. (Apr. 20, 1998). Name of the game is branding. *Electronic Media*, pp. 16, 37.

Schleuder, J. D., White, A. V., and Cameron, G. T. (1993). Priming effects of television news bumpers and teasers on attention and memory. *Journal of Broadcasting and Electronic Media 37*: 437–452.

Singh, S. N., and Cole, C. A. (1993). The effects of length, content, and repetition on television commercial effectiveness. *Journal of Marketing Research 30*: 91–104.

Slattery, K. L., Hakanen, E. A., and Doremus, M. E. (1998). The expression of localism: Local TV news coverage in the new video marketplace. *Journal of Broadcasting and Electronic Media 42*: 403–413.

Thorson, E., and Lang, A. (1992). Effects of television videographics and lecture familiarity on adult cardiac orienting responses and memory. *Communication Research 19 (3)*: 346–369.

Walker, J. R. (1993). Catchy, yes, but does it work? The impact of broadcast network promotion frequency and type on program success. *Journal of Broadcasting and Electronic Media 37*: 197–207.

Walker, J. R., and Ferguson, D. A. (1998). *The Broadcast Television Industry*. Boston: Allyn and Bacon.

Wilke, M. (June 2, 1997). Stations still getting their feet wet in online strategies. *Advertising Age*, p. S12.

Wilkinson, J. S., and Eastman, S. T. (1997). Network and syndicated radio programming. In S. T. Eastman and D. A. Ferguson (eds.), *Broadcast/Cable Programming: Strategies and Practices, 5th ed.* (pp. 337–350). Belmont, CA: Wadsworth.

Williams, G. A. (1989). Enticing viewers: Sex and violence in TV guide program advertisements. *Journalism Quarterly 66*: 970–973.

Williams, G. C. (1998, April). Money, music, and marketing: Promoting local radio with cash. Paper presented to the Broadcast Education Association, Las Vegas, NV. www.promolounge.com

Yoon, K., Bolls, P. D., and Lang, A. (1998). The effects of arousal on liking and believablitiy of commercials. *Journal of Marketing Communications 4:* 101–114.

Yoon, K., Bolls, P. D., Lang, A., and Potter, R. (1997). The effects of advertising pacing and arousal on ad and brand attitudes and behavioral intention. In M.C. Backlin (ed.), *The Proceedings of the Conference of the American Academy of Advertising*, pp. 169–171.

Index